SHARED GROUND
AMONG JEWS AND CHRISTIANS
A SERIES OF EXPLORATIONS

VOLUME I

Jews and Christians

Exploring the Past, Present, and Future

Editor
James H. Charlesworth

Assistant Editors
Frank X. Blisard, Jeffrey S. Siker

CROSSROAD • NEW YORK

1990
The Crossroad Publishing Company
370 Lexington Avenue
New York, NY 10017

Copyright © 1990 by The American Interfaith Institute

Printed in the United States of America

Library of Congress Cataloging-in-Publication Data

Jews and Christians : exploring the past, present, and future/
    editor, James H. Charlesworth ; assistant editors, Frank X. Blisard,
    Jeffrey S. Siker.
        p.   cm.
    "An American Interfaith Institute Book."
    Includes bibliographical references.
    ISBN 0-8245-1012-7
        1. Judaism—Relations—Christianity—Congresses. 2. Christianity
    and other religions—Judaism—Congresses. 3. Judaism (Christian
    theology)—History of doctrines—Congresses. I. Charlesworth,
    James H. II. Blisard, Frank X. III. Siker, Jeffrey S.
    BM535.J48 1990
    261.2′6—dc20   89-48199
                                                                        CIP

Contributors
and Participants

J. Christiaan Beker
Richard J. Dearborn Professor
  of New Testament Theology
Princeton Theological Seminary
Princeton, New Jersey

Irvin J. Borowsky
Chairman
American Interfaith Institute
Philadelphia, Pennsylvania

James H. Charlesworth
George L. Collord Professor
  of New Testament Language
  and Literature
Princeton Theological Seminary
Princeton, New Jersey

A. Roy Eckardt
Professor of Religion Studies,
  Emeritus
Lehigh University
Bethlehem, Pennsylvania

Richard K. Fenn
Maxwell M. Upson Professor
  of Christianity and Society
Princeton Theological Seminary
Princeton, New Jersey

Hans J. Hillerbrand
Professor of Reformation
  History
Southern Methodist University
Dallas, Texas

Carlo Maria Martini
Cardinal of Milan
Milan, Italy

Robert T. Osborn
Professor of Religion
Department of Religion
Duke University
Durham, North Carolina

John Priest
Professor of Religion
  and Classics
Florida State University
Tallahassee, Florida

Jeffrey S. Siker
Assistant Professor
  of New Testament
Loyola Marymount University
Los Angeles, California

D. Moody Smith
G. W. Ivey Professor
  of New Testament
The Divinity School
Duke University
Durham, North Carolina

Grover A. Zinn
Danforth Professor
  of Religious Studies
Oberlin College
Oberlin, Ohio

Contents

Contributors and Participants   5

Foreword   9
Irvin J. Borowsky

Preface   12
James H. Charlesworth

Acknowledgments   16

Abbreviations   17

1. Christianity and Judaism: A Historical
   and Theological Overview   19
   (Italian Original)   27
   Cardinal Carlo Maria Martini
   Discussion   34

2. Exploring Opportunities for Rethinking Relations
   Among Jews and Christians   35
   James H. Charlesworth
   Discussion   54

3. The New Testament View of Judaism   60
   J. Christiaan Beker
   Discussion   70

4. Judaism and the Gospel of John   76
   D. Moody Smith
   Discussion   97

5. History and Interpretation: "Hebrew Truth,"
   Judaism, and the Victorine Exegetical Tradition   100
   Grover Zinn
   Discussion   123

Illustrations   Following 126

6. Martin Luther and the Jews   127
     Hans J. Hillerbrand
   Discussion   146

7. Salient Christian-Jewish Issues of Today:
   A Christian Exploration   151
     A. Roy Eckardt
   Discussion   178

8. Holocaust as a Pathological Act of Secularization   185
     Richard K. Fenn
   Discussion   207

9. The Christian Blasphemy: A Non-Jewish Jesus   211
     Robert T. Osborn
   Discussion   239

List of Illustrations   240

A Selected Bibliography on Jewish-Christian Relations   242
     Jeffrey S. Siker

Index of Names   249

Index of Passages   255

Foreword

Irvin J. Borowsky

At no time in the history of Christian and Jewish dialogue has there ever been such a concentrated effort by both religions to build sincere bridges of communication.

The latest statistics report that there are one billion, eight hundred million Christians and just over twelve million Jews in the world including three million trapped in Russia. That leaves less than ten million Jews living in the free world. These are the survivors of the pogroms and the Holocaust. The number of Jewish survivors is shockingly low and, at the rapid rate of assimilation, the number is decreasing every decade.

And, yet, despite their dwindling numbers, the distrust and hatred of the Jewish people continues in the Western world.

It is no secret that, in the past 800 years, the Jews have suffered one pogrom after another. Half of the total Jews born into the world were murdered. These facts may be treated as ancient history.

In the last 48 years alone, one out of every three Jews has been killed. Their crime was having Jewish parents. That issue must be confronted as a current event. During the past eight hundred years, the Jewish people were expelled at one time or another from most European nations, including England, France, Spain, and Portugal. Again, these statistics are sometimes sadly shelved as ancient history.

Today there are very few Jews left in Germany, Austria, Czechoslovakia, Spain, and Portugal. In these countries Jews once enjoyed life in thriving communities and contributed significantly to their homelands. In Poland, for instance, the home of three million Jews only 50 years ago, now a mere handful survive. That fact also must be acknowledged as a current event.

During the most recent pogrom—the Holocaust—Jews could find *no* place or country to which they could flee. *No* country would take them in. Sometimes, Jews having succeeded in escaping their persecutors, and leaving behind an adopted homeland, were turned back on the high seas and forced back into the fury of the Holocaust. It is hard to realize that less than 50 years ago boatloads of Jewish refugees were denied entrance into the United States; denied entry into Cuba and every Latin American country. They were forced to return to Europe, where they were murdered by the Nazis. The ones who were able to reach the Swiss or Spanish borders were also told "No Jews wanted or allowed." Would the murder of these millions, including babies and children, have occurred had their executioners been taught that Jesus and all the founders of Christianity were Jewish?

True Christians cannot and do not show disrespect for the religion of Jesus. He was a Jew; and he was devoted to Judaism.

For centuries, educated Christians and Jews had hoped that hatred of the Jewish people would fade away. That hope sadly ballooned into a fantasy. This hatred of Jews is neither emotional nor accidental. It is planted in the pages of the translations of the New Testament. Hatred of Jews increased over the centuries. Unfortunately, two cardinal themes are repeated in Christian anti-Semitism:

- Jews are identified with the power of evil ("Ye are of your father the devil, and the lusts of your father ye will do. . . ." Jn 8:44).

- The Jews themselves are made to admit their collective responsibility for the crucifixion of the Son of God ("Then answered all the people, and said, His blood be on us, and on our children." Mt 27:25).

How broadly were "the Jews" responsible? Were Jews in Alexandria or those in Athens or Galilee involved? Are the enslaved Jews to be implicated? The Sandhedrin numbered 71; add 50 leading priests and the crowd in Jerusalem of about 100. Can the total have been more than 250?

Within Christendom since the time of Hitler, there has existed a widespread reaction of shock and soul-searching concerning the Holocaust. Today, church leaders, divinity schools, and Christian communities in abundance have expressed their disavowal of anti-Semitism. These expressions all have two persistent themes: the recognition that anti-Semitism and Christianity are inconsistent, and the charge that true Christians must fully repudiate anti-Semitism. At the highest levels, statements have been issued that repudiate the charge of deicide.

For 1900 years, the concept of Jews killing Jesus has been so formulated in the Christian tradition that responsibility has rested not only on Jews in the age of Jesus but on Jews of all ages, of all times, in every geographical area. It is this deicide charge that Christians are, only now, rejecting. It is this deicide charge that has had an unholy influence; that has led to evil that denies the very words and work of Jesus.

Over the centuries, acts of violence against the Jewish people were seldom directly inaugurated or promoted by church officials. These acts were the work of bigots who incited mobs. The Church as an institution never killed Jews.

We congratulate the contributors who make this book a reality. They represent the most progressive thinking and the reality of the strong bridges of communication that are being built between the two religions.

Preface

James H. Charlesworth

After the crucifixion of Jesus of Nazareth, a Jew, at the hands of the Romans in 30 C.E., his predominantly Jewish followers found themselves fighting for their survival primarily against fellow Jews—not only in Palestine (*Acts*) but also in the Roman capital and elsewhere (Suetonius, Tacitus; *Romans, Corinthians, Galatians*). After the destruction of Jerusalem and the burning of the Temple by the Romans in 70 C.E., the fissure in Judaism became a chasm. Eventually the second generation of Jesus' followers broke with the members of the other form of Judaism that survived the devastation of 70. Jesus' Jewish group became labeled "Christian" because his followers claimed he was "Christ," the Greek equivalent of the Hebrew and Aramaic word, "Messiah." The other surviving Jewish group became Rabbinic Judaism, heavily shaped and influenced by the followers of the great Rabbi Hillel, a contemporary of Jesus in pre-70 Palestine.

Eventually hatred came to characterize the "bond" that would link Jews and Christians during the centuries and millennia subsequent to their common origins. Some impressive and recently unearthed evidence reveals that churches and synagogues were often close to one another (the evidence of archaeology). Scholars have learned that centuries after 70, Christians were known to admire and attend Jewish synagogal services (John Chrysostom, *Homilia adversus Judaeos*).

Each of these twin survivors of the variegated cosmopolitan religion that was pre-70 Judaism (or, more accurately, varieties of Judaism) lost many of the envigorating earlier traditions as some of those elements (in essence, at least, if not *in toto*) were appropriated by the other survivor. Eventually the two descendants parted ways. Christianity became the state religion of the "Holy Roman Empire." Under Constantine "the Great," in the fourth century, the ruling Christians, some of whose ancestors had themselves been fed to the lions in coliseums, began vehemently castigating and persecuting "Jews" and labeled them "Christ killers."

Jews, in turn, coined their own castigations. A malediction against the Notzrim ("Christians") was added in some post-70 Jewish communities to the twelfth "benediction" of the *Eighteen Benedictions*. Some medieval Jewish sources record the charge that Jesus had been born not of a virgin, but illegitimately from a tryst between Mary and a Roman soldier, sometimes named Panteras; hence, Jesus son of Joseph (Jn 1:45) is occasionally referred to as *bn pnṭyr'* in the Talmudim and Midrashim.

To be sure, polemics did become more rooted in Christian theology than in Jewish thought, as Professor Robert Osborn unfortunately feels compelled to emphasize. Recent research, however, has uncovered some surprising exceptions to such a rule. The twelfth-century Victorines—especially the later ones, like Andrew of St.-Victor and Herbert of Bosham (a scholar in the entourage of Thomas Becket)—were influenced by Jewish oral and written traditions, especially exegesis of Scripture. Remarkably, however, some of these medieval Christian scholars at times preferred Jewish exegesis to Christian. Some even questioned the messianic exegesis of certain psalms and rejected the usual Christian interpretation of *Isaiah* 7:14ff. as predicting the birth of Jesus through a virgin. Moreover, medieval art was not always anti-Jewish. Professor Grover Zinn, in his contribution to the present volume, draws attention to a little known work of medieval art which seems to *reverse* the thrust of customary anti-Jewish iconography.

Martin Luther, as is well known, made some very harsh and shocking statements about the Jews. But can Luther really be held accountable for the anti-Semitism of the later nineteenth century and the Holocaust? Professor Hans Hillerbrand urges that Luther's comments on the Jews must be seen in the context of other, earlier anti-Jewish sentiments pervading Christianity; in terms of Luther's horrendous denunciations of Roman Catholics and Anabaptists; in relation to the positive evaluation of

Judaism in German Pietism; and in light of the recognition that anti-Semitism sprang up in many European countries and centers in which Lutheranism was not dominant.

The Enlightenment produced a serious critique of Christianity's dogmas, especially the absolute uniqueness of Jesus, and, in the process, removed many barriers separating Jewish and Christian theologies. But, again, these cultural currents scarcely affected the development of critical scholarship. The great nineteenth-century scholar Adolph von Harnack denied the Semitic roots of Christianity and even wanted to excise the "Old Testament" from the Christian canon. Similarly, the gifted and influential nineteenth-century scholar of Christian origins, Emil Schürer, described early Jewish prayer as bound in the fetters of a rigid legalism.

The present century is marked by numerous unprecedented phenomena in the history of Judaism and Christianity. Of singular importance are the following: the Holocaust; the establishment of the state of Israel; the distressing resurgence of anti-Semitism throughout the world over the last decade; and the recognition by international experts, Jewish and Christian, as well as others, that Christianity—in its history and in its theology—is deeply rooted in Judaism.

The history of hatred among long lost brothers is chronicled by international experts in the present volume. Moving rapidly, like a helicopter over the Grand Canyon, they survey for us the high and low topographical features of the relations among Jews and Christians from the first to the twentieth centuries.

My thanks are extended to the distinguished scholars who gathered with me in Philadelphia in May of 1987 privately to discuss and debate the tortured yet intertwined histories of Jews and Christians. Their papers, revised, and the subsequent discussions, considerably abbreviated, are collected and presented in the following pages. Regrettably, Professor John Priest withdrew his paper, owing to an illness. His Eminence Carlo Maria Martini, Cardinal of Milan, could not attend, but sent his paper in the original Italian, which, together with the translation by J. F. Hotchkin, leads this collection. Professor Robert T. Osborn graciously allowed me to add his significant paper to this symposium.

Jeff Siker helped in the earlier stages of this work. Frank Blisard has served diligently as the final editorial assistant. I am grateful to each of them for the hours poured into this book.

This volume is the first in a series to be published by the American Institute for the Study of Religious Cooperation, under the chairmanship of Irvin J. Borowsky. May this descendant of Judah, whose parents were rescued from Poland in the bottom of a hay wagon by Christians, continue to help build bridges to the eternal city of brotherly love.

J.H.C.
July 4, 1988
Philadelphia, Pa.

Acknowledgments

Professor Robert T. Osborn's paper appeared in the *Journal of the American Academy of Religion* 53 (1985). We are grateful to the editors of that journal for the permission to republish this work, in a revised form.

We are also grateful to those who have helped us obtain and permitted us to reproduce the important and attractive illustrations. Most notably we now thank the following: the directors of the Kunstgeschichtlichen Institut der Philipps-Universität, Marburg; William W. Clark and Grover Zinn; the directors of the Cathedral, Freiburg im Breisgau; and the librarian of the Bibliotheek der Rijksuniversiteit te Leiden.

List of Abbreviations

I. Ancient Documents

Bible and Apocrypha

Gen	Genesis	Dan	Daniel
Ex	Exodus	Hos	Hosea
Lev	Leviticus	Joel	Joel
Num	Numbers	Amos	Amos
Deut	Deuteronomy	Obad	Obadiah
Josh	Joshua	Jonah	Jonah
Judg	Judges	Micah	Micah
Ruth	Ruth	Nah	Nahum
1Sam	1 Samuel	Hab	Habakkuk
2Sam	2 Samuel	Zeph	Zephaniah
1Kgs	1 Kings	Hag	Haggai
2Kgs	2 Kings	Zech	Zechariah
1Chr	1 Chronicles	Mal	Malachi
2Chr	2 Chronicles	2Ezra	2 Ezra
Ezra	Ezra	Tob	Tobit
Neh	Nehemiah	Jdt	Judith
Esth	Esther	AddEsth	Additions to Esther
Job	Job	WisSol	Wisdom of Solomon
Ps(s)	Psalms	Sir	Sirach
Prov	Proverbs	1Bar	1 Baruch
Eccl (Qoh)	Ecclesiastes	LetJer	Letter of Jeremiah
Song	Song of Songs	PrAzar	Prayer of Azariah
Isa	Isaiah	Sus	Susanna
Jer	Jeremiah	Bel	Bel and the Dragon
Lam	Lamentations	1Mac	1 Maccabees
Ezek	Ezekiel	2Mac	2 Maccabees

Mt	Matthew	1Tim	1 Timothy
Mk	Mark	2Tim	2 Timothy
Lk	Luke	Tit	Titus
Jn	John	Phlm	Philemon
Acts	Acts	Heb	Hebrews
Rom	Romans	Jas	James
1Cor	1 Corinthians	1Pet	1 Peter
2Cor	2 Corinthians	2Pet	2 Peter
Gal	Galatians	1Jn	1 John
Eph	Ephesians	2Jn	2 John
Phil	Philippians	3Jn	3 John
Col	Colossians	Jude	Jude
1Thes	1 Thessalonians	Rev	Revelation
2Thes	2 Thessalonians		

Pseudepigrapha

For abbreviations of documents cited, see list of abbreviations in J.H. Charlesworth, ed., *The Old Testament Pseudepigrapha* (Garden City, New York, 1983) vol. 1, pp. xlv-l.

II. Modern Works

RSV   *The Holy Bible.* Revised Standard Version.

WA   Luther, Martin. *Werke. Kritische Gesamtausgabe* [Weimarer Ausgabe].

CHAPTER ONE

Christianity and Judaism A Historical and Theological Overview

Cardinal Carlo Maria Martini

A Historical Overview

The New Testament Epoch

In its origins Christianity is deeply rooted in Judaism. Without a sincere feeling for the Jewish world, therefore, and a direct experience of it, one cannot understand Christianity. Jesus is fully Jewish, the apostles are Jewish, and one cannot doubt their attachment to the traditions of their forefathers. In announcing and inaugurating the messianic Passover, Jesus, the universal redeemer and the suffering servant, did not do so in opposition to the covenant of Sinai; rather, he fulfills the sense of Sinai. True, one does find anti-Jewish polemics in the New Testament. These have to be understood at different levels.

1. On the *historical* level, they can be seen within the atmosphere of sectarian assaults aimed at different groups (Pharisees, Sadducees, Qumranites, Essenes).

2. On the *theological* level, the term "the Jews," particularly as found in the *Gospel of John*, is a category used to describe anyone who refuses salvation. This categoric use of the term was well demonstrated by Karl Barth (see, e.g., his *Commentary on Romans*).

3. On the *eschatological* level, the goal of the structures that flow from the covenant came to be seen as necessitating the Kingdom, when God reigns "over all and in all."

4. On the *ecclesiastical* level, these polemics are a reaction

to the demands advanced by Judaizers in circles of Christians with pagan backgrounds.

But all this does not mean that from the start Christianity and the New Testament had an anti-Semitic character. The strong emphasis Paul places on the tradition and the covenant with the patriarchs in his *Epistle to the Romans* counters such a view. It even seems intended to counter a certain current of opposition to Jews that was then manifesting itself among some Christians in Rome with their background in the Greco-Roman world.

The Patristic Period

Yet to be completed is a study of the Church Fathers to determine their understanding of the relationship between the Judiasm of 'Eres Yisra'el (the Land of Israel) and that of the Diaspora (particularly as this was expressed in the Talmud). Moreover, the study of first-century heresies, especially those of Asia Minor and the Middle East, as well as their relationship with Jewish currents, would be valuable in helping to understand the birth of Islam.

Until the fifth century the term "Jew" did not have a pejorative sense in the writings of the Church Fathers. Semitic thought categories and mentality continued to penetrate Christian thought especially up until the Council of Nicea (325). But even later the fruits of such Semitic thinking can be seen in Syrian authors such as Saint Ephraem. Because of these writers, and Saint Ambrose as well, these fruits are to be found also in the West. This is even more the case when it comes to liturgical life and prayer, since this was essentially related to the experience of the synagogue, as we see in Alexandria at the time of Origen. This intimate connection began to break down in Visigoth Spain (seventh century), when church councils pressured Jewish converts to abjure and abandon every earlier tradition.

Augustine, for his part, introduced a negative element into judgment on the Jews. As one who was always seeking to collect grains of truth (the *logoi* of the Stoics), even those found in pagan authors, he advanced the so-called "theory of substitution" whereby the New Israel of the church became a substitute for ancient Israel. But still we have not arrived at a situation of gross intolerance.

Evidence of Christian appreciation of Judaism can be found even in Rome, for instance, in the early Christian mosaic in the Church of Santa Sabina. Next to a figure representing the "Church of the Nations," the mosaic depicts the "Church of Circumcision" as a *noble* matron. Later, in the Middle Ages, this image would be replaced by that of the blindfolded synagogue [as illustrated in this book and in Dr. Zinn's paper].

The Medieval Period

Poliakov has shown in an exhaustive study that up until the Crusades the situation of Jews in Europe generally remained one of serene coexistence with the Christian population.

A brutal and bloody turn was provoked by the fanatical masses who mobbed together in the armies directed at the Holy Land. They were responsible for ferocious massacres of entire Jewish communities in Germany, notwithstanding the opposition of bishops and of counts. The Jews were left with a choice only between baptism and martyrdom, and by the thousands they chose the latter, proclaiming their own fidelity to God. After 1144 the accusation of ritual homicide circulated. Still later came the charge of a hateful plot being carried out against the human race by the Jews, who were cursed because they were "God-killers." The consequences were very grave, especially at the popular level. The Jews came to be regarded virtually as a symbol of satanic evil to be implacably extirpated by every available means.

The church did not partake of these aberrations; yet, it felt the effects of this atmosphere. Thus in 1215 the Fourth Lateran Council imposed on Jews the distinctive "sign."

Still, in the thirteenth and fourteenth centuries one finds a particularly flourishing Jewish community in Rome. The Council of Vienna (1310–1311) decreed that throughout Europe chairs of Hebrew and Aramaic should be established for the study of the Talmud, although this reform of higher studies never actually came about. In Spain, France, and Italy there was deep collaboration between Jews and Christians at the cultural level. This atmosphere shows through in Boccaccio's novella on "Melchisedeck the Jew and Saladin" (*Decameron* I, 3).

For the Jews, "the Middle Ages" continued in Europe up until the time of the French Revolution, marked by two very

serious events—the expulsion from Spain (1492) and the establishment of the ghetto, decreed by the papal bull *Cum Nimis
Absurdum* (1555), accompanied by burnings of the Talmud,
harassments, religious trials, and cultural degradation. These
persecutions ought to inspire us to serious research to determine the causes. It is certain that religious prejudice, fed by
inflammatory popular preaching (e.g., Saint Bernard), easily
offered pretexts to those who sought to draw political or economic advantage from the insecure and menaced Jews.

It is humble wisdom to recognize the errors of a badly informed religiosity, or worse, a blind fanaticism. Religious intolerance can mask even an irreligious mentality, and an unwary
religiosity can be used to other, nonreligious ends. Examples
of this are not lacking in Scripture. For this reason Jesus calls
for a conversion of the heart, in order to adore the Father "in
spirit and in truth" (Jn 4:23).

The Modern Period and the Present

After their emancipation, the Jews became active participants
in the scientific, literary, philosophical, political, economic, and
artistic fields in nations born in the modern era. Meanwhile,
currents favoring return to the "land" in Palestine flourished,
inspired either by religious or by purely political-ideological
motives.

In the same period, however, the church experienced a season of uneasy relationships with the new social order and new
mentality. Is it conceivable that had fraternal relations been established between Christianity and Judaism, we would not
have experienced certain sad misunderstandings between the
church and the modern world?

New pogroms in Russia at the end of the nineteenth century,
however, again linked fanaticism, intolerance, and religious
prejudices with political motivations. The programmatic exter-
mination of European Jews carried out with systematic and absurd ferocity by the Nazis is a tragic and indescribable horror.
This new idolatrous state tyranny ably exploited secular prejudices against the Jews that were widespread among the pop-
ulace. The horror this instills in us is joined with vivid sorrow
when we consider what indifference, or worse, what spite,
often separated Jews and Christians in those years, even

though one can still remember the heroism of many who came to the aid of persecuted Jews.

Pius XI was preparing an encyclical condemning anti-Semitism; but sadly his death, in 1939, interrupted this project.

The period after the war saw the rebirth of a "Jewish" state with its own autonomy and a democratic character. The majority of Jews saw it as an answer to their prayers, saluting it as "the beginning of the flowering of the Redemption." The church, for its part, took on an attitude of dialogue with the world, attentive to discern the "signs of the times" in a spirit of service to humanity still lacerated by grave contradictions. The Second Vatican Council gave full expression to the passion of the church for the salvation of the world and for peace. It repudiated the accusation of "deicide" and "the teaching of contempt" (Jules Isaac) with respect to the Jews. To the contrary, it underlined our great common inheritance of faith in the mysterious plan of salvation willed by God (*Nostra Aetate*, n.4). The signs of these major openings, such as the visit of John Paul II to the synagogue of Rome or the grand prayer for peace in Assisi, have been before the eyes of all of us. The Holy Father has proclaimed blessed a daughter of the Jewish people who at Auschwitz offered herself with Christ "for true peace" and "for her people."

A Theological Overview

These brief historical notes are intended to serve only as a stimulus in order to show how necessary it is to have a more accurate critical analysis of the past. The church will always be grateful to anyone who offers it such a serious cultural contribution, since this is very valuable for interpreting history in the light of the principles of faith.

I would like only to indicate some of these principles. A fatiguing and until now sorrowful historical journey has brought them to the fore in theological reflection. They appear as well in documents published by the Commission for the Religious Relations with the Jews, which seeks to apply the teachings of the Second Vatican Council. This commission was established in 1974, and for several years I was a consultant to it. Our journey must continue, and theology is invited more insistently now, since the *Shoah*, to "be confronted with the

history and the experience of faith of the Jews at Auschwitz"
(J. B. Metz).

The Common Roots That Make Us Brothers

John XXIII, the Second Vatican Council, Paul VI (in his encyclical *Ecclesiam Suam*), John Paul II, that is to say, the entire recent universal magisterium of the church, together with
documents from episcopal conferences and individual local
churches, all unanimously drive home the point that the
church and the Jewish people are bound by a deep bond "at
the level of their own religious identity." This bond does not
destroy but validates the two communities and their individual
members in their specific differences and in their common
values.

Here I would like to offer a brief—and by no means exhaustive—summary of these *common elements* as they are found in
Scripture and tradition:

1. the faith of Abraham and of the patriarchs in the God
who has chosen Israel with irrevocable love;

2. the vocation to holiness ("Be holy, because I am holy";
Lev 11:45) and the necessity for "conversion" (*teshubhah*) of
the heart;

3. the veneration of Sacred Scripture;

4. the tradition of prayer, both private and public;

5. obedience to the moral law expressed in the commandments of Sinai;

6. the witness rendered to God by the "Sanctification of
the Name" in the midst of the peoples of the world, even to
the point of martyrdom if necessary;

7. respect and responsibility in relationship to all creation,
committed zeal for peace and for the good of all humanity,
without discrimination.

And yet, these common elements are understood and lived
out in the two traditions in profoundly different ways.

Differences

These deep values that unite us do not suppress certain
characteristics that distinguish us and that come to be seen so
clearly at the establishment of an honest dialogue: in Jesus who

died and rose we Christians adore the only begotten Son beloved of the Father, the Messiah, Lord, and Redeemer of all people, who draws together in himself all creation. Nevertheless, with this act of faith we retain and confirm the Jewish values of the Torah, as Paul asserted (Rom 3:31). Our dynamic and eschatological exegesis of the Scriptures places us in a line of continuity and yet discontinuity with the Jewish interpretation.

There remains for us the urgent duty of undertaking ecclesiological research in order to clarify how the two communities of the covenant—church and synagogue—are not simply amalgamated by their participation in a common mission of service to God and man. Saint Ambrose, in speaking of the relationship between the two "covenants" (Old Testament–New Testament), spoke of a "wheel within a wheel." The image is an attractive one. Saint Paul used the vivid image of the cultivated olive tree and the wild olive branches (Rom 10:17–24).

History, on the other hand, has shown us how much damage this mission has suffered because excessive and sometimes tragic polemical counterpositions have divided us.

One Hope and a Common Goal

It is not only the sources and many elements of our journey that we hold in common; even the final goal can be expressed and understood in convergent terms. Hope in a messianic future, when God alone will reign, King of justice and of peace; faith in the resurrection of the dead, in the judgment of God rich in mercy, in the universal redemption—these are all common themes for Jews and Christians. Perhaps even more than it would seem, the very differences that distinguish us from each other on these points can be regarded as reciprocally complementary.

Collaboration and Fraternal Cooperation

It is on the basis of these principles—which certainly deserve further, more attentive, and deeper study—that there is already apparent a broad area for a responsible common commitment. This is especially so at the spiritual and ethical level, in the field of human rights, and in an assistance to people and persons in need of solidarity, both for peace and for the integral development of humanity. And I believe this will become even more apparent. More and more frequently there appear kindred points of contact that broaden our mutual responsibilities towards other devout monotheists, particularly towards Islamic faithful.

For this reason the shared commitment of Jews, Christians, and Muslims to seek a balanced solution that will bring a "just and complete" peace to Israel (John Paul I, September 6, 1978), to the Palestinian people, and to Lebanon becomes ever more urgent. Jerusalem is, as it were, the center and the symbol of these common religious, historical, ethical, and cultural values which must be harmoniously gathered together and respected.

As Jesus wept at the sight of Jerusalem "in order that it might obtain pardon through the tears of the Lord" (Saint Ambrose, *De Paenitentia*, I.ii), so let all of us hope that from Jerusalem there will flow forth a river of peace and a torrent of pardon and love.

(This translation was not made by Cardinal Martini's staff. The original, which follows on the next page, was translated by J. F. Hotchkin, who was recommended by the Secretariat for Catholic-Jewish Relations in Washington.)

CHAPTER ONE (ITALIAN ORIGINAL)

Christianity and Judaism

Cardinal Carlo Maria Martini

.

Sguardo Storico

Epocha del N.T.

Il cristianesimo delle origini è profondamente radicato nell'ebraismo, e non può essere compreso senza avere contemporaneamente una sincera simpatia e una esperienza diretta del mondo ebraico. Gesù è pienamente ebreo, ebrei sono gli apostoli, e non si può dubitare del loro attaccamento alla tradizione dei Padri. La Pasqua messianica che Gesú, redentore universale e servo sofferente, annuncia e realizza, non si oppone all'Alleanza del Sinai, ma ne completa il senso. Le polemiche antiebraiche presenti nel N.T. si comprendono a diversi livelli:

1. a livello *storico*, nell'atmosfera delle lacerazioni settarie che opponevano i diversi gruppi (farisei, sadducei, qumram, esseni, . . .);

2. a livello *teologico*, particolarmente in Giovanni: i "Giudei" sono una categoria per esprimere chi rifiuta la salvezza. Questa terminologia categoriale fu ben chiarita da Karl Barth (cf.p.es. il "Commento ai Romani");

3. a livello *escatologico*, per cui la "fine" delle strutture dell'Alleanza viene sentita come una necessità del Regno, quando Dio regna "tutto in tutti";

4. a livello *ecclesiale*, come reazione alle pretese giudaizzanti che si affermavano in ambiente di cristiani provenienti dal paganesimo.

Ma tutto questo non significa che il cristianesimo originario e il N.T. abbiano carattere antisemita. Il grande rilievo che Paolo dà alla tradizione e all'Alleanza dei Padri nella lettera ai Romani sembra anzi voler contrastare la corrente di una certa opposizione agli ebrei che si manifestava presso alcuni cristiani di Roma provenienti dal mondo greco-romano.

Periodo Patristico

Lo studio dei Padri per coglierne il rapporto con l'ebraismo di 'Erez Israel e della diaspora (come si esprime in particolare nel Talmud) non è stato ancora compiuto; anche lo studio delle eresie dei primi secoli, specialmente in Asia e in Oriente, e il loro rapporto con le correnti ebraiche, sarebbe prezioso per capire la nascita dell'Islam.

Il termine "Judaeus" non ha, fino al secolo V, un senso peggiorativo presso i Padri; le categorie di pensiero e la mentalità semita continuano a penetrare il pensiero cristiano specialmente fino a Nicea, ma anche dopo fecondano specialmente gli autori siri, come S.Efrem, e attraverso di essi—anche grazie a S.Ambrogio—sono presenti in occidente. Questo vale ancor più per la vita liturgica e la preghiera, per la quale è essenziale il rimando all'esperienza sinagogale, come vediamo ad Alessandria al tempo di Origene. Questa familiarità comincerà a incrinarsi nella Spagna visigota (sec.VII) quando i Concili imporranno agli ebrei convertiti di abiurare e di abbandonare ogni tradizione precedente.

Agostino, peraltro, sempre attento a cogliere i semi di verità (i *lògoi* stoici) anche dai pagani, introduce però un elemento negativo nel giudizio sugli ebrei: è la cosiddetta "teoria della sostituzione" dell'Antico Israele da parte del Nuovo Israele, la Chiesa. Ma non siamo ancora a una situazione di pesante intolleranza, come testimonia anche, proprio a Roma, il mosaico paleocristiano di S.Sabina che raffigura accanto alla "Ecclesia ex Gentibus" la "Ecclesia ex Circumcisione" come una nobile matrona, immagine che nel Medio Evo verrà sostituita da quella della Sinagoga bendata.

Periodo Medievale

Il Poliakov ha esaurientemente mostrato che, fino alle

Crociate, la situazione degli ebrei in Europa è ancora in genere di serena convivenza con la popolazione cristiana.

Una brusca e sanguinosa svolta è provocata dalle masse fanatiche che si muovono disordinatamente insieme agli eserciti diretti in Terra Santa: esse sono responsabili di feroci massacri di intere comunità ebraiche in Germania, nonostante le opposizioni di Vescovi e di conti; agli ebrei veniva solo lasciata la scelta fra battesimo e martirio, e a migliaia scelsero quest'ultimo proclamando la propria fedeltà a Dio. Dal 1144 si diffonde anche l'accusa di omicidio rituale, e più tardi quella di un odioso complotto degli ebrei—maledetti perchè deicidi—contro il genere umano. Le conseguenze, specie a livello popolare, saranno gravissime: gli ebrei diventano quasi simboli del male satanico, da estirpare implacabilmente con ogni mezzo.

La Chiesa non partecipa di queste aberrazioni, tuttavia risente di questa atmosfera: così, nel 1215, il Concilio Lateranense IV impone agli ebrei il "segno" distintivo.

Il secolo XIII–XIV vede però a Roma una comunità ebraica particolarmente fiorente, e nel 1310–1311 il Concilio di Vienne decreta l'istituzione in tutta Europa di cattedre di ebraico e aramaico per lo studio del Talmud, anche se questa riforma di studi non venne mai attuata. Comunque in Spagna, Francia e Italia la collaborazione a livello culturale fra ebrei e cristiani è profonda; questa atmosfera traspare nella novella di Boccaccio (*Decamerone* I, 3) su "Melchisedèa Giudeo e il Saladino."

Il medioevo, per gli ebrei, continuerà in Europa fino alla rivoluzione francese, marcato da due eventi gravissimi: l'esilio dalla Spagna (1492) e l'istituzione del Ghetto, determinata dalla Bolla pontificia "Cum nimis absurdum" (1555), accompagnata dai roghi del Talmud, vessazioni, processi religiosi, decadimento culturale. Queste persecuzioni debbono ispirarci una seria riflessione per coglierne le cause, e certo i pregiudizi religiosi, alimentati da accese predicazioni popolari (cf.S. Bernardino), offrirono facilmente pretesti a chi cercava di trarre vantaggi politici od economici dagli ebrei insicuri e minacciati. Riconoscere gli errori di una malintesa religiosità o, peggio, del cieco fanatismo, è umile saggezza. L'intolleranza religiosa maschera spesso l'irreligiosità, e una religiosità meno attenta può essere strumentalizzata ad altri fini: non mancano esempi nella Scrittura, e Gesù perciò esorta alla conversione del cuore, per adorare il Padre "in spirito e verità" (Jv 4,23).

Periodo Moderno e Contemporaneo

Gli ebrei dopo l'emancipazione sono attivamente presenti in campo scientifico, letterario, filosofico, politico, economico, artistico, nelle nazioni nate nell'epoca moderna, mentre fioriscono correnti favorevoli al ritorno alla "terra," in Palestina, ispirate da motivi religiosi o puramente politico-ideologici.

Nello stesso periodo, invece, la Chiesa sperimenta una stagione di non facili rapporti con il nuovo ordine sociale e la nuova mentalità. Possiamo forse pensare che se ci fossero state relazioni fraterne fra cristianesimo ed ebraismo non avremmo sperimentato certe dolorose incomprensioni fra Chiesa e mondo moderno?

Nuovi *pogrom* si susseguono in Russia sul finire del secolo XIX: anche qui fanatismo, intolleranza e pregiudizi religiosi si uniscono con le motivazioni politiche. Tragico e indiscrivibile è l'orrore dello sterminio degli ebrei d'Europa programmato con sistematica e assurda ferocia dai nazisti: questa nuova tirannide statolatrica sfruttava abilmente i secolari pregiudizi antiebraici diffusi a livello popolare. All'orrore si unisce in noi un vivo dolore, se consideriamo quanta indifferenza, o peggio, quanto astio separava spesso ebrei e cristiani in quegli anni; ma va pure ricordato l'eroismo di molti per soccorrere gli ebrei perseguitati.

Pio XI stava preparando una enciclica di condanna dell'antisemitismo, e solo la morte interruppe questo progetto.

Il dopoguerra vede il risorgere di uno stato "ebraico" con una propria autonomia e con caratteri democratici, per il quale la maggior parte degli ebrei pregano salutandolo quale "inizio della fioritura della Redenzione." La Chiesa si pone in atteggiamento di dialogo con il mondo, attenta a discernere i "segni dei tempi," in spirito di servizio all'umanità ancora lacerata da gravi contraddizioni. Il Concilio Ecumenico Vaticano II esprime tutta la passione della Chiesa per la salvezza del mondo e per la pace e ripudia l'accusa di "deicidio" e "l'insegnamento del disprezzo" (Jules Isaac) nei riguardi degli ebrei, sottolineando al contrario il grande patrimonio comune di fede nel mistero del piano salvifico voluto da Dio (*Nostra Aetate*, n.4). I segni di queste grandi aperture, come la visita di Giovanni Paolo II nella Sinagoga di Roma o la grande preghiera per la Pace in Assisi, sono sotto gli occhi di tutti noi. Proprio quest'anno, 2 maggio, il Santo Padre proclamerà beata una figlia del popolo ebraico che ad Auschwitz si è offerta con Cristo "per la vera pace" e "per il suo popolo."

Sguardo Teologico

Queste brevissime note storiche vogliono solo essere uno stimolo per mostrare quanto sia necessaria una sempre più accurata analisi critica del passato: la Chiesa sarà sempre grata a chi le offrirà un serio contributo culturale, prezioso per interpretare la storia alla luce dei principi di fede.

Vorrei solo indicare alcuni di questi principi, che un faticoso e talora doloroso cammino storico ha fatto emergere nella riflessione teologica e nei documenti applicativi del Concilio emanati dalla "Commission for the Religious Relations with the Jews," istituita nel 1974, di cui fui per diversi anni consultore. Questo cammino deve continuare, e la teologia è invitata, con più insistenza, dopo la *Shoah* a "confrontarsi con la storia e l'esperienza di fede degli ebrei ad Auschwitz" (J. B. Metz).

Le Radici Comuni che Ci Rendono Fratelli

Giovanni XXIII, il Concilio, Paolo VI (Enciclica *Ecclesiam Suam*), Giovanni Paolo II, cioè tutto il recente magistero universale della Chiesa, così come i documenti di Conferenze Episcopali e di singole chiese locali, concordemente ribadiscono che Chiesa e popolo ebraico sono legati da un profondo vincolo "a livello della propria identità religiosa," un vincolo che non distrugge anzi valorizza le due comunità e i singoli membri nelle loro specifiche differenze e nei lor valori comuni.

Vorrei qui tentare solo un rapido sommario non esaustivo di questi elementi comuni, secondo la Scrittura e la Tradizione.

1. La fede di Abramo e dei Patriarchi nel Dio che ha scelto Israele con irrevocabile amore;

2. La vocazione alla santità: "Siate santi, perchè io sono Santo" (Lev 11,45) e la necessaria "Conversione" (*Teshuvah*) del cuore;

3. La venerazione per le Sacre Scritture;

4. La tradizione di preghiera, tanto privata quanto pubblica;

5. L'obbedienza alla legge morale espressa nei Comandamenti del Sinai;

6. La testimonianza resa a Dio nella "Santificazione del Nome" in mezzo ai popoli, fino al martirio se necessario;

7. Il rispetto e la responsabilità nei confronti di tutto il creato, l'impegno per la pace e il bene dell'umanità intera, senza discriminazioni.

E tuttavia questi elementi comuni sono intesi, vissuti nelle due tradizioni con modalità profondamente differenti.

Differenze

Questi profondi valori che ci uniscono non sopprimono certe le caratteristiche che ci distinguono e che vanno esposte con altrettanta chiarezza, a fondamento di un onesto dialogo: in Gesù morto e risorto noi cristiani adoriamo il Figlio unigenito prediletto del Padre, il Messia Signore e Redentore dei popoli tutti che ricapitola in sè tutto il creato. Tuttavia con questo atto di fede noi riteniamo di confermare i valori ebraici e la Torah, come afferma Paolo (Rom 3,31). La nostra esegesi dinamica ed escatologica delle Scritture ci pone in una linea di continuità-diversità con la interpretazione ebraica.

Rimane il dovere urgente, per la riflessione ecclesiologica, di chiarire come le due comunità dell'Alleanza, Chiesa e Sinagoga, non si confondano pur partecipando di una missione comune a servizio di Dio e dell'uomo. S.Ambrogio, parlando dei rapporti fra le due "Alleanze" (Vecchio Testamento-Nuovo Testamento) parla di "rota intra rotam" e l'immagine è attraente. S.Paolo aveva usato l'immagine viva dell'ulivo buono e dell'oleastro.

La storia passata, d'altra parte, ci ha mostrato quanto danno questa missione ha patito a causa della eccessive e talvolta tragiche contrapposizioni polemiche che ci hanno divisi.

Una Speranza e un Fine Comune

Non solo le radici e molti elementi del nostro cammino sono comuni, ma anche la mèta finale può essere espressa e intesa in termini di convergenza. La speranza nel futuro messianico, quando Dio solo regnerà, Re di giustizia e di pace; la fede nella risurrezione dei morti, nel giudizio di Dio ricco di misericordia, la redenzione universale, sono temi comuni per ebrei e cristiani. Le stesse diversità che su questi punti ci contraddistinguono potrebbero essere viste, forse più spesso che non sembri, anche nel senso di una reciproca complementarità.

Collaborazione ed Emulazione Fraterna

Sul fondamento di questi principi, che certo andranno attentamente studiati e approfonditi, appare già ora e apparirà credo più chiaramente come esista un ampio spazio per un doveroso impegno comune, specialmente a livello spirituale, etico, nel campo dei diritti umani e nell'assistenza a popoli e persone bisognosi di solidarietà per la pace e lo sviluppo integrale dell'umanità. Sempre più spesso appariranno anche punti di contatto affini che allargheranno queste responsabilitá comuni ad altri credenti, in particolare ai fedeli dell'Islam.

A questo proposito, l'impegno comune di ebrei, cristiani e musulmani per una soluzione equilibrata che porti la pace "giusta e completa" (Giovanni Paolo I, 6/IX/78) a Israele, al popolo palestinese e al Libano, si fa sempre più urgente. Gerusalemme è come il centro e il simbolo di questi comuni valori religiosi, storici, etici e culturali, che debbono essere armonicamente composti e rispettati.

Come alla vista di Gerusalemme, Gesù pianse "affinchè ottenesse il perdono per le lacrime del Signore" (S. Ambrogio, *De Paenitentia*, I.ii), così noi tutti speriamo che da Gerusalemme sgorghi un fiume di pace e un torrente di perdono e di amore.

DISCUSSION

Cardinal Carlo Maria Martini could not attend the symposium in Philadelphia, so there was no discussion with him. Moreover, his paper arrived after the conference, hence it could not be discussed or cited in the other papers or discussions. I am certain that all participants would have applauded his main insights and arguments. It is encouraging to hear a leading scholar and cardinal in the Roman Catholic tradition speak in an openly and informed manner about the distressing anti-Judaisms in the New Testament, and the need to build bridges among Jews and Christians today. [J. H. C.]

CHAPTER TWO

Exploring Opportunities for Rethinking Relations among Jews and Christians

James H. Charlesworth

Introduction

We can no longer ignore the barriers that isolate Jews and Christians from one another. No one can rest unconcerned about this vexing problem, which often entails portraying the other as the feared one or even the hostile enemy. To become informed about the shared origins of Judaism and Christianity is to gain an awareness of gross injustices committed over the course of almost two millennia. This awareness demands a commitment to change. There is no alternative. Either one becomes enlightened and morally focused or one stumbles in the night of ignorance and moral decadence.

Concerning the Prejudice of Scholars

Biblical scholars must not hide from the tensions, misunderstandings, and fears that continue to separate Jews and Christians. To plead for the need to be objective in all endeavors may at first seem warranted, because of a continuing history of excessive emotion and subjectivity; but not all endeavors are to be judged by such scholarly norms. There is no refuge from confrontation with our past. It is no longer acceptable to ignore the unfortunate fact that at times the paradigms of biblical criticism have been founded on unexamined "anti-Semitisms," and even on a pervasive unconscious anti-Jewish mentality. For example, only recently have biblical scholars become shocked that Emil Schürer's *A His-*

tory of the Jewish People in the Time of Jesus Christ (1898) is, in
places, almost as anti-Semitic—that is anti-Jewish[1]—as H. St.
Chamberlain's *Foundations of the Nineteenth Century* (1910),
which was a virtual Magna Carta for the Nazis. While discussing the piety of Jews during Jesus' time, Schürer claimed that
Jewish prayer "was bound in the fetters of a rigid mechanism,
vital piety could scarcely be any longer spoken of. This fatal
step had also been already taken by Judaism in the time of
Christ."[2] He even went on, in what was once thought to be a
parade example of historical and objective reporting, to conclude that the *Shema* (Hear, O Israel) and the *Shemoneh Esreh*
(Eighteen Benedictions) were by the time of Jesus "made the
subjects of casuistic discussions, and their use was thereby de-
graded to an external function."[3] These words from the zenith
of nineteenth-century scholarship usher us into the century
that saw the rise of both the historical-critical method—
now used by all biblical scholars—and of the neologism "anti-
Semitic."

Far too often theologians and scholars have been merely
learned rather than erudite, subjective rather than objective,
and anti-Semitic rather than historically sensitive to the Jewish
roots of Christianity. To refuse to participate in the dialogue towards better relations among Jews and Christians is not the
mark of an objective biblical scholar; it is a tacit commitment to
the impossibility of being scholarly, and an assent to prejudicial
methods and warped conclusions.

This short essay attempts only to explain why a new basis
has appeared for rethinking the relations among Jews and
Christians. The basis is seen thanks to an improved perception
of the origins of Rabbinic Judaism and Earliest Christianity.

A Paradigm Shift in Understanding Origins

A new understanding of Early Judaism (ca. 250 B.C.E. to 200

---

[1]See J. H. Charlesworth, "Neologisms: Their Origins—'Anti-Semitism,'" in *Explorations: Rethinking Relationships Among Jews and Christians*, 1.1 (1987) 4. For the conveni-
ence of those interested in reading further on the points about to be made, I have
added brief notations to reliable works, usually in English.

[2]E. Schürer, *A History of the Jewish People in the Time of Jesus Christ*, trans., S. Taylor
and P. Christie (Edinburgh, 1898) division 2, vol. 2, p. 115.

[3]*Ibid.;* here Schürer notes his indebtedness to Weber's *System der altsynagogalen palä-
stinischen Theologie*, pp. 40–42.

C.E.) is now appearing in scholarly publications. The old view of first-century (C.E.) Judaism was simplistic: The Jewish religion was centered in Jerusalem, with the Temple as the magnet of world Jewry. From this citadel emanated the proper interpretation of the Torah (the embodiment of God's will, Law). The Jewish religion was affirmed to be immune from pagan influences. It was monolithic, orthodox, and normative; and diversity within the system was expressed through only four sects, two of which (the Sadducees and the Pharisees) belonged to "normative Judaism."

Now this historical reconstruction has collapsed. The discovery of many early Jewish documents—especially the Dead Sea Scrolls[4]—as well as the renewed appreciation of the Old Testament Pseudepigrapha,[5] the refined study of the Mishnah and the recognition of its post–second-century editorial nature,[6] the startling achaeological discoveries relating to pre-70 Palestine, especially in and near Jerusalem,[7] and the improved methodology for studying Early Judaism have cumulatively caused a major paradigm shift. There was not one ruling, all-powerful group in Early Judaism; many groups claimed to possess the normative interpretation of Torah. Jerusalem and the Temple were not only a centralizing force; they also spawned and sustained other varieties of Judaism, most notably the Samaritans and the Essenes. Palestinian Judaism was neither dormant nor orthodox; it was vibrantly alive, and impregnated by the most recent advances in technology, art, literature, astronomy, cosmology, calendrical chronology, and symbolism in all the contiguous cultures. There were not four sects, but at least a dozen groups and many subgroups. We should not think in terms of a monolithic first-century Palestinian Judaism; perhaps we should attempt to contemplate a post-70 Pharisaic type of Judaism and a variety of pre-70 "Judaisms."

[4]For popular and reliable accounts, see the following recent publications: J. C. Trever, *The Dead Sea Scrolls: A Personal Account* (Grand Rapids, Mich., 1977); P. R. Davies, *Qumran* (Grand Rapids, 1982); M. A. Knibb, *The Qumran Community* (Cambridge, New York, 1987). Qumran is the name of the place in which the Dead Sea Scrolls were probably copied or composed.

[5]J. H. Charlesworth, ed., *The Old Testament Pseudepigrapha*, 2 vols. (Garden City, N.Y., 1983–85).

[6]See the numerous works by J. Neusner, especially his *Judaism: The Evidence of the Mishnah* (Chicago, 1981).

[7]See N. Avigad, *Discovering Jerusalem* (Nashville, 1983).

After 70 C.E., and the destruction of Jerusalem by the Romans, there was little variety in Judaism; basically, only a Hillelite-dominated Pharisaism survived, and—especially after the defeat of the pseudo-Messiah Bar Kokhba in 135—it was drained of its earlier apocalyptic fervor. Before 70, Judaism was characterized by rich diversities and creative responses to God's will embodied in Torah. One of the Jewish groups was the Palestinian Jesus Movement, based in Jerusalem, loyal to Jesus of Nazareth, and developing boundaries that clarified how and why its understanding of Torah was appreciably different from all the other Jewish groups.

The Palestinian Jesus Movement—strictly speaking—came to an end with the catastrophe of 70. Only after 70 can one talk about "Christianity" and the shift of this religion's central base from burned Jerusalem to imperial Rome, which had been central to Paul's westward missionary activity and became the geographical center of the religion by the end of the second century C.E. The new religion gradually, not immediately as once was thought, separated itself from its Jewish roots. Along the way Jewish documents were transported to our day with massive additions by Christians; a good example of such edited works is the *Martyrdom and Ascension of Isaiah*, which is composed of separate Jewish and Christian documents.[8]

Nineteenth-century scholars would be astounded to learn that today we are more reluctant to judge some documents as either originally composed by a Jew but later expanded by a Christian, or composed by a Christian but extensively based on early Jewish traditions. The best example is the *Testaments of the Twelve Patriarchs*.[9] Is this document essentially a Jewish or a Christian work? The debate is unresolved. For our present purpose the dead-end is in fact a display window—we see through this debate and this document the shared origins of Christianity and Judaism.

Long ago we learned that the noun *Meššiaḥ*—"the Anointed One" or "Christ"—appears in both Jewish *and* Christian writings, and that it is only the interpretation and application of

---

[8]For a translation and introduction, see Charlesworth, *Old Testament Pseudepigrapha*, vol. 2.

[9]For a translation and introduction, see Charlesworth, *Old Testament Pseudepigrapha*, vol. 1. Also, see M. de Jonge, ed., *Studies on the Testaments of the Twelve Patriarchs* (Leiden, 1975).

the title "Messiah" that clarifies whether a document is to be classified "Jewish" or "Christian." Usually there are no keys that can be used to swing open the door of the debate. Recently, however, we have discovered that the belief in the *return* of the Messiah is not only a Christian but also a Jewish concept. Well known is the early Christian belief that Jesus will return to earth as the triumphant Messiah, an event usually referred to as the "parousia" (after the Greek term, meaning "presence," "coming," or "advent," used in this connection in *Matthew*, the Pauline writings, and some later epistles).

Now we have learned that some early Jews believed that the Messiah had been on earth with Adam in Paradise and that he would return again here on earth sometime in the foreseeable future. For example, R. H. Charles, the greatest expert on the Old Testament Pseudepigrapha at the beginning of this century, translated *2 Baruch* 30:1 as follows: "And it shall come to pass after these things, when the time of the advent of the Messiah is fulfilled, that He shall return in glory."[10] His comment on this passage was as follows: "This seems to mean that after His reign the Messiah will return in glory to heaven."[11] Perhaps Charles was correct, but his interpretation may well miss what the author had intended. Note the new translation of *2 Baruch* 30:1, which is rendered by A. F. J. Klijn as follows: "And it will happen after these things when the time of the appearance of the Anointed One has been fulfilled and he returns with glory, that then all who sleep in hope of him will rise."[12] Like other preexistent divine agents of redemption, especially Melchisedek (cf., *2 Enoch*),[13] the Messiah will return to earth to restore God's fallen creation. The perspective is clearly Jewish; the Christian concept of the parousia of Jesus may be linked with it. The origins of Judaism and Christianity are indisputably intertwined. To study only one in isolation is to lose the potential of understanding it. One search informs us of the other; the mutual benefit is enormous.

To study early Jewish liturgy is to study the origins of Chris-

---

[10]R. H. Charles, ed., *The Apocrypha and Pseudepigrapha of the Old Testament in English* (Oxford, 1913; republished many times) vol. 2, p. 498.

[11]*Ibid.*

[12]Charlesworth, *Old Testament Pseudepigrapha*, vol. 1, p. 631.

[13]For a translation and introduction to *2 Enoch*, see Charlesworth, *Old Testament Pseudepigrapha*, vol. 1.

tian liturgy. It is misleading to state only that the disciples of
Jesus were Jews; it is more helpful to clarify that all of his disciples were Jews, and that the liturgy used by Jesus and his earliest followers was Jewish.

An early hymnbook, the so-called *Odes of Solomon*,[14] has been
identified as Jewish by some renowned scholars, but as Christian (or Jewish Christian) by equally well-trained specialists. An
alleged Jewish hymnbook has been discovered embedded in
the *Apostolic Constitutions,* which dates from the late fourth century C.E. This manual for training and initiating converted
Christians seems to contain earlier Jewish synagogal prayers
which have been revised by a Christian. This discovery is remarkable; it demonstrates that at the time when anti-Judaism
had clearly arisen in the church, Jewish prayers were being
added to a major Christian catechism.

With the renewed appreciation of early Jewish literature
comes the recognition that some documents once elevated as
"Christian" are now admitted to be "Jewish." The most famous
examples are the *Prayer of Manasseh* and *Joseph and Aseneth.*[15]

Surely one of the most sensational developments in the field
of Early Judaism and Christian Origins is the recognition that
a book called the *Parables of Enoch* (1En 37–71)[16] is not a third-
century Christian composition, as most New Testament scholars tended to assume for almost the last quarter of a century.[17]
It is characteristically Jewish; and it probably was written by a
Jew in Palestine sometime before the destruction of the nation
in 70 C.E. This astounding conclusion is now advocated by most
international experts on this work (namely Isaac, Black, Nickelsburg, Stone, Collins, Uhlig, Suter, and VanderKam).

What remains to be explored is the following: A main reason
for dating this book, the *Parables of Enoch,* long after the New
Testament documents is the claim that its author apparently
knew and drew upon the New Testament writings. Now, how-

---

[14]For translations and introductions, see Charlesworth, *Old Testament Pseudepigrapha,*
vol. 2, and H. F. D. Sparks, ed., *The Apocryphal Old Testament* (Oxford, 1984).

[15]Translations and introductions to these documents are found in Charlesworth, *Old
Testament Pseudepigrapha.*

[16]For a translation and introduction, see Charlesworth, *Old Testament Pseudepigrapha,*
vol. 1.

[17]See the report of the discussions in the SNTS seminars in Tübingen and Paris:
J. H. Charlesworth, *The Old Testament Pseudepigrapha and the New Testament* (Cambridge,
1985, 1987).

ever, there is an obvious need to investigate the extent to which
the New Testament authors were themselves significantly influenced by the ideologies, terms, and symbols preserved only
or primarily in this pre-70 Jewish work.

It should now be clear that the study of Early Judaism and
Christian Origins has been revolutionized. Truly amazing
changes have occurred in this field.

Jewish and Christian Origins

The old—and in some circles still dominant—view of Christian Origins is unacceptable. It portrayed (or portrays) Christianity as a Greek-oriented religion clearly distinct from
Judaism, the latter being understood solely in terms of Rabbinic
Judaism. The origin of each religion was seen as radically different. Jewish and Christian scholars tended to assume that
Judaism originated in about the fifth century B.C.E., shortly
after the Babylonian Exile, and that Christianity developed out
of this religion but soon became dominated by Greek thoughts
and norms.

In no way supportive of this fabricated history is the fact that
many citizens of the late (post-325 C.E.) Roman Empire, especially Christians, saw Christianity as partially derivative from
but—and the emphasis was put on discontinuity—distinctly
superior to Judaism. This view of Christian Origins is as misleading as portraying pre-70 Judaism in terms of post-135
Judaism: it is retrospective—reading back anachronistically
into an early period a specific type of religion that originated
only in a later period.

This distortion of history arose from the repeated failure to
ask honest questions about Jewish and Christian Origins;
from an uncritical reading of the Mishnah, as if it were un-
edited records of the Jewish world antedating the destruction
of 70 C.E.; from an ignorance of the Old Testament Apocrypha
and Pseudepigrapha and of the New Testament Apocrypha
and Pseudepigrapha; and from a failure to recognize the open
canon of early Christians. Christian portraits of this history
were also marred by Christian triumphalism and sporadic outbursts of anti-Judaism.

Now, we know that Rabbinic Judaism and Early Christianity
are twin offspring of the same religion, Early Judaism.[18] Both

religions developed at the same time (the first and second centuries C.E.) out of the same geographical region (primarily Palestine—which, however, was not isolated from but in contact with and enriched by the great surrounding cultures).

I am convinced that Rabbinic Judaism developed out of one group in Early Judaism, namely the Pharisees, especially the branch influenced by Hillel, but drained, especially after 135, of the earlier apocalyptic eschatology that had influenced many early Pharisees. Christianity, on the other hand, developed out of many groups in Early Judaism, especially the Hillelite branch of Pharisaism, but with profound indebtedness to Jewish apocalypticism.

Today it is necessary to emphasize two insights: (1) both modern Judaism and Christianity have the same "mother," Early Judaism; (2) Early Judaism was far more varied, rich, and cosmopolitan than can be discerned by looking only at Rabbinic Judaism and post–second-century Christianity.

Since they have the same parent, we must again stress that the origins of Rabbinic Judaism and Early Christianity must not be studied in isolation. To study the origins of Judaism is to take seriously the references to and indebtedness to Early Judaism preserved in the intracanonical and extracanonical Christian documents. To study the origins of Christianity is to examine intently and sympathetically the origins of Rabbinic Judaism and the full world of Early Judaism. In a profound sense both Rabbinic Judaism and Earliest Christianity not only preserve but are a part of Early Judaism. Christianity, especially in the late first century when the Gospels were written, was clearly influenced by post-70 Judaism; but it is far from clear whether post-70 and pre-200[19] Judaism was influenced by Christianity.

To speak analogically about a "mother" and her "offspring" has its limitations, as do all analogies. For fruitful dialogues among Jews and Christians, however, it is essential to acknowledge the common origin of Judaism and Christianity: Early Judaism.

Building upon this base we can continue by exploring the im-

---

[18]See A. F. Segal, *Rebecca's Children: Judaism and Christianity in the Roman World* (Cambridge, Mass., London, 1986).

[19]Around 200 C.E., Rabbi Judah the Prince compiled the Mishnah.

plications of the emerging new views of Jesus, of Paul, of the *Gospel of John*, and of the *Gospel of Matthew*. These subjects, examined together, focus our attention on the major areas that have thus far undermined an honest, informed, and promising dialogue among Jews and Christians.

Jesus

An old implicit view of Jesus was articulated by H. St. Chamberlain at the end of the nineteenth century. He contended that Jesus was not a Jew, that he had been born in Galilee where there was not a pure race of Jews, that he was in fact an Aryan, and that he was rejected by and eventually killed by the Jews.

The old explicit view of Jesus recognized that he was by birth a Jew, but many Jewish and Christian scholars—for different reasons—went on to enunciate that he was really very different from his fellow Palestinian Jews. He was unique. Jews viewed this uniqueness as pejorative; he was peculiar. Christians went on to stress his unique and divine qualities to such an extent that all connections with history, his humanity (despite being affirmed explicitly in the great creeds of the Church), and his Jewishness were usually, at least tacitly, severed.

Today there is among scholars, both Jewish and Christian, of all denominations, a universal recognition that Jesus was a Jew.[20] No qualifications are added. He was a devout Jew who fit right into the religious scene of pre-70 Palestinian Judaism. For at least two decades, however, specialists have endeavored in vain to place Jesus within one of the four famous "sects" of Judaism.

S. G. F. Brandon incorrectly concluded that Jesus was linked in some way with the Zealots, who sought to kill Romans and free "the Land" from pagans.[21] Jesus was a revolutionary; but his revolution was not focused on this world's political struc-

---

[20]See the forthcoming volume in this series, titled *Jesus' Jewishness*.

[21]S. G. F. Brandon, *Jesus and the Zealots* (New York, 1967).

[22]See O. Cullmann, *Jesus and the Revolutionaries*, trans. G. Putnam (New York, 1970), and M. Hengel, *Victory over Violence: Jesus and the Revolutionists*, trans., D. E. Green (Philadelphia, 1973). More recently, R. A. Horsley has argued that the Zealots, as a "sect" within Early Judaism that was militantly opposed to Rome, never existed, and that Jesus neither was a pacifist nor advocated violence: ". . . there is no evidence that Jesus himself advocated, let alone organized, the kind of armed rebellion that would have been necessary to free the society from the military-political power of the Roman empire" (p. 321). See Horsley, *Jesus and the Spiral of Violence* (San Francisco, 1987).

tures.[22] His actions in the Temple were zealous for purity and righteousness, and perhaps denoted the need for restoration, but they were not the actions of a Zealot. After knocking over the tables of the money changers, he quietly withdrew from the Temple. It is now impossible, however, to link Jesus with the Zealots, because they did not appear as a major party in Judaism until the Great Revolt against Rome which began in 66 C.E. and ended with the burning of the Temple in 70.[23]

Many scholars, in the last two hundred years, have erroneously concluded that Jesus should be associated with the Essenes, and may have been an Essene. With the discovery of the Dead Sea Scrolls, beginning in 1947, this hypothesis was taken up and affirmed by some excellent scholars. Today, it is safe to report that most scholars stress not only the similarities but also the differences between Jesus and the Essenes. Jesus' association with individual Jews who were declared to be unclean by Essenes and Pharisees, and his amazingly liberal interpretations of the Torah, raise a barrier against categorizing him as an Essene.[24]

G. Vermes claims that Jesus must be seen within the Galilean group of miracle workers who were also charismatic.[25] This suggestion helps us take more seriously the complex intellectual world of Jesus' day; but it fails to do justice to the full evidence regarding the Jesus of history. There is abundant evidence that, while Jesus *was* a miracle worker, he did *not perceive* himself primarily as a miracle worker. First and foremost he presented himself as one who had been called to declare and proclaim the nearness of God's Rule (the Kingdom of God). His early followers also did not portray him as a miracle worker, but as "the Messiah" or "Son of God," as we know from studying the *Gospel of Mark*.

E. P. Sanders wisely attempts to see Jesus within the dynamic world of Early Judaism.[26] He concludes that Jesus should be seen as one who was influenced by the theology of restoration presumably prevalent in Palestinian Judaism, and that he attempted to announce and initiate the restoration of

---

[23]See D. M. Rhoads, *Israel in Revolution 6–74 C.E.* (Philadelphia, 1976).
[24]For more discussion, see Charlesworth, "The Jesus of History and the Archaeology of Palestine," in *Jesus Within Judaism* (Garden City, N.Y., 1988).
[25]G. Vermes, *Jesus the Jew* (London, 1973).
[26]E. P. Sanders, *Jesus and Judaism* (Philadelphia, 1985).

them and on the Jesus tradition inherited by the Evangelists cumulatively succeed in placing Jesus within the complex context of pre-70 Palestinian Judaism, but not within one of the so-called sects. He belongs only to pre-70 Palestinian Judaism; he does not fit into post-70 Judaism or even into pre-Herodian Palestinian Judaism.

Paul

The old view of Paul was that he was, at least in some ways, an antithesis to the Jesus of history. Jesus was a Jew; Paul was a Christian. Unlike Jesus, Paul wrote in Greek, was culturally very Greek, and was not influenced by Jewish apocalypticism. Jesus was theocentric; Paul Christocentric. Jesus called Jews to prepare for God's Rule; Paul claimed that all Jews were lost and could be saved only by faith in Jesus the Christ. This old view was never so neatly articulated; but it can be found piecemeal beneath the surface as unexamined presuppositions in many publications that antedate World War II.

A new view of Paul has begun to emerge. Paul, like Jesus, is now portrayed as very Jewish.[33] Like Jesus, Paul was influenced primarily by Jewish thought; when he quoted from or alluded to Greek philosophical thought, it was to reach his Greek audience, not to alter or reveal the essential source of his thought. Thanks to the insightful work of E. Käsemann[34] and J. Christiaan Beker,[35] Paul is now seen to be significantly dependent upon Jewish apocalyptic thought and eschatology. Like Jesus, Paul is now seen to be theocentric; he is preoccupied with Christology, precisely because it was there that the big questions were being raised and where the need for reflection and development was demanded by polemical and apologetic social confrontations. The real questions raised by Paul focused on the development and alterations of Jewish thought necessitated by the life, teachings, death, and resurrection of

---

[33]The turning point may be discerned in the classic work by W. D. Davies titled *Paul and Rabbinic Judaism: Some Rabbinic Elements in Pauline Theology* (London, 1948, 1955 [2d ed.]). Also, see Davies, *Jewish and Pauline Studies* (Philadelphia, 1984).

[34]E. Käsemann, *New Testament Questions of Today*, trans., W. J. Montague and W. F. Bunge (Philadelphia, 1969); see esp. pp. 82–107, 108–37, 168–82, 188–95; Käsemann, *Perspectives on Paul*, trans., M. Kohl (Philadelphia, 1971).

[35]J. Christiaan Beker, *Paul the Apostle* (Philadelphia, 1980), and Beker, *Paul's Apocalyptic Gospel* (Philadelphia, 1982).

Jesus. Parallels to each of these can be found in Early Judaism, including the belief in the bodily resurrection of the righteous by God either sometime after death or at the time of the final judgment.

The importance of the new view of Paul as a basis for a better relationship among Jews and Christians is even more profound than just indicated. The old view portrayed Paul as one who frantically attempted to convert Jews to Christianity, as the pioneer and expert on the mission to the Jews. Now, however, a different reading of Paul is beginning to emerge.[36] Paul wrote that all Israel would be saved (Rom 11:26), he celebrated the superiority of Israel over the Gentiles (Rom 11), and he proudly confessed: "I myself am an Israelite, a descendant of Abraham, a member of the tribe of Benjamin. God has not rejected his people whom he foreknew" (Rom 11:1–2; RSV). He emphasized that his fellow Jews "are Israelites, and to them belong the sonship, the glory, the covenants, the giving of the law, the worship, and the promises; to them belong the patriarchs, and of their race, according to the flesh, is the Christ" (Rom 9:4–5; RSV).

These passages need to be given more prominence in the thorny question of a possible Christian mission to the Jews. I am convinced that this mission has been based on misinterpretations of Paul's writings;[37] moreover, conversion of Jews to "another religion" incorrectly assumes that Jesus attempted to establish a new religion different from "Judaism" to which Jews could convert.

Let me reiterate, for emphasis, and expand this crucial point. Paul is often exasperatingly unclear, unrepresentative of many aspects of Early Judaism, and even self-contradictory. A mission to the Jews should not be based on Paul's letters.[38] He

---

[36]See, for examples, the important articles by J. C. Hurd, L. Gaston, P. Richardson, E. P. Sanders, and D. Fraikin in P. Richardson, with D. Granskou, *Anti-Judaism in Early Christianity*, 2 vols. (Waterloo, Ontario, Canada, 1986).

[37]In addition to Beker's books, already cited, see the following brilliant publications: K. Stendahl, *Paul Among Jews and Gentiles and Other Essays* (Philadelphia, 1976); E. P. Sanders, *Paul and Palestinian Judaism* (Philadelphia, 1977); Sanders, *Paul, the Law, and the Jewish People* (Philadelphia, 1983).

[38]L. Gaston claims that for "Paul, Jesus was neither a new Moses nor the messiah, nor the climax of the history of God's dealing with Israel, but the fulfillment of God's promises concerning the gentiles, and this is what he accused the Jews of not recognizing" (p. 66). See Gaston's "Paul and the Torah," in A. T. Davies, ed., *Antisemitism and the Foundations of Christianity* (New York, 1979).

never knew that his letters would be canonized, scrutinized, and taken as if they represented his ultimate treatises. Not even the *Letter to the Romans* is free from the contingencies that helped shape Paul's thought. I am convinced that to continue to use Paul to promote a mission to convert the Jews is unrepresentative of Paul (and Jesus) and borders on a fanatical attempt to assume God's own role (theodicy).

Two very different paradigms must be clarified: (1) the attempt of a first-century Jew (Jesus or Paul) to "convert" *fellow* Jews to a particular understanding *of Judaism*; (2) the attempt of a twentieth-century Gentile to "convert" Jews to a religion that has been shaped by almost two thousand years of development utilizing some non-Jewish categories and anti-Jewish polemics. The verb "to convert" has been forced to convey two appreciably different meanings. Fortunately, a new era is dawning in which these differences are taken seriously.[39]

John

A dramatic shift has occurred in the study of the *Gospel according to John*. The old scholarly view was that it was the latest gospel, and the most Greek-oriented one. Before World War II, scholars tended to argue that the author of *John* thought in Greek, was certainly not an apostle, was ignorant of Palestine, and was anti-Semitic.

A new view has emerged, thanks to the researches of many scholars, including R. E. Brown, J. L. Martyn, and D. M. Smith.[40] Portions of the *Gospel of John* may preserve some of the earliest Gospel records. This gospel is in many ways the most Jewish of the Gospels. It is not impossible that in some ways the earliest tradition in it may be related to the apostle John. The author certainly knew Jerusalem; only he describes the Pool of Bethsaida, with its five porticoes. Now this pool with its unique architecture has been discovered by archaeologists, just north of the Temple mount, precisely where the Fourth

---

[39]See *Explorations* 1.3 (1987).

[40]See especially the following: R. E. Brown, *The Gospel According to John*, 2 vols. (Garden City, N.Y., 1966–70; London, 1971); J. L. Martyn, *History and Theology in the Fourth Gospel* (New York, 1968, rev. ed. Nashville, 1979); Martyn, *The Gospel of John in Christian History* (New York, 1978); D. M. Smith, *Johannine Christianity* (Columbia, S.C., 1984).

Evangelist had situated it. It also seems to be mentioned in the Dead Sea Scroll inscribed on copper.[41]

Most important is the improved understanding of "the Jews" in this gospel. While in *Matthew, Mark,* and *Luke,* Jesus is seen warring against the demons, in *John* he is portrayed fighting "the Jews."[42] Many of the passages in *John* appear to be anti-Judaic. But recent research has shown that this gospel was produced by a group, perhaps a school,[43] of well-educated Christians, some of whom had been born Jews. In that community the Jews who "believed in Jesus" were being expelled from the synagogues in which they desired to worship and celebrate the high Jewish holidays. Only in *John* do we find the phrase *aposynagōgos,* "to be put out of the synagogue" (Jn 9:22, 12:42, 16:2), which denotes the Jews who were thrown out of the synagogue. It seems, therefore, that the hostile portrayal of the Jews in *John* was occasioned by a harsh social situation: Jews levelling invectives at other Jews. *John* emerges out of a historical situation marred not by non-Jews versus Jews, but by some Jews fighting with other Jews. If this is an accurate perception, as many specialists on *John* now conclude, then it is misleading to base a Jewish-Christian dialogue on a document that is the byproduct of a social crisis; and it is misinformed—and unjust—to justify distrust of Jews on the basis of alleged "anti-Judaisms" in the *Gospel of John.*

---

[41]See Charlesworth, *Jesus Within Judaism.*

[42]See the important discussion by J. T. Townsend on "The Gospel of John and the Jews," in Davies, ed., *Antisemitism and the Foundations of Christianity,* pp. 72–97.

[43]See R. A. Culpepper, *The Johannine School* (Missoula, Mont., 1975).

[44]Schniewind, Schlatter, Allen, Bultmann, and many other scholars before World War II contended that the *Gospel of Matthew* comes from a setting in which converted Jews were in the majority. In the early sixties W. D. Davies emphasized the Jewish setting of Matthew's Gospel; see Davies, *The Setting of the Sermon on the Mount* (Cambridge, 1964). Recently, D. Hill claimed that *Matthew* comes from "a predominantly Jewish-Christian community which lived so close to antagonistic Judaism that it needed to understand the relation of its faith and Gospel to Judaism and the best way to defend it against attack" (pp. 54-55). See Hill, *The Gospel of Matthew* (Grand Rapids, Mich., London, 1972, 1984). A similar view was developed by D. R. A. Hare, *The Theme of Jewish Persecution of Christians in the Gospel According to St. Matthew* (Cambridge, 1967).

Long ago E. von Dobschutz argued that the Evangelist Matthew was a converted rabbi. See his "Matthew as Rabbi and Catechist," which appeared in 1928 and is translated by R. Morgan and reprinted in G. Stanton, ed., *The Interpretation of Matthew* (Philadelphia, London, 1983) pp. 19–29. M. D. Goulder, under the influence of von Dobschutz, argues that Matthew was not a rabbi but a provincial scribe. See Goulder, *Midrash and Lection in Matthew* (London, 1974). See, finally, the careful advice of G. Stanton, "Matthew's Gospel: A New Storm Centre," in *The Interpretation of Matthew,* pp. 1–18.

Matthew

Less dramatic shifts have occurred in the study of the *Gospel of Matthew*.[44] Many scholars recognize that it is a very Jewish document.[45] More than any of the four Evangelists, Matthew seeks to prove that Jesus is the long-awaited Jewish Messiah, because the "messianic prophecies" in the Hebrew Scriptures were fulfilled in the life and teachings of Jesus. His attempt is at once obvious and overdone. In order to fulfill Zechariah's prophecy about the triumphal entry into Jerusalem of the ideal king (Zech 9:9), Matthew inexplicably has Jesus riding on two animals at the same time. This point is impossible to miss in the Greek; Jesus is said to have sat upon "them" (Mt 21:7). For Matthew and his community, Jesus is clearly the Messiah who was promised by God to the Jews.

Research on Matthew's use of the Old Testament and his method of interpreting Scripture has been compared with the biblical commentaries *(pesharim)* found among the Dead Sea Scrolls. Krister Stendahl, formerly dean of Harvard Divinity School and now bishop of Stockholm, in a pioneering study of *Matthew* concluded that the *Gospel of Matthew* emerged from a school which interpreted the Hebrew Scriptures in a fashion similar to that known from the Dead Sea Scrolls.[46]

Most scholars today have concluded that the Evangelist Matthew, who wrote about 85 C.E., was dependent on the *Gospel of Mark*, which was written around 70. If that is a reliable conclusion, and I think it is, then Matthew has added some striking verses that are horrifyingly anti-Jewish. Added to the Passion narrative by Matthew—and found only in his account —are these words: "So when Pilate saw that he was gaining nothing, but rather that a riot was beginning, he took water and washed his hands before the crowd, saying, 'I am innocent of this man's blood; see to it yourselves.' And all the people answered, 'His blood be on us and on our children' " (Mt 27:24–25; RSV). Matthew was eventually interpreted in such a way

---

[45]For a decidedly different opinion, that the *Gospel of Matthew* was put into its present form by a Gentile Christian group, see K. W. Clark, "The Gentile Bias in Saint Matthew," *Journal of Biblical Literature* 66 (1947) 165–72; P. Nepper-Christensen, *Das Matthausevangelium, ein judenchristliches Evangelium?* (Aarhus, 1958); W. Trilling, *Das Wahre Israel* (Munich, 1964 [3rd ed.]); G. Strecker, *Der Weg der Gerechtigkeit* (Göttingen, 1971 [3rd ed.]).

[46]K. Stendahl, *The School of Matthew* (Philadelphia, 1954, 1968).

that "all the people" denoted "all the Jews." It was incorrectly assumed that Matthew accurately preserved what had actually occurred.[47]

Scholars have shown that these verses were added by Matthew as an expression of a crisis between Matthew's group of Jews who accepted the gospel's message and other Jews who rejected as preposterous the claim that Jesus was the Messiah. These editorializing embellishments in the *Gospel of Matthew* must not be used to reconstruct what had happened around 30 C.E. in Jerusalem after Jesus' arrest.[48]

One of the major obstacles to an honest and promising dialogue among Jews and Christians can now be put aside. Jews today are not in any way guilty of Jesus' horrible death.[49] Jesus was a devout Jew, who died at the hands of Roman executioners, had many Jewish followers, and was greatly admired by other Jews. Some of the leading priests may well have been behind his arrest. The week of Passover also was accompanied by chaotic and frantically crowded conditions in Jerusalem.

In no way should any intelligent person continue to think that Jesus' blood is now on the hands of the Jews and their children. It should sicken anyone to have to write or read such a notion, especially when it should no longer be necessary. The problem, of course, is that these verses are preserved in the manuscripts of *Matthew* and it has been canonized. To write commentaries to warn against misinterpreting these words will hardly suffice; most Christians when they read the gospels assume them to be factual accounts of what happened. This legacy can be passed on only with grave trepidation. The problem must not be ignored.

The *Gospel of Matthew*, in summation, does preserve some unique traditions that are shockingly anti-Jewish; but these can

---

[47]E. Buck rightly points to the editorial additions found in these verses, and stresses that these "Matthean assertions . . . strain historical probability." Buck, "Anti-Judaic Sentiments in the Passion Narrative According to Matthew," in P. Richardson with D. Granskou, eds., *Anti-Judaism in Early Christianity*, vol. 1, p. 177.

[48]See the judicious comments by D. R. A. Hare in *Antisemitism and the Foundations of Christianity*, pp. 27–47.

[49]See the following informed works by Jewish scholars: P. Winter, *On the Trial of Jesus* (Berlin, New York, 1974 [2d. ed.]); E. Rivkin, *What Crucified Jesus?* (Nashville, 1984). There are many careful and informed studies on the trial and death of Jesus by Christian scholars; see the numerous studies edited by E. Bammel and C. F. D. Moule in *Jesus and the Politics of His Day* (Cambridge, 1984).

now be shown to have been added by Matthew in the heat of adverse social and polemical conditions in post-70 settings.[50]

Conclusion

The bridge for an honest and fruitful relationship among Jews and Christians is now being laid on these seven foundations: (1) Jewish and Christian scholars have begun to recognize the common origin of Rabbinic Judaism and Early Christianity. (2) Some early writings can no longer be categorized as either Jewish or Christian. (3) It is now recognized that Jesus was a devout Jew who lived in Palestine before the Roman destruction of 70 C.E. (4) The New Testament documents were written primarily by Jews; they should not be studied in isolation from the history of Judaism. (5) The apparent anti-Judaisms in the New Testament are usually additions to the tradition, and reflect the social hostility between two distinct Jewish groups, especially after 70. (6) Paul and most of the New Testament authors were theocentric, pro-Jewish, depended on the so-called Old Testament, and inherited from the theology of Early Judaism the great dreams of a messianic age soon to dawn. (7) The Scriptures of the early Rabbinic Jews and earliest Christians were the same—the "Old Testament" or *Tanach*; and both groups inherited the same liturgical book, the Psalms of David, and other statutory prayers now preserved in the Mishnah. Of course, Christians early added liturgical hymns and prayers that emphasized Jesus' place in the drama of salvation. The Lord's Prayer, taught by Jesus to his followers, is a very Jewish prayer. Jews and Christians alike call God "Father," praise his creation, yearn for the dawning of his will and kingdom here on earth, call for forgiveness that can come only from him, and praise his loving-kindness.

The foundation for a better relationship among Jews and Christians has been laid by the labors of Jewish and Christian historians. May bridges be constructed by all who care.

---

[50]See especially the comments and insights by E. Buck and B. Przybylski in *Anti-Judaism in Early Christianity*, vol. 1. In particular Przybylski argues insightfully for the position that the final edition of *Matthew* reflects "a predominantly Jewish Christian" community, which was in polemical relationship with post-70 Pharisaic and scribal synagogal Judaism. Hence, the anti-Judaisms in *Matthew* result from "a limited internal Jewish dispute" (p. 198).

DISCUSSION

ECKARDT: I'd like to pursue the point made by Dr. Charlesworth, that almost all the New Testament documents were written by Jews and so cannot be studied in isolation from Early Judaism. That point bears directly on the charge that sometimes is made that the New Testament is anti-Semitic. It is one thing if these were Gentile writers—then one could suppose that these Gentiles were anti-Semitic—but it is a different ballgame if one maintains that they were Jewish writers who were, as Dr. Charlesworth put it, *apparently* "anti-Semitic" yet *substantively* perhaps not. Thus this question of authorship is fundamental to the whole discussion of the New Testament and anti-Semitism.

CHARLESWORTH: The material that has been taken to be anti-Semitic or anti-Jewish is primarily in two documents, namely, the *Gospel of Matthew* and the *Gospel of John*. Those passages that have come to be regarded, especially in the past 100 years, as the most shockingly anti-Semitic and anti-Jewish were forged by the interaction of two processes: redaction of Christian traditions, the internecine strife within Judaism. [See Professer Beker's argument in the following chapter that 1 Thes 2:14–16 is a later redaction.] An example of the redaction of traditions (or editorial expansions upon earlier sources) is when Matthew adds, "Let his blood be on us and on our descendents." It is only in *Matthew*. Matthew adds it to *Mark*, and only *Matthew* has Pilate washing his hands, in effect saying, "I pass this on to you."

The other document is *John*, and we will hear a lot more about that from Professor Smith, so I won't go into detail. But in *John* we find Jesus warring against "the Jews" rather than against the demons, as had been the case in *Matthew, Mark,* and *Luke.* And only in *John* do we have *aposynagōge*, which means being thrown out of the synagogue. So again it is a very Jewish document, yet it reflects a tremendous struggle by Jews against fellow Jews. We need to remember that by this time (ca. 85) the history of Israel has come to an end. The Jews have been transported to Rome and elsewhere, and the Temple has been burned. And all this occurred in "the promised land"? I would say if you are really going to try to understand *Matthew* and

John, you should read 4 *Ezra,* which is one of the most powerful struggles with theodicy ever written.

But Dr. Eckardt is right: not only were the New Testament documents written by Jews but the most horrifyingly "anti-Semitic" material is found in sections that were redacted under the pressure of social crises—Jews versus Jews. The second point I want to make is that my experience of the study of the New Testament has almost always been in terms of the history of Christianity. No one in my circles ever asked the question, Should the New Testament writings be studied as part of the history of Judaism? I want thorough discussion of that question to take place, and I do not want the question to be resolved prematurely.

BEKER: If I may interrupt. . . . I think that once a Christian starts saying that the Messiah is "Jesus Christ," at that point dogma enters the picture and the dialogue becomes very difficult. That, it seems to me, is the central problem.

ZINN: What do you mean by the central problem?

BEKER: The concept of the Messiah was very nebulous in first-century Judaism; but once you start to make that concept very definite and the basis of a faith statement—namely, the faith statement of the resurrection—you are dogmatically asserting the Messiah Jesus Christ and you have, *in nuce,* the whole dogmatic development of Christianity.

PRIEST: It may not be a major point, but I think it is worth noting that the anti-Semitic or anti-Jewish statements in *Luke,* in particular the parables, can be explained by the shift of audience; that is, in one aspect of Jesus' public life, he was speaking to one broad group, probably the crowd, and in *Luke* the focus has been shifted—and narrowed—to the disciples. Thus the attack on the Jews and the anti-Semitism evident in many of the Lukan parables were addressed to groups of Jews who were themselves oppressed by certain segments of Jewish leadership. It is not a blanket anti-Jewishness. It is, in the first instance, a siding with the riff-raff of society against the leadership; then, when focus shifts to the disciples, it is the making of a distinction between "You Jews who are my followers" and "All other Jews." There is a shift, then, between the original reference to Jewish leaders and the later reference to Jews in general.

In *Luke* the reference is to the Jewish leadership throughout. But with the shift of audience in the parables, the distinction made is not one between Jewish leaders and Jewish people. The distinction now becomes one between Jew and Christian, as the disciples epitomize the church.

SMITH: If I may just comment on one other problem that Dr. Beker has raised—the distinct emergence of what we call Christian dogma—a related problem to keep in view, and to examine, is the emergence in the first century of communities that are distinct and new that are not synagogues. Now, this is already happening with Paul—and, of course, this is very problematic in interpreting Paul—but it may also be problematic later, in interpreting the Johannine corpus and particularly the *Gospel of John*. There is this disjuncture or splitting of communities taking place a generation later than Jesus.

BEKER: This phenomenon has always surprised me, and it is very difficult for me to visualize the scenario in *Matthew* and *John*. In one way, it seems to me, Matthew is still fighting with the synagogue across the street. The Matthean community seems to be struggling, working out its own identity in relation to the synagogue. Whether the Matthean community is already separated from the synagogue or not is very hard to say. In fact, what is the difference really between *John* and *Matthew* in this respect? The two scenarios seem very similar, except that in *John* the conflict seems to have become much more aggravated.

SMITH: Also, it is my impression that the last layer of Johannine tradition or redaction really isn't concerned with the relationship to the synagogue anymore, but solely with the internal Christian community.

BEKER: But it seems that a lot of the hostility we are talking about is similar to that seen whenever groups start to separate themselves from the mother group and start to form their own identities. Does identify formation always take place in terms of a negative stance against the mother?

FENN: I think you are asking about something that, from a sociological point of view, would be called Jewish anti-Semitism.

ECKARDT: Yes, self-hatred.

HILLERBRAND: The new group, it seems to me, needs to rationalize its existence by a negative stance against the establishment or against whatever is rejected. And, quickly scanning the centuries, I cannot really think of any exception to that. If one were not profoundly critical, one would not dissent.

BEKER: In *Matthew* it is very concrete—there is a community that still pays the temple tax, still keeps the Sabbath, and at the same time has a hostile relationship to its parents. Now, what is going on in such a community? It is very, very peculiar. In certain ways, I would maintain, the Matthean community is still almost part of the synagogue.

ZINN: Let me join the historian over here for a minute. I am a little perplexed that where we find what Dr. Charlesworth has identified for us as somehwat Jewish groups in conflict with each other, according to early Christian documents, we have to say that it is self-hatred or Jewish anti-Semitism. Second- and third-century Christians were also engaged in the process of differentiating themselves, as reflected in Irenaeus and his satire of the gnostics. Do we call that Christian self-hatred? Or look at the 16th century and later, when the left-wing Reformation tried to sort itself out with what the Swiss Mennonites did in the course of the Amish split. I think this is, as we've said, a universal phenomenon of differentiation within groups. Perhaps we are rushing to find a label for this phenomenon.

ECKARDT: I would tend to agree with Dr. Beker—we cannot say that this was a matter of self-hatred on anyone's part, but it certainly was a matter of experiencing the resurrection faith, which was a positive thing and which became the basis of Christian existence.

BEKER: See, my radical point is simply this—that once that happens, once the resurrection faith about Jesus "the Christ" becomes the criterion for what it means to be a Christian, then to what extent are you already out of the dialogue? To what extent have you really lost the grounds for a meaningful dialogue?

HILLERBRAND: I follow Dr. Beker all the way except for the last question. I would state the question raised by this dogmatization a little differently, namely, Can the faith be stated not only negatively, against what is rejected, but also positively? The creeds of the church clearly indicate that the latter is a real possibility. The Apostle's Creed talks about a triune God, talks about a son, and does not really dwell on whether that son is the Messiah. And so I must presume it *can* be stated positively. I think the historic, intriguing question is, Why did the negative cling and persist. In other words the dialogue has ended, so the Messiah doesn't really make that much sense anymore. You have credal statements that are stated quite differently, yet somehow or other this negative anti-whatever-it-is persists.

CHARLESWORTH: I want to address Dr. Beker's point. I don't like the word dogma, and I try to avoid using it. For me, it conveys all kinds of freight that I find horrifying (closemindedness and the like), and it smacks of the 19th-century triumphalist approach to Christian origins. But when you ask whether we have moved away from a Jewish dialogue with the proclamations (a) that Jesus is Messiah and (b) that he has been raised, I would answer emphatically, No, because both of those are very clearly developed paradigms for dialogue and discussion and difference within only one religion that we know of—the Jewish religion. The belief in the coming of a Messiah is a Jewish idea and that is problematic and perplexing in itself, and to claim that Jesus is the Messiah is to use Jewish norms for articulation. Moreover, the belief that God raises the individual after death or at the final judgment was *not* a uniquely Jewish idea, but it *was* a profoundly Jewish idea. As we know from the *Eighteen Benedictions,* "Blessed are you, O Lord, who raise the dead," and a very important related passage in the *Gospel of John* (chapter 11) has Martha turning to Jesus and saying, "Yes, I know that Lazarus will be raised at the end of time" (i.e., the final judgment). Jesus responds by saying in effect, No, that's not what I'm about. Jesus, according to *John* 11, raises Lazarus immediately. But I think it is a very important passage, without doubt. According to this passage, we have precious evidence that at least one of Jesus' followers already believed in the Jewish doctrine of resurrection.

SMITH: I wonder whether what Dr. Beker was saying is that the perception of reality was so altered by belief that the resurrection had already occurred, that a separation came about because of radically different perceptions of reality—perhaps determined on the basis of where humanity is on the eschatological timeline.

BEKER: That's very helpful. But let me ask Dr. Charlesworth what he means in his paper by the meaning of the verb "return." Are you saying that certain first-century Jewish groups believed not only in a preexistence of the Messiah but also a dwelling on earth of the Messiah and even a return of the Messiah?

CHARLESWORTH: What I am saying is that we used to have a very clear paradigm: if we found a passage that talked about the Messiah returning to earth, it was clearly Christian because it must be referring to the parousia of Jesus. Some Jewish documents give me the impression we have clear evidence of a belief that the Messiah was with Adam in paradise, that he was then hidden, and that he would return to the earth (see my discussion in *The Messiah*, forthcoming). In other words, if we find a passage referring to "the return" of the Messiah on earth, we can no longer say it must be Christian.

CHAPTER THREE

The New Testament View of Judaism

J. Christiaan Beker

Introduction

This paper was originally prepared for the Committee of Jewish-Christian Relations for the Presbyterian Church, of which I am a member, and which has been appointed to draw up a document on Jewish-Christian relations for the General Assembly. I submitted this paper recently to a very small group and I thought it would be helpful to present it again here and solicit your reactions to it.

One of the most terrible things in Jewish-Christian dialogue which I encounter regularly is the confusion among theologians who use the New Testament simply to collect contingent statements about the gospel and compare them to each other in order to confer normative status upon various situational statements that can be properly understood only within the particular situations in which they arose. It seems to me that as long as the Christian is not willing to take another look at what basically constitutes the authority of scripture we will not get anywhere, because the expressions of hostility about God will also receive normative status. It also seems to me that in a lot of Jewish-Christian dialogue there is a certain falseness, because we say, "Well, it really isn't all that bad," and we all say, "Shalom" and then go about business as usual.

My intent was—and is—simply to invite a radical questioning, primarily by Christians, about Christians' handling of their own scriptures in relation to Judaism.

Methodology in Jewish-Christian Dialogue

My hermeneutical perspective is guided by the following principles and insights:

1. The intention of any New Testament view of Judaism must honor the integrity of Judaism as a religion *sui generis.* Thus the dialogue must take place without false harmonizations and must not allow intellectual rigor and honesty to be compromised by Christian guilt-feelings about Christianity's anti-Semitic heritage.

2. Christian interpreters must be clear as to what model will guide them in constructing the relation between Tanakh (the Hebrew Scriptures) and the New Testament. Conciliatory gestures about the relation of the New Testament toward Judaism do not suffice when focal issues are overlooked. In Christian thought, various models—however eirenically disguised—have operated and still operate: (A) the law/gospel model; (B) the allegorical/typological model[1]; and (C) the promise/fulfillment model.

It is evident that the promise/fulfillment model has been the most prominent one in recent years. Are we, however, really convinced that the promise/fulfillment model is appropriate for Jewish-Christian dialogue today? And even if it turns out to be the normative model for some if not all of the New Testament writings, can we still work with it fruitfully in our present situation?

The Tanakh, especially in its exilic and post-exilic development, opens up two distinct ways in which Israel's tradition was appropriated. We may call them, in a rather simplified manner, the way of *wisdom and Torah* and the way of *eschatological Messianism.* The interrelation of these ways in various modalities constitutes the plurality of Judaisms in the first century C.E. However, at the time of the codification of the Mishna (ca. 200 C.E.), the interrelation of the two ways disintegrated into two separate structures of thought: (1) formative or classical Judaism chooses the way of the Torah, while suppressing the eschatological Messianic tradition, whereas (2) Christianity —now predominantly Gentile—has radically reinterpreted and transvalued its original eschatological heritage and chooses a

---

[1] See the *sensus plenior* model of Roman Catholic scholarship.

Christological protology over its original apocalyptic eschatology. Christianity consolidates and undergirds its confession of Jesus as the Christ with a Greek philosophical model so that Jesus the Messiah eventually becomes the ontological Son of God. From that point on, a dialogue with Judaism—already displaced by missionary and ecclesial strategies of suppression and vilification—becomes *intellectually* impossible.

However, there can be no doubt that the point of departure of the Christian movement is marked by the eschatological-apocalyptic movement of John the Baptist and Jesus—a movement which, because of its radicality and the implicit or explicit Messianic claims of Jesus, is of a different texture than the way of the Torah which eventually became the normative way of Judaism.

I point this out because the failure to perceive the two so different appropriations of the Tanakh tradition by Jews and by Christians in the first century C.E. hampers any meaningful dialogue in our own time.

From its first beginnings until now, Christian theology has had to do battle continuously with its own apocalyptic-eschatological provenance; and notwithstanding repressions of this modality in the history of Christian thought, the apocalyptic-eschatological beginnings repeatedly rise to the surface in Christian theology. For Judaism, this trend is much less problematic: Messianism is here "framed within the methods of an essentially ahistorical teleology."[2]

The issue of the two ways (complexly and confusedly inter-related in the Judaisms of the first century, to which the early Christian movement belongs) is important for the dialogue between contemporary Jews and Christians. It teaches us, for example, that the question of the Messiah is much less important for Jews than for Christians. In fact, there is no such thing as "*the* Messiah" in Judaism, no formal doctrine in any way comparable to Christian reflections about "the Christ." This fact shows that in Judaism Messianism functions as a *supplement* to its central concern—Israel's sanctification in obedience to the Torah.[3] And therefore, a Jewish-Christian encounter cannot, from the Christian side, impose a specifically Christological

---

[2]J. Neusner, *Messiah in Context* (Philadelphia, 1984) p. ix.
[3]See Neusner, *Messiah in Context*, pp. 227–31.

grid on the discussion, especially when the Nicene creed is the silent or explicit partner in the dialogue and the determining factor behind Christian interpretations of the Old Testament and the New Testament.

How shall we formulate *"the* New Testament attitude" toward Jews and Judaism? Inasmuch as the New Testament is a library of diverse books written for a variety of audiences on a variety of occasions, there is no single "canonical" normative answer available, however necessary it may be for the systematic and biblical theologian to present a coherent biblical picture. This fact presents an enormous problem for the Protestant Christian theologian. For Judaism, the canon is not a crucial theological problem; it is the source of the tradition, but it is continuous with the flow of the ongoing tradition and not sharply separated from it.[4] For the Protestant Christian theologian, however, the canon has an exclusive position inasmuch as it is the normative "apostolic" witness to the exclusive "once-for-all" event of Christ. This view entails an implicit dogmatic claim about the unity of the witness of the canon, notwithstanding its historical and literary diversity.

But how can such a unified claim be asserted with reference to the New Testament attitude toward Judaism? In the context of Jewish-Christian relations, the atomistic selection of New Testament texts from a diversity of books suggests to me a false harmonization of the New Testament witness and a false assumption about the essential unity of Scripture. Are those engaged in present-day Jewish-Christian dialogues sufficiently aware of this issue?

Whatever constitutes the *coherence* of the New Testament witness with respect to God's revelation in Christ, soteriology, anthropology, ecclesiology, etc., there exists no such coherent view with respect to its relation to Judaism. We recognize that the confrontation between the Christian movement and Judaism in the New Testament is dominated by *contingent situational factors*, such as the search for a Christian identity apart from the synagogue, and Jewish accusations and polemics against the earliest Christians. For Christians today, the crucial question is whether, in their present theological reflections on Judaism, they shall accord normative canonical status to those

---

[4]Witness the confluence of the written and oral traditions.

contingent factors. A false literalism threatens to collapse the coherent-normative elements of the gospel into its contingent expressions, thus elevating those contingent expressions to a normative canonical status. Such a view—whether explicitly or implicitly held—compels well-intentioned Christian partners in the dialogue to "soften up" in a superficial manner the obviously anti-Jewish sentiments of the New Testament.

In other words, a sensible Jewish-Christian dialogue depends on a crucial *theological* decision: Where do we locate the authority of scripture? Only in its coherent-normative view of the gospel, or in its contingent-contemporaneous expressions as well? The Christian theologian, then, must face this issue: Does not our theological situation today compel us to recognize clearly the anti-Semitisms not only of the Christian tradition but also of the New Testament itself? And further, in recognizing them, to ask whether they are in any way commensurate with the essential coherence of the gospel, that is, with the revelation of God's grace and welcome in Christ to a warped human condition which embraces both Jews and Gentiles, both Jews and Christians?

Thus the task of the Christian theologian with respect to "the Jewish question" is a foundational task. If we freely *criticize* Christian *tradition* in terms of its response to Judaism, can we *exempt* the *New Testament* from that critique? And do not we, too, often resort to an artificial rescue mission which amounts to intellectual dishonesty, artificially softening the clearly anti-Jewish statements of the New Testament rather than coming to terms with them?

The New Testament Canon Apart from Paul

Before focusing on the Pauline witness, I offer some general observations about other New Testament witnesses.

A total of around fifteen authors produced the twenty-seven books of the New Testament. It is interesting to notice the significant shifts of scholarship in our century in describing first-century Judaism and early Christianity. We know today far less about first-century Judaism and early Christianity than scholars like R. H. Charles assumed at the beginning of the twentieth century. Today's recognition of the plurality of Judaisms goes hand-in-hand with the recognition that most New Testament authors were not Gentiles (though that was widely assumed earlier) but were Jewish-Christians of an indeterminate type. The author of *Luke-Acts* and the author of *2 Peter* are probably the only Gentile authors in the New Testament. In the context of our discussion it is especially important to know which of the New Testament authors show knowledge of pre-70 C.E. incipient Rabbinism. By this criterion, it seems that Paul and Matthew are the only New Testament writers who qualify.

For a fruitful Jewish-Christian dialogue, the least promising New Testament books are nine: *Matthew, Mark, Luke-Acts* (2), the Johannine writings (4), and *Hebrews.* There are four books that have little or nothing to contribute for this purpose: *Jude, James, 1 Peter,* and *2 Peter.* This leaves fourteen remaining books: Paul and the Pauline tradition (13), and *Revelation.*[5]

I call the nine books mentioned first above "least promising" because they present, for a variety of reasons, such a polemical view of Judaism that no Jew can recognize their picture in it as an authentic description.

In *John* the Jews are equated with a fallen world and its darkness. A satanic genealogy (8:44) is ascribed to them and Jesus is portrayed as a metaphysical miracle without concrete relationship to the Jewish community. *John's* Jesus is a stranger within Judaism (10:34); the true people of God are the pneumatics, who are Jesus' "own"—his "disciples" or "friends"—and they simply displace Israel as God's people. The incidental and enigmatic reference in 4:22, "for salvation is from the Jews," cannot exonerate the basic tenor of this gospel.

The structure of *Matthew, Mark,* and *Luke* impresses on the reader the final judgment of God upon the *nation* of Israel, not just its leadership. Notwithstanding the occasionally appreciative attitude of Jesus towards Pharisees, scribes, and Jews, the Synoptic gospels all climax in an acrimonious polemic against Judaism: just before the Passion story, all three have Jesus narrate the Parable of the Wicked Husbandmen (Mk 12:1–12; Mt 21:33–46; Lk 20:9–19)—an allegory of Israel's final judgment by God:

> What will the owner of the vineyard do? He will come and destroy the tenants, and give the vineyard to others. . . . And they

---

[5]I shall not here discuss *Revelation.*

tried to arrest him, but feared the multitude, for they perceived that he had told the parable against them. (Mk 12:9–12 [RSV])

And *Matthew* 21 concludes:

He will put those wretches to a miserable death, and let out the vineyard to other tenants who will give him the fruits in their seasons. (Mt 21:41; cf. also Lk 20:16 [RSV])

Matthew is indeed the manual of a Hellenistic-Jewish church that is conscious of its Jewish heritage—of Torah and Halakah —of the need to correlate in some way the traditional Torah and the messianic Torah of Jesus. However, *Matthew* is also self-conscious about the status of the church as the true Israel because Jesus and his new law have fulfilled the ancient promises.[6] *Matthew* is much more Jewish and sympathetic to the Torah than Paul, yet much more hostile in his treatment of the Jews as a people. In the crucifixion scene the "crowd" (Mt 27:15, 24) suddenly becomes "the people [of Israel]" (Mt. 27:25), so that the people of Israel as a whole become responsible for Jesus' death and verbally seal their own judgment (Mt 27:25).

The *Gospel of Luke* is marked by the increasing hostility between Jesus and the Pharisees and Sadducees which foreshadows the hour of their final condemnation.[7] The *Acts of the Apostles* reports the final doom of the Jews; the climax of the book announces that the gospel is forever denied to the Jews and now travels to the Gentiles (28:26–28), because the Jews stubbornly refuse to accept the message of Jesus and his resurrection (23:6–10).

Moreover, an interpretation of *Hebrews* which would argue that it does not really address the relationship between Jewish and Christian communities of the time, because *Hebrews* is more concerned with interpreting the Hebrew Scriptures, is a peculiar argument—notwithstanding its eirenic intent. The use of the Hebrew Scriptures is common to virtually all New Testament documents; what is at stake is the method of their use. An epistle which uses typology—if not allegory—to celebrate the uniqueness of the high-priesthood of Christ in such a way as to demonstrate the superior against the foil of the inferior,

---

[6]See the various "fulfillment" quotations in Mt.
[7]See especially Lk 19:26–27, the conclusion to the travel narrative.

can hardly please any Jewish reader. *Hebrews* 8:13 is often misinterpreted in the context of Jewish-Christian dialogues in light of statements like 10:1 and 10:9. Then it becomes clear that *Hebrews* does not operate simply on the modality of continuity/fulfillment, but also on that of discontinuity/abolition.[8]

The Pauline Corpus

With respect to "the Jewish question," the Pauline corpus provides us with the only body of material in the New Testament where the *coherence* of the gospel does not utterly contradict its *contingent* expression.

To be sure, *1 Thessalonians* 2:14-16 is a contingent polemical expression:

> . . . the Jews, who killed both the Lord Jesus and the prophets, and drove us out, and displease God and oppose all men by hindering us from speaking to the Gentiles that they may be saved— so as always to fill up the measure of their sins. (RSV)

This pronouncement of (pen)ultimate judgment upon the Jews utterly contradicts the gospel of God's ultimate mercy and glory. However, in the Pauline letters it stands as an exceptional statement; indeed it is therefore considered by many recent interpreters to be a non-Pauline interpolation.

For Paul, Israel has not only a *positive* function in *past* salvation history, but also a *positive* function in *future* salvation history. In other words, Israel's protological election by God will be confirmed by Israel's eschatological salvation. Paul's wrestling with "the Jewish question" in *Romans* 9–11 is not a nationalist survival or an appendix to his thought but an integral part of it, as the literary structure of *Romans* with its emphasis on "to the Jew first" reveals (Rom 1:16; 2:9–10). According to Paul, the position of Israel in salvation history is crucial, because:

1. There will be no final eschatological deliverance for the world without the salvation of all of Israel (Rom 11:25-26).

2. The church of the Gentiles has no authenticity or identity unless it realizes that it is "grafted, contrary to nature, into a cultivated olive tree," i.e., into Israel, "beloved for the sake of their forefathers" (Rom 11:24, 28).

---

[8]See the abolition of the first covenant in Heb 10:9.

3. The promises of God for the Gentiles become null and void, unless God's promises towards Israel become realized. In other words, the gospel cannot have any authentic validity or legitimation apart from the People of Israel, because the theological issue of God's faithfulness and righteousness determines the truth of the gospel (Rom 3:3).

This stance toward Israel is unique in the New Testament and post-apostolic literature. For Paul, Israel remains a distinct entity in the future of God's purpose and is not absorbed into the church.

But how can Israel's *priority* be maintained in the light of Paul's claim—a claim that undergirds his apostolate to the Gentiles—of the *equality* of Jew and Greek in Christ on the basis of justification by faith alone (Rom 3:28–31)? Moreover, why is Paul *negative* about Torah-keeping, as that which defines Israel, yet *positive* about Israel as God's people? How does he handle this seemingly outright contradiction?

Paul answers these twin questions in one basic theological move. The priority of Israel and the universality of the gospel can be maintained simultaneously, because they both have a *theocentric foundation*, manifested in a radical way by the Christ-event. The Christ-event, according to Paul, makes clear that Israel's priority does not lie in its empirical achievement of "covenant-keeping," but solely in God's faithfulness to His own promises, i.e., in God's grace. Because Israel has failed its own Torah in its transgressions—transgressions which, for Paul, reveal not only Israel's shortcomings, but the contrariness of its heart (Rom 10:21) and the misdirection of its zeal (Rom 10:2)—Christ is "the end of the Torah" (Rom 10:4), that is, the end of the Torah's own condemnation of Israel.

The question remains whether this answer is convincing, even on logical grounds. For how can one speak about Israel's abiding priority and authenticity, if one denies what makes Israel, that is, the Torah? To what extent then can Paul posit the continuity between *Israel* and the Gospel, when the Christ-event marks the discontinuity between *Torah* and Gospel?

Even if one grants that for Paul the Christ-event manifests God's apocalyptic judgment on humankind (on both Jew and Greek—Rom 3:9) so that henceforth all humankind must equally depend on God's mercy in Christ, where precisely does Paul locate the Jewish failure *before* the coming of Christ? *Ro-*

mans 9:30-33 seems to give a purely Christological answer, as if the Jews failed in their own past by not submitting to Christ:

> . . . Israel who pursued the righteousness which is based on law did not succeed in fulfilling that law. Why? Because they did not pursue it through faith, but as if it were based on works. They have stumbled over the stumbling-stone [i.e., Christ]. . . . (RSV)[9]

Obviously, historic Israel never eliminated "faith" from "Torah-keeping"; so "faith" in *Romans* 9:33 must refer to faith in Christ. What is so shocking about this argument is that Paul does not argue here, as he does elsewhere in *Romans* (e.g., 2:1–29), that the Jews failed in their *keeping* of the Law, i.e., by their actual transgressions. Rather, the very *striving* of the Jews to keep the Law is here under indictment. But one may ask, How can the Torah and its *mizvoth* (commandments) be kept by faith alone without "works"?

Nevertheless, it seems to me that Paul, the ex-Pharisee—notwithstanding the frequent misunderstandings and accusations by Judaism in branding him an apostate and betrayer—provides us with the most positive scenario in the New Testament for a Jewish-Christian dialogue. In Paul the coherence of the gospel (the normative claim of God's act of mercy in Christ) finds frequent and adequate expression in the contingencies of Paul's positive wrestling with "the Jewish question." As such, Paul remains for us a catalytic figure, who can sponsor important and abiding questions for a fruitful Jewish-Christian dialogue.

I say specifically "a catalytic figure," because the promise of Paul for the Jewish-Christian dialogue does not lie in a literalistic appropriation of his thought, nor even in the solutions he offers, but in the questions he poses. Paul, then, raises the hope that both Israel and the church in their separate ways may nevertheless together rejoice in the God of their destiny.

---

[9]See Isa 28:16 in Rom 9:31–33 and 10:11.

DISCUSSION

CHARLESWORTH: Dr. Beker has introduced to New Testament research the technical terms *contingency* and *coherence*. Would he please explain for us why he chose this paradigm and how he defines it? I have no problem with it, but I'm sure there are other people here who are not quite so sure.

BEKER: These terms seem to be very appealing, probably because they are such nice alliterations. But what I'm basically trying to say is that the gospel can only be a word of truth, a word of God, when that word becomes the word "on target," when it concretizes itself in the context of the actual sociological and economic conditions of real people. If scripture were simply coherent, the statement of the truth of the gospel would become mere monologue imposing itself on every human situation. If it is purely contingent, as we see in a lot of churches today, the question simply is an opportunistic one—What will the market buy, and how can I frame the gospel in such a way that it corresponds with the current cultural fads? The important thing, to me, is that the New Testament authors talk about gospel in terms of the dialectic between contingency and coherence, that although the gospel may not always be relevant to the human situation, relevance cannot be bought at the expense of the gospel's truth claim. That's what I really wanted to pursue.

PRIEST: This, I feel, may be a valid and necessary function for the so-called biblical historicist: to raise—within the context of the church rather than merely of the classroom—the historical question, "Why did Paul write this at this particular time?" Then we may ask the question, "Is it true?"—not "Is it true in terms of factual truth?"—"Is it something that transcends a time-conditioned situation and is relevant today?" Is that what you mean by the coherence of God?

BEKER: Yes.

PRIEST: So historicism does have an initial function.

BEKER: This is where I try to apply it to Jewish-Christian dialogue, because when I did that before in a Presbyterian setting, there was a terrible outrage about it. Why? Because they felt I was tampering with the authority of scripture. You see, my point is simply this: if we do not start moving with this sensitivity and methodology we will kill the Jewish-Christian dialogue in its tracks by allowing terribly anti-Jewish statements to dominate the canon. The question is, How can the people in the pew really understand that these statements are no longer "canonical"? That is the central issue. And I think that the leadership of the church has a very poor understanding of this issue, because they continue to let these canonical statements stand while attempting to soften them with various kinds of effrontery—saying, in effect, "It really isn't all that bad. . . . Jesus was a Jew, too. . . . We all know a little bit of Hebrew. . . . We kept the Old Testament, after all."

PRIEST: That is why I am so opposed to canonical criticism conceived of other than as a historical method. Canonical criticism as an extension of comparative midrash is all right, as far as I'm concerned. But when it becomes a theological issue, that is when I begin to have a problem with canonical criticism. And certainly, in the context of Jewish-Christian relations, that is an inevitable wedge.

SIKER: To me the central question seems to be, Does the coherent core of the gospel militate against the integrity of Israel apart from Christ? Scholars such as Gaston and Gager, for instance, talk about Christ coming to the Gentiles; so, for them, Christ's coming has no direct bearing on Israel. It is just how God includes the Gentiles—which seems at times to be playing fast and loose with some of what Paul says. But the central question really is whether the gospel itself militates against the integrity of Israel as a continuing faithful people of God apart from Christ. It is Israel's status apart from Christ that has provided the basis for Christianity's having historically viewed Israel as a rejected people. Right?

ZINN: Put it another way: Can Israel be Israel apart from Christ?

BEKER: That is why I raise the question about Paul: can the church be the church apart from Israel? To put it simply, I don't think a Christian can honestly look at the Jewish faith without being extremely grateful, because without the Jewish faith he would still be a pagan.

SMITH: Dr. Beker, E. P. Sanders, at the conclusion of his *Paul and Palestinian Judaism*, says something to the effect that, for Paul, there is only one thing wrong with Judaism—it's not Christianity. How do you react to that?

BEKER: I think Sanders avoids the issue with his holistic methodology. He simply sees Christianity and Judaism as two very distinct religions and he never explores why or how Christianity arose from Early Judaism(s), or what were the numerous conflictual situations. The question Sanders totally avoids is, What, on psychological grounds, was the Judaism that made Paul a "Christian"? To me it is an incredibly difficult question—unless, of course, one subscribes to a meteor-from-heaven interpretation of Paul's "conversion," to wit: Paul, a happy Jew, is just walking along and suddenly gets bumped on the head by Jesus, who says "You'd better turn around and become a Christian" or some such thing. Sanders avoids this whole question. He does not discuss it; he assumes Paul is a Christian and proceeds from there. To me, the real puzzle is: do we have to say with Luther that Paul was an unhappy Jew and that therefore when he got the aspirin of Christ he swallowed it gratefully, or do we have to say Paul was an anti-Semite who didn't realize he was a Semite until he somehow met Christ? And it seems to me a very, very difficult question. I'm still very puzzled about it. How can Paul say, on the one hand, "I was blameless under the Law," and, on the other hand, "I reach farther than my Jewish compatriots in keeping Torah"?

ECKARDT: What then is the necessity of Christianity? If Paul is a happy Jew, then Christianity is not necessary.

BEKER: Correct.

ZINN: Do you mean, in the moral and theological sense?

BEKER: Yes. On the other hand, if you hold to the psychological reductionism, it also follows that Paul hated being a Jew, so the super-ego evolved: he hated being a Jew, he hated his parents, he hated the striving—the classic Jew-in-Despair motif. Going this route, we end up with a Wandering-Jew-in-Despair notion of Paul who at some point suddenly becomes convinced in Jesus as a means of throwing this whole Judaism to the wind. That psychological explanation is also a reductionism. But in reality, I find it very, very difficult.

SMITH: Dr. Beker, I'm extremely fascinated with this question too. Would it help to state—not to solve, but to state—the question as follows: What was it in Paul's pre-conversion theological makeup that—given the Damascus road experience, whatever that was—made becoming a Christian justifiable to him theologically, as something rooted in his theological past?

BEKER: What could it have been? You see, for me, the nagging question is this: Does Paul—a Christian—really ever understand Judaism? This is a puzzle. Did he have any understanding of his own tradition, or was first-century Judaism so corrupt that he didn't realize that in authentic Judaism faith and works were inseparable? Why does he have this terrible polemic against works of the Law? These are very difficult questions to answer.

ECKARDT: Could we say he was sort of mixed up?

BEKER: Well, of course, that's a very easy way out.

ECKARDT: Well, then, what *is* the way out?

ZINN: Indeed. And where does that leave the Torah community? This brings us back to Dr. Charlesworth's question. I favor this distinction between coherence and contingency, although I think it could become too facile a device because once you make something contingent, you tend to cease to wrestle with it.

BEKER: Exactly.

ZINN: But if the coherence of the gospel really is the Christ, then what does that do to the relationship between the two traditions in an empirical sense? Where does that leave the Torah tradition?

BEKER: I don't want to suggest an end. I'm only suggesting that Paul raised some interesting questions. I don't want to simply paraphrase Paul's answer and call it ours. But it seems to me a weird inconsistency to deny Torah and be pro-People of Israel. That would be a more-than-profound theology; I would call it a dialectic—or is it simply nonsense?

SMITH: Paul sees the problem himself, doesn't he? Don't you think it bothers him a lot?

CHARLESWORTH: I want to pursue several of Dr. Beker's points. First of all, we can never have an articulation of the coherence of the gospel that is not in some way contingent.

BEKER: Correct.

CHARLESWORTH: Then the question becomes, To what extent does contingency impinge upon coherence?

BEKER: What is remarkable to me in the coherence-contingency schema, with respect to Israel and Paul, is that we expect Paul, of all people in the New Testament, to say "To hell with the Jews" and "To hell with the Torah," yet he, in the first two centuries, is the only one to sound a genuinely positive note about Israel—and for theological reasons.

SMITH: And that is what Sanders tends to play down: he rearranges the picture in a different way, yet the elements of the picture remain the same; whereas, after Paul, the elements change.

CHARLESWORTH: Would you agree with the following line of reasoning, Dr. Smith? As I read Paul, he's fascinated by two phenomena that he cannot deny and that seem to shape him as well as his thought—namely, the crucifixion of Jesus, who is obviously very unique and special for him, and the resurrection of Jesus, which is not part of his belief but part of his experience, according to his claims. This relates to the idea of coherence in Paul's life pre- and post-conversion. I see him— long before the year 30—struggling as a student under Gamaliel, saying, I can't understand suffering in the world and how the resurrection that we strive to believe in has anything to do with resolving the contingent problem in my life of suffering.

SMITH: You're talking about Paul?

CHARLESWORTH: Yes. I'm talking about Paul as a student trying to study Torah, being very sensitive about suffering and saying, I don't accept the idea that suffering can be negated by asserting that those of us who are righteous are going to be raised from the dead someday. If my scenario makes sense, then we have a continuing coherence in Paul's life and thinking that simply shifts with the contingency—his "conversion" experience—so that he can begin to relate to Jesus' suffering.

SMITH: So it is important not only that the Messiah has come, as Sanders says, but that Jesus was the Messiah.

BEKER: But in terms of suffering, Paul remains an apocalyptic theologian. It seems to me that Paul remains very much a Jew in his resolution of the problem of suffering. The suffering is not solved once and for all by the death of Christ, because death remains the last enemy.

ZINN: You talk about faith in Christ and faithful obedience to the Torah. Now, aren't those two different uses of the word *faith*?

BEKER: Yes. That's what I'm trying to say. Faith in Christ is faith in a miracle which is not evidential, unless you want to prove the resurrection. Faith in the Torah is very different—you do not have to believe in a miracle. You may have to believe in the miracle of the existence of the People of Israel, but such faith is a continuing faith*fulness* to the Torah. Once you say faith in Christ is faith in a miraculous happening which cannot be proven, then you are in a dogmatic tradition. [Many of Beker's thoughts find recent expression in his "Paul's Theology: Consistent or Inconsistent?" *New Testament Studies* 34 (1988) 364-77. J. H. C.]

CHAPTER FOUR

Judaism and the Gospel of John

D. Moody Smith

Introduction

The *Gospel of John* seems on the face of it a poor basis for Jewish-Christian dialogue. The Protestant New Testament scholar Eldon Jay Epp in 1975 advanced the thesis that

> the attitude toward the Jews that finds expression in . . . the Gospel of John coacted with the extraordinary popularity of that gospel so as to encourage and to buttress anti-Semitic sentiments among Christians from the second century C.E. until the present time. This leads to the conclusion that the Fourth Gospel, more than any other book in the canonical body of Christian writings, is responsible for the frequent anti-Semitic expressions by Christians during the past eighteen or nineteen centuries, and particularly for the unfortunate and still existent characterization of the Jewish people by some Christians as 'Christ-killers.'[1]

Similarly, the Roman Catholic theologian Rosemary Ruether characterized *John* as the gospel in which the Jews "are the very incarnation of the false, apostate principles of the fallen world, alienated from its true being in God." Moreover, "because they belong essentially to the world and its hostile, alienated principle of existence, their instinctive reaction to the revelation of the spiritual Son of God is murderousness" (Jn 8:40, 44).[2] If modern exegesis deemphasizes "the Jews" so as to understand the term to mean the unbelieving—as contrasted with the believing—mode of existence, rather than having any concrete historical referent or significance, well and good. "This indeed is . . . the only authentic way to read the antithesis between the 'believer' and 'the world' (qua 'the Jews') in *John*."[3] Theologically speaking, it is a proper reading. Nevertheless, Christians, historically, have not read *John* in this way, says Ruether, because the gospel does not, in fact, demythologize the Jews. Rather, it mythologizes the distinction between two modes of existence, the believing and authentic over against unbelieving and unauthentic, by identifying them with two historically and empirically distinct communities, the Christian and the Jewish.

Whatever may be said about *John* on this score, modern exegetes agree that it does not represent the views of Jesus or his original disciples. "Jesus was a Jew, and so were his first disciples. In fact, the earliest Christians did not think of themselves as members of a new religion separate from Judaism. Yet from the beginning Jesus and his disciples represented something new."[4] That "something new," however, was not conceived of as the end of Judaism and the beginning of something called Christianity. As to the Law, Jesus did not reject it, but set about interpreting it anew for a new day. The famous statement in *Matthew* 5:17 ("Do not think that I have come to destroy the law and the prophets; I have come not to destroy but to fulfill.") may not actually have originated with Jesus. It can reasonably be argued that on Jesus' lips such a statement would have been superfluous. He and his followers, as well as his hearers, would have assumed as much. However that may be, Jesus certainly reckoned most seriously with the Jewish belief that God had spoken, that his will was concretized in Law, and that the Hebrew Scriptures were a faithful account of his speaking.

---

[1] E. J. Epp, "Anti-Semitism and the Popularity of the Fourth Gospel in Christianity," *Journal of the Central Conference of American Rabbis* 22 (1975) 35. "Anti-Semitism," which has distinctly racial overtones, is inappropriate to describe the attitude of the Fourth Gospel, where the roots of conflict were theological and in all probability lay within the synagogue, between Jews who believed in Jesus and the majority, who did not. Nevertheless, the *reading* of *John* has contributed to the growth of anti-Semitism among Christians and others. See the excellent discussion of this matter and the entire question in R. A. Culpepper, "The Gospel of John and the Jews," *Review and Expositor* 84 (1987) 273–88, esp. pp. 282–85. Culpepper's citation of the literature is a useful bibliographical aid. Note particularly the important article by J. Ashton, "The Identity and Function of the *Ioudaioi* in the Fourth Gospel," *Novum Testamentum* 27 (1985) 40–75.

[2] R. R. Ruether, *Faith and Fratricide: The Theological Roots of Anti-Semitism* (New York, 1974) p. 113.

[3] *Ibid.*, p. 116.

[4] R. A. Spivey and D. M. Smith, *Anatomy of the New Testament*, 3d ed. (New York, 1982) p. 13.

The new thing that Jesus proclaimed was the realization of the Rule of God, certainly no novel concept. But Jesus believed that its time had come and that his mission was to proclaim that the ancient faith in God as king was becoming reality in his own mission and message. Such an expectation and faith did not, of course, negate the Law and the prophets; rather, it was understood as their proper fulfillment. The Rule of God, expressed already in his Law, was to find effectual and final fulfillment. The question of exactly how Jesus conceived this fulfillment is one that has motivated and stimulated much New Testament scholarship, but probably admits of no final conclusion. In the Synoptic Gospels and tradition the kingdom impinges upon the present and is enormously relevant to decisions people make here and now. Yet at the same time it is not an inner spiritual experience or dimension, but the reality that everyone will have to reckon with ultimately, for it will impose itself upon us.

The revival of scholarly historical interest in Jesus of Nazareth has for good reason centered upon his Jewishness, that is, upon his rootedness in the traditions of Israel. Apart from that rootedness he cannot be understood. There is, of course, a sense in which "Jewish" is an anachronistic term, and one imposed from without. It is a term that does not appear on the lips of Jesus in the Synoptic Gospels. Ancient Jews did not ordinarily understand or refer to themselves as such, except when assuming an outsider's perspective. (For example, the ancient lintel inscription from Corinth reads "Synagogue of the Hebrews.") Although the term "Jew" and the conceptualization of Judaism and Jewishness were certainly antecedent to the rise of Christianity, they have taken on a new and somewhat different significance as the two religions have separated from and interacted with one another. Nevertheless, it is not incorrect or misleading to speak of the Jewishness of Jesus as a way of indicating where he belongs historically and theologically. In one important sense, Bultmann was correct to see Jesus as a "presupposition" of New Testament theology and to place him within Judaism.[5] Insofar as Jesus may become the

---

[5]R. Bultmann, *Theology of the New Testament*, vol. 1, trans., K. Groebel (New York, 1951) p. 1: "The message of Jesus is a presupposition for the theology of the New Testament rather than a part of that theology itself."

subject matter of New Testament theology, however, scholars must take seriously that theology's Jewishness. (Possibly because of Bultmann's own modern, existentialist, and Lutheran presuppositions, he was unable to accomplish this adequately.)

The Meaning of "the Jews" in the Gospel of John

The Jewishness of Jesus shines through the Synoptic Gospels, even though they are all distinctly Christian documents, because it is enshrined in the traditions on which they draw. Those traditions, however much they may reflect—in their selection, arrangement, and editing or formulation—the interests of the early church, nevertheless enshrine the attitudes and emphases of Jesus. This fact becomes particularly clear in light of certain data of vocabulary and terminology, and especially when those data are compared with evidence from the *Gospel of John*.

In the Synoptic Gospels, there are only sixteen occurrences of the term *Ioudaios* (pl., *Ioudaioi*), "Jew(s)." They are found mostly in the passion narratives, where the Roman authorities are interested in the question of whether Jesus is the king of the Jews. Otherwise, the term rarely appears, and where it does it also, as in the passion narratives, betrays an extra-Jewish (whether Christian or Gentile) perspective (e.g., Mt 2:2; Mk 7:3). In the Synoptic Gospels' narrative of Jesus' ministry, the term "Jews" is superfluous because everyone is a Jew, unless otherwise designated, and the perspective of the narrator lies within the Judaism of first-century Palestine, or so it seems. Although modern redaction criticism has rightly emphasized the underlying, and sometimes explicit, Christian perspective of the authors, a critically innocent or naive reading of the texts sees in them a narrative of events transpiring within the world of Judaism and of the historical Jesus, as problematic as direct historical inferences from the narrative may be. It has often been observed that parties to discussion with Jesus are not called Jews, but are Pharisees, Sadducees, Herodians, scribes, disciples of John the Baptist, and chief priests. Jesus may even have had a Zealot among his disciples (Lk 6:15; Acts 1:13). Of these the Sadducees, Herodians, scribes, and Zealots do not appear at all in *John*.

On turning to *John*, we notice immediately that in contrast to synoptic usage, the Jews are spoken of quite frequently. There are seventy-one occurrences of the term in *John*, surpassed only by the eighty-odd occurrences in the *Acts of the Apostles*. (In the remainder of the New Testament, "the Jews" appears fewer than thirty times.) The preponderance of the term in *John* and *Acts* is interesting and significant. In both, disciples of Jesus (i.e., Christians) are clearly differentiated from Jews. This is not the case in the Synoptic Gospels, and not for the most part in the letters of Paul, who contrasts Jews and Greeks, not Jews and Christians. The situation in *John* and *Acts* seems almost prescient of later usage and determines the traditional Christian reading of the New Testament and understanding of the apostolic generation in ways that are not always historically felicitous.

It is fair to say that in *John* the Jews stand over against Jesus and his disciples, who are distinguished from them. Yet the Evangelist obviously knows that Jesus is a Jew (4:9) from Nazareth, the son of Joseph (1:45). His disciples, some of whom were followers of John the Baptist (1:35), were Jews as well (cf. 18:15). Despite his knowledge of the historical facts, John insists on characterizing the Jews as somehow clearly different and distinguishable from the band of Jesus and his disciples. Understandably, when Jesus tells the Samaritan woman that "salvation is of the Jews" (4:22), modern exegetes ask whether the Evangelist could have written such a thing and suggest it may be a later editorial insertion. (Just what purpose it might have served, however, is not immediately clear.) By and large, "the Jews" in *John* are the opponents of Jesus.

As such, they are quite often identified with the Pharisees (e.g., *John 9*), who appear frequently in the synoptic narratives as well. In the synoptics the Pharisees are, of course, a group within Judaism, whereas in *John* they sometimes seem to be identical with Judaism, or at least with its essence. We shall later consider the possible historical reasons for this significant difference. For the moment it is sufficient to note it and to observe that it may be significant in coming to terms with the nature and identity of "the Jews" in the *Gospel of John*. In *John* the Pharisees seem to be taking over Judaism. It is quite interesting and typical that the familiar synoptic linkage of the Pharisees to the Scribes is entirely missing from *John*. Instead, more than once the Pharisees are in league with the chief priests (7:45; 11:47). Probably they were unlikely political or religious bedfellows in the time of Jesus. Such a linkage occurs also in *Matthew* (21:45; 27:62), where a historical setting similar to *John's*, but different from Jesus' own, may be in view. It is not found in *Mark* and *Luke*, and when Pharisees and chief priests (or Sadducees) appear together in *Acts*, they are more often than not at odds with each other (Acts 5:34; 23:6-9).

In view of the prominence of the Pharisees, and their apparent identification with "the Jews," in John's Gospel it is all the more striking that they do not appear prominently in the passion narrative. True, only in *John* do the Pharisees appear in the party that goes out to arrest Jesus just before his trial and crucifixion (18:3). Yet thereafter they disappear completely (although there are Jews aplenty in the trial narratives). In this respect *John* agrees with the other gospels: despite the prominence of the Pharisees as Jesus' opponents throughout his public ministry, they do not figure in the events leading up to his execution. This striking fact is more likely a reflection of history and tradition than of the author's mentality, however, for he tends to identify the Pharisees with the Jews, who are already presented as the mortal enemies of Jesus. (Christians have long felt that "Pharisaic legalism" opposed Jesus and essentially did him in. This questionable view is encouraged by the presentation of them in *John*, but even there at the crucial point the Pharisees disappear from the scene. Jesus falls victim to Temple or priestly authorities.)

Who are these Jews? We address this question first of all from the standpoint of the phenomenology of the text. They are clearly Jewish people, but they are not all Jewish people. To begin with, Jesus and his disciples are not among "the Jews," although they are plainly Jewish. Moreover, no Galilean or Samaritan is called a Jew, except in chapter 6. That "the Jews" are residents of Judea is probably the case in most instances, but simply to translate *Ioudaioi* as "Judeans" will not do. They are both more and less than "Judeans." From *John* 9:22 one may infer that they are religious leaders exercising authority in the synagogues to which at least some followers of Jesus belonged. From *John* 12:42 the same inference may be made, except in this case the most authoritative figures are called "Pharisees." They are powerful or influential enough to exercise authority over other Jews, who are called "rulers" or "officials" of these synagogues. Particularly in view of the fact that both *John* 9:22 and 12:42 deal with expulsion from the synagogues, it is likely that the "Jews" in the one case and the "Pharisees" in the other are the same authorities. It is important to notice that they are authorities who exercise significant power over other Jewish people. At least in these contexts, "Jews" may be "Pharisees," but they are not to be identified or confused with the totality of the Jewish people.

Thus Jesus, his followers, Galileans, and perhaps Samaritans are Jewish, but they are not "the Jews." There are also people explicitly called "Jews" who are not enemies of Jesus. Prominent among them is Nicodemus, a ruler of the Jews (3:1), who keeps coming back to Jesus, speaks for him (7:50), and helps bury him (19:39). We never read that he believed in Jesus, though some Jews (or Pharisees) do (9:16; cf., 8:31). The people who mourn Lazarus with Mary and Martha are said to be Jews, although they also are not hostile to Jesus. Moreover, throughout John's Gospel "Israel" and "Israelite" are used in a positive sense. Thus Nathanael can be called "truly an Israelite in whom there is no guile" (1:47) and Jesus is hailed as "king of Israel" (1:49), a title whose entirely positive connotations contrast with "king of the Jews," which has a negative and sarcastic ring on the lips of Romans (e.g., 19:3).

"The Jews" is, then, a term used of a group of Jew*ish leaders* who exercise great authority among their compatriots and are especially hostile to Jesus and his disciples. A recent study of the gospels' use of *Ioudaioi* confirms the view that when it is used in a peculiarly Johannine sense, that is, not with reference to Judeans or to Jewish customs, feasts, and so forth, it refers to certain authorities rather than to the people as a whole.[6] It is these authorities, not Jewish people generally, who are portrayed as hostile to Jesus throughout *John* and make that gospel appear anti-Jewish. This being the case, it is reasonable—and probably correct—to contend that the anti-Jewish aura of the Fourth Gospel is a misreading of the text and, presumably, of the intention of its author(s). Nevertheless, it is a misreading that has all too easily and understandably arisen in the his-

---

[6]U. C. von Walde, "The Johannine Jews: A Critical Survey," *New Testament Studies* 28 (1982) 33–60.

tory of Christian exegesis, and it may be well-nigh impossible to put it to rest in all the circles in which the gospel is read and treasured.

Before dealing with this larger issue, however, it will be useful to inquire further into the historical setting and putative purpose of the portrayal of "the Jews" in the *Gospel of John*. We proceed on the assumption that only a setting different from the immediate historical setting and purpose of Jesus himself will explain the statements and perspective of the Fourth Gospel. Jesus of Nazareth did not distinguish himself from the Jews in the way the Johannine Jesus does. Nor did he dwell upon his messianic role. If he ever acknowledged the claim that he was the messiah (cf., Mk 8:27–30), he did not give it the emphasis it receives in the Fourth Gospel.

Expulsion from the Synagogue

The absence of Zealots, Sadducees, and Herodians in the *Gospel of John* and the tendency for Jews to be equated with Pharisees suggests that *John* appeared after the Roman War, that is, after 70 C.E. Following the war, the so-called Council of Jamnia began the process of retrenching and redefining Jewish life and collecting and codifying traditions that would eventuate in the emergence of Rabbinic Judaism as the heir of Pharisaism. The language of John's Gospel apparently reflects this state of affairs when the Pharisees are equated with the Jewish authorities, precisely the authorities who are able to say who belongs within the synagogue and who must be excluded. They are in the Fourth Gospel, as in broader Jewish history, defining what Judaism shall be. In putting Johannine Christianity beyond the pale, the Pharisees of the Fourth Gospel affirmed a religion of law and absolute monotheism. They rejected a sectarianism based on charismatic inspiration and seemingly limitless transferral of divine prerogatives and attributes to a crucified messianic claimant whose followers believed had risen from the dead. Almost certainly John's Gospel reflects this post-70 situation in Judaism, as well as in what we might call Jewish-Christian relations.

Can the setting and purpose of the Fourth Gospel be defined more precisely? Nearly two decades ago, J. Louis Martyn made an ingenious proposal based primarily on the three instances in the Fourth Gospel in which the threat of expulsion from the synagogue is reflected or predicted (9:22; 12:42; 16:2).[7] If such a threat was not made and was scarcely even conceivable in Jesus' own day, Martyn asks when and under what circumstances it may have been found. His underlying assumption is that the statements in *John* mirror an actual historical situation and set of circumstances. In this respect the *Gospel of John* affords primary testimony for the circumstances under which it was written (as argued by many, esp. Bultmann, Wellhausen). These in turn have been retrojected into the time of Jesus and his disciples. (It is thus only secondarily testimony for the times and events it purports to narrate.) This process took place without deliberate design and forethought over a period of years.

Martyn thought it likely that a primitive narrative gospel consisting of a collection of miracle stories and probably also a rudimentary passion narrative was used by Jewish followers of Jesus to attract adherents to their movement within the synagogue. Such a gospel had been analyzed from the canonical text by Martyn's student Robert T. Fortna on other, chiefly unrelated, grounds.[8] It was a missionary gospel, and its original conclusion (now found in Jn 20:30–31) reflects this fact. As Christian missioners using such narratives, or such a primitive gospel, attained success in persuading their fellow Jews that their Jesus was, in fact, the Messiah of Israel, a backlash or reaction among the majority who were not convinced set in. In

---

[7]J. L. Martyn, *History and Theology in the Fourth Gospel*, rev. ed. (Nashville, 1979). The book was first published in 1968. See R. E. Brown, *The Gospel of John* (Anchor Bible 29; Garden City, N.Y., 1966) vol. 1, pp. LXX–LXXV, LXXXV, who also linked the origin of the Fourth Gospel to a similarly conceived synagogue controversy. Although their proposals were made independently, Martyn and Brown have subsequently carried on a mutually fructifying discussion. Brown's own position is set out most fully in *The Community of the Beloved Disciple* (New York, 1979).

[8]Cf. R. T. Fortna, *The Gospel of Signs: A Reconstruction of the Narrative Source Underlying the Fourth Gospel* (SNTS MS 11; Cambridge, 1970), originally a dissertation with Martyn at Union Theological Seminary.

[9]The form of the benediction, as reformulated, accepted by Martyn (*History*, p. 58) is as follows:

> For the apostate let there be no hope
> And let the arrogant government
>   be speedily uprooted in our days.
> Let the Nazarenes (*notzrim* = Christians) and the *Minim*
>   (heretics) be destroyed in a moment
> And let them be blotted out of the Book of Life and not
>   be inscribed together with the righteous.
> Blessed art Thou, O Lord, who humblest the proud!

The malediction against the Nazarenes and Minim is thought to be the work of Samuel the Small (80–90 C.E.).

this connection the Twelfth Benediction of the *Shemoneh Esreh* was reformulated, in such a way as to condemn sectarians (*minim*) and Nazarenes (*notzrim*).[9] Presumably its purpose was to smoke out Christ-confessors within the synagogue, who could not pronounce this benediction, or malediction, against themselves. This reformulation of the Twelfth Benediction took place in the Rabbinic Academy at Jamnia. According to tradition, it was done by a sage called Samuel the Small under the auspices of Rabbi Gamaliel II, and it has been dated in the ninth decade of the first century. The status of the synagogue ban as a general edict or decree of Jamnia is inferred from the statement of *John* 9:22, that "the Jews had already agreed. . . ."

There is actually no direct evidence that the Twelfth Benediction was reformulated or originally used for the purpose of identifying Christ-confessors specifically and expelling them from the synagogue. If a dating in the 80s is correct, it would antedate the publication of the Fourth Gospel by about a decade (just the right amount of time) if that gospel were composed— as is usually thought—between 90 and 110. Before Martyn's book appeared, W.D. Davies had already proposed such a date and use of the Twelfth Benediction in his work on Matthew.[10] Davies also cited the several places in Justin Martyr's *Dialogue with Trypho* that can be construed as allusions to the use of the Twelfth Benediction to drive Christians out of the synagogue. The evidence is indirect and circumstantial, but impressive, particularly when it is correlated with the fears and predictions of expulsion from the synagogue found in the *Gospel of John*. As we have noted, this state of affairs scarcely corresponds to a setting in the ministry of Jesus, and one is impelled by its prominence in the Fourth Gospel, together with other evidence bearing on Jewish-Christian conflict, to seek a plausible setting for it. Martyn's proposal is then a logical—as well as a brilliant —intuition of the historical imagination.

Nevertheless, it is a proposal and not a demonstration, as subsequent discussion has revealed, and, indeed, as Martyn had recognized from the beginning. Between the initial publication of Martyn's work and the appearance of the second, revised edition a decade later, he had entertained, in conversation and correspondence, the objections and reservations of

---

[10]W. D. Davies, *The Setting of the Sermon on the Mount* (Cambridge, 1964) pp. 275–79.

Wayne A. Meeks and Morton Smith.[11] Meeks and Smith were unwilling to assign the reformulation of the Twelfth Benediction as early a date as Martyn had proposed. Hence they raise questions about a direct connection between the Benediction and passages such as *John* 9:22 that Martyn had made. (Nevertheless, Meeks and Smith agree with Martyn that the Twelfth Benediction and the Johannine *aposynagōgoi* are manifestions of the same or related historical developments.) Subsequently, others have more sharply questioned the early dating of the reformulated Twelfth Benediction that Martyn had accepted, its relation to the Fourth Gospel, and its possible reflection in patristic texts such as Justin's *Dialogue with Trypho.*[12] The authority of Jamnia to promulgate what in effect was a decree against Jewish Christians has also been challenged. Later Rabbinic sources afford precious little evidence of its use in this way. On the contrary, the evidence of the fourth-century bishop John Chrysostom indicates that Christians were then welcome in synagogues and, in Chrysostom's view, had to be warned away from them. Moreover, even the question of when Samuel the Small altered *the text* of the Twelfth Benediction may presuppose a textual stability that did not exist at that time.[13] It can reasonably be argued that at most the evidence suggests local rather than universal measures against Christ-confessors in the synagogue and that these were, moreover, a passing phase. One sadly notes that Christian-Jewish conflict has apparently left bolder evidence than Christian-Jewish harmony or tolerance, which may have been as common in the pre-Constantinian era.

Martyn and others involved in the scholarly discussion are working on a problem of ancient historiography, and their hon-

---

[11]Cited by Martyn, *History*, nn. 69 and 75; cf. also no.81, in which he responds to D. R. A. Hare.

[12]For example, R. Kimelman, "*Birkat ha-Minim* and the Lack of Evidence for an Anti-Christian Jewish Prayer in Late Antiquity," in E. P. Sanders et al., eds., *Jewish and Christian Self-Definition*, (Philadelphia, 1981) vol. 2, pp. 226–44; also S. T. Katz, "Issues in the Separation of Judaism and Christianity after 70 C.E.: A Reconsideration," *Journal of Biblical Literature* 103 (1984) 43–76. The near consensus at the end of the 1970s was stated well by J. T. Townsend, "The Gospel of John and the Jews: The Story of Religious Divorce," in A. Davies, ed., *Antisemitism and the Foundations of Christianity* (New York, 1979) pp. 72–97.

[13]According to the assessment of most recent scholarship by A. L. Nations, "Jewish Persecution of Christians in the Gospel of John" (unpublished paper read before the Fourth Gospel Section of the Society of Biblical Literature national meeting, Atlanta, November, 1986).

esty and integrity as historians can only be honored and admired. The possible bearing of this attempted historical reconstruction and objections to it upon modern Jewish-Christian dialogue is, however, interesting. The implication of Martyn's thesis is that the *Gospel of John* is not, as might first appear, a generally and vehemently anti-Semitic (more accurately, anti-Jewish) document, but a response to a specific crisis in Jewish-Christian relations that had been initiated, or at least exacerbated, by the promulgation of the revised Twelfth Benediction. (Of course, according to Martyn's thesis, the controversy began within the synagogue, among Jews, and that intramural status still pertained at the point of the reformulation of the Benediction.

Ironically, the objections by Jewish scholars such as Kimelman and Katz, which are substantial, in distancing the Fourth Gospel from the Twelfth Benediction and its postulated function, tend to push it back in the direction of a generally anti-Semitic or anti-Jewish writing. Obviously, a scholarly historical issue cannot be decided on the basis of the needs of contemporary Jewish-Christian dialogue. Nor is it helpful, and it is probably not accurate, to say that the truth lies somewhere in between. It would perhaps be more accurate to say that the sources available to us do not permit us to say exactly what transpired to produce the tension between Johannine Christianity and Judaism that is evident in the Fourth Gospel. If the problem with the Martyn thesis is the lack of positive and explicit, as opposed to suggestive, evidence in the rabbinic sources particularly, the problem with simply dismissing it is the evidence—in *John,* and elsewhere in the New Testament and early Christian sources—of strong tension between Jews and Christians, and occasional persecution.

However that may be, it is unnecessary and hazardous hurriedly to draw parallels or relations between this ancient situation and the present, or between it and instances of Jewish-Christian tension and persecution in intervening centuries. If, in fact, Johannine Christians were persecuted by some Jews or Jewish authorities, as Saul at first persecuted the Christian sectarians, this is obviously no justification for Christians' persecuting Jews subsequently. Such persecution, or threat thereof, makes historically understandable certain statements in the *Gospel of John* that otherwise appear to be the product of a gratuitous anti-Judaism. If *John* is properly read only in the latter way, the consequences for Jewish-Christian dialogue are unfortunate, particularly in view of the virtual certainty that Christians will continue to accord *John* a high, canonical authority in their own religion and theology. But the seemingly anti-Jewish statements in the *Gospel of John* are disastrous theologically only on the basis of a rather narrow and literalistic conception of the authority of the New Testament Scriptures.

"The Jews" in Other Johannine Writings

The prominence of "the Jews" in the Fourth Gospel bespeaks a real, historical situation and confrontation, wherever and whenever it may have occurred. The *Gospel of John*, however, is only one of five "Johannine" writings in the New Testament. In none of the others do Jews or Judaism figure in the same way; in fact, even in a long section of the gospel (chaps. 13–17) this confrontation fades completely into the background. The *Revelation of John* stands at the periphery of the Johannine circle, and, in the judgment of some, wholly outside it. As I have suggested elsewhere, however, there are a sufficient number of points of contact and similarity to warrant the assumption of a significant relationship or consanguinity.[14]

Revelation, interestingly enough, reflects less hostility toward Jews than does John's Gospel. The term *Ioudaioi* appears only twice in *Revelation* (2:9; 3:9), in both cases in an indirectly positive sense. That is, members of the "synagogue of Satan" are said to claim to be Jews although in reality they are not. The presumption is that it is good to be a Jew. "Jew" is still used in a positive sense, even as it is in Paul's *Letter to the Romans* (2:17, 28, 29; cf., 3:1). This remains the case even if the "synagogue of Satan" means Jews in Smyrna, or Philadelphia, or even contemporary Jews generally. In that case, they have defected from proper Judaism, from what it should mean to be a Jew. It is not certain, however, that by the "synagogue of Satan" John means all Jews or Judaism generally, as many Christian exegetes have assumed.[15] He may mean only Jews in

---

[14]D. M. Smith, "Johannine Christianity: Some Reflections on Its Character and Delineation," *New Testament Studies* 21 (1975) 222–48, esp. pp. 233, 234. See R. E. Brown, *The Community of the Beloved Disciple*, p. 6, n. 5.

the aforementioned localities who have persecuted or driven out the followers of Jesus who are being addressed. In that case we may be very near the milieu of the *Gospel of John*.[16] It is not necessary to assume that John regards all Jews as necessarily members of the Synagogue of Satan, as the author of the Fourth Gospel would, at least if the evidence of passages such as *John* 8:44 is determinative. In other words, the Fourth Gospel may represent the expansion or tendency to generalize attitudes only nascent in *Revelation*. *Revelation* 2:9 and 3:9 may not be derived from, or inferred from, the broader condemnation of Jews and Judaism rather common in the Fourth Gospel. In *Revelation*, "Jew" is still a good word; in the Fourth Gospel, it is not, having been displaced by "Israelite." *Revelation*, if basically earlier than this gospel (as, for example, Barrett argues), may represent a period prior to the *Gospel of John*. Possibly *Revelation* 3:9 still contemplates the conversion of such Jews.

On the other side of the Fourth Gospel, then, one would locate the Johannine epistles. *Ioudaios/oi* appears not once in any of them, a remarkable fact in view of its frequency in *John*, which is in many respects so closely related theologically to them. There is an obvious reason for this. The opponents, who come frequently into view in the letters, are not Jews but other Christians, whose life-style, ethics, and theology do not meet with the author's approval. To hear him tell it, they are loveless heretics who falsely claim to be without sin and perhaps for that reason are especially incorrigible. If, as on other grounds appears likely, the Johannine epistles are later than the Johannine gospel and presuppose it, a significant change in fronts has occurred. The struggle with Jews seems to be a thing of the past. Perhaps significantly, the vehemence of the opposition is still by no means diminished for that reason. If the Christian opponents are not "children of Satan," they are children of this world, "anti-Christs" (1 Jn 4:3, 5; 2 Jn 7). This is not significantly better.

The farewell discourses of *John* are in some respects closer to the Johannine epistles than to the rest of that gospel, in which

---

[15]For example, R. H. Charles, *The Revelation of St. John*, International Critical Commentary (Edinburgh, 1920) vol. 1, pp. 56–57, 88–89.

[16]On the possible relation of the conflict between Jews and Christians in *Revelation* to the *Birkat ha-Minim* and thus to the *Gospel of John*, see C. J. Hemer, *The Letters to the Seven Churches of Asia in Their Social Setting* (Sheffield, England, 1986) pp. 4, 9, 12, 149.

such open opposition to Jews is manifest. In chapters 13 through 17 *Ioudaioi* occurs only in 13:33, where Jesus tells his disciples what he says to them he has already told the Jews. The reference to being put out of the synagogue and being killed (16:2) would seem to have Jewish opposition in view, and Jesus' discussion of the world's hatred (15:18–16:4) doubtless includes Jewish opposition. But otherwise, the farewell discourses are concerned with distinctly Christian theological and related issues, not with external opposition. For good reason it has been argued that the farewell discourses are in some respects, or in some part, closer to these epistles than to the rest of this gospel.[17] The farewell discourses, then, represent a Johannine Christianity that has weathered the synagogue controversy and moved on to other concerns.

One cannot fail to note an anomaly present in both this gospel and these epistles. In no other New Testament opus is there stronger emphasis on God's love, as expressed in Jesus his Son (3:16; 1 Jn 4:10, 14, 16) or on the command to love as the expression of true discipleship. Only those who truly love one another can claim to be recipients of God's love or, for that matter, can claim to love God (1 Jn 4:20). Yet love is expressed only within the circle of believers: "Love one another" (Jn 13:34–35; 15:12–13; 1 Jn 3:23; 2 Jn 5). Commandments and exhortations to love the neighbor (Mk 12:31)—and even the enemy (Mt 5:44)—are absent from the Fourth Gospel and the Johannine Epistles. Outsiders, whether because they have not believed or because they have believed wrongly, are not necessarily to be loved. While the *Gospel of John* does *not* teach that Christians should *hate* their enemies (cf. Mt 5:43), *1 John* comes close: "the world"—those outside the faith (or the church)—is not to be loved (1 Jn 2:15); "the world" will hate believers (Jn 15:18, 19). Believers are not told to love the emissaries of the world as if they too are children of God. In fact, the only true children of God are believers (1:12). The Johannine Jesus gives no instructions to disciples about how they should behave toward those who hate them. Perhaps a position of relative powerlessness is assumed. They are simply warned so that they will be pre-

---

[17]F. F. Segovia, *Love Relationships in the Fourth Gospel: Agape/Agapan in 1 John and the Fourth Gospel* (Atlanta, 1982), especially pp. 21–24, 217–19, argues that the final redaction of the discourse is the work of the author of *1 John* or someone closely related to him in theology and ecclesiastical setting.

pared for the world's hatred and be able to overcome it. Even the command to love is subsumed within John's dualism, and does not overcome it. Only God does that: the world may hate God (Jn 15:23), but God nevertheless loves the world—in spite of, perhaps because of, its sinfulness. However that may be, believers are not—at least not explicitly—urged to emulate God in this respect.

Here we see a collision between the quasi-metaphysical dualism of the Fourth Gospel and its basic theological-ethical affirmation. That is, the dualistic conceptual framework seems to impede, if not prevent, the universal extension of the love of God and humanity which is the fundamental axiom of *John*. This impediment obviously has to do with the role of belief (i.e., reception of that love). When revelation meets unbelief all bets are off and love's expression is thwarted, at least among human beings. Nevertheless, in John's view, the love of God is not defeated. Whether human love ought to stop at the boundary of belief and unbelief is a question that merits reflection. In the view of the synoptic Jesus, who in this respect is also more likely the historical Jesus, it should not. The fact that in *John* human love does stop at this boundary is, as we have seen, related to the author's and the community's dualism. How it is related is a good question. Does that dualism set limits conceptually so as to override *John's* intent? Is the love of which the author of *John* speaks effective only within the limits set out by a fideistic, if not ontological, dualism? Or is that dualism itself a product of the social situation of *John*, in that the rejection of the community's claims, of its evangelical effort, results in an ossification of boundaries? In that case, one might ask whether John's response is the only, or the best, one in the face of the rejection of missionary witness. John seems to know, however, that the expression of love, even within the community, is the most effective form of witness to those outside (15:12; cf. 17:20–23). If love within the community is a powerful witness, how much more might the expression of love towards those outside the community witness to them?

Implications of the Issue for Contemporary Jewish-Christian Dialogue

A generation ago, scholarship tended to gloss over the Jews

in the *Gospel of John*. For Bultmann the Jews were a surrogate for the world, their presence apparently accounted for by the historical setting of Jesus' ministry within Judaism.[18] John had no great interest in polemicizing against historical, empirical Jews in his own life-setting, although Bultmann notes that insofar as "the situation of the Church is reflected in the Gospel of John, its problem is the conflict with Judaism, and its theme is faith in Jesus as the Son of God."[19] Bultmann's interest was definitely the theological theme rather than the setting. His English contemporary and counterpart, C. H. Dodd, much more than Bultmann, took into account the Jewish and Old Testament conceptual background of John. Yet Dodd found in the Hermetic literature—of fundamentally pagan origin—the closest affinities with the Fourth Gospel.[20] Dodd saw *John* as a book addressed not primarily to Christians, much less to Jews or Jewish Christians, but to a non-Christian public, to "devout and thoughtful persons . . . in the varied and cosmopolitan society of a great Hellenistic city such as Ephesus under the Roman Empire."[21] For Dodd, even less than for Bultmann, a rather vociferous internecine conflict among Jews, or between Jews and Christians, was not the substratum of Johannine thought; and the exegete did not need to take it into account in order to understand *John*.

Developments of the past two decades, epitomized by Martyn's thesis, have wrought a significant change in Johannine exegesis and interpretation. In different ways, Raymond Brown, Wayne A. Meeks, Marinus de Jonge, Klaus Wengst, Oscar Cullmann, Georg Richter, and others have underscored and demonstrated the significance of the Jewish or Jewish-Christian milieu and affinities of the Fourth Gospel. The second edition of Barrett's justly famous commentary is an accurate barometer of this change.[22] Scholars seeking to understand and interpret the *Gospel of John* may no longer bypass or downplay

---

[18]R. Bultmann, *The Gospel of John: A Commentary*, trans., G. R. Beasley-Murray, et al. (Philadelphia, 1971) pp. 86–87. R. A. Culpepper, *Anatomy of the Fourth Gospel: A Study in Literary Design* (New Testament Foundation and Facets; Philadelphia, 1983) pp. 128–31, brings out the important element of truth in Bultmann's position: "Through the Jews, John explores the heart and soul of unbelief" (p. 129). See also Ashton, "*Ioudaioi* in the Fourth Gospel," *Novum Testamentum* 27 (1985) 68.

[19]*Theology of the New Testament*, trans., K. Grobel (New York, 1955) vol. 2, p. 5.

[20]C. H. Dodd, *The Interpretation of the Fourth Gospel* (Cambridge, 1953) p. 5.

[21]*Ibid.*, p. 9.

this dimension of its historical setting or horizon, as had Bultmann and Dodd. Rather, the Jewishness of the Fourth Gospel has been established in such a way as to press upon us the importance of Jewish-Christian relations—*and* Jewish-Christian disagreements—as ingredients of any historically responsible exegesis.

By the same token, the Jewish dimension of the origin and purpose of the Fourth Gospel can scarcely be acknowledged as something that, while real, belongs essentially to the past. In vital respects the issues upon which the Fourth Gospel focuses with such unremitting starkness and clarity remain before us. That is, Christians in the contemporary world, like the Christians of the Johannine community, live in the presence of Jews who do not accept the theologically daring—even extreme— propositions about Jesus that the author of *John* set forth. They could not do so and remain Jews in the now generally accepted sense of the term. Thus the Fourth Gospel seems to offer little hope or basis for dialogue between Christians and Jews. At the same time, the fact that *John* belongs to the Christian canon of scripture—to the New Testament—makes such dialogue all the more necessary.

As we have noted, the harshness of the alternatives as posed by the Jesus of the Fourth Gospel—and equally by "the Jews" mentioned in it—is somewhat mitigated by an appreciation of the dire historical circumstances of those ancient Jews and Christians. Both lived under conditions of great stress and duress. The stress under which those Jews lived is not always recorded in as direct or obvious a fashion as is that which beset the Johannine Christians (although, of course, in *John* theirs is also recorded indirectly, as if it applied to Jesus rather than his disciples). The portrait of late first-century Judaism is buried in the difficult, laconic, and often obscure statements of rabbinic sources. It comes to light in the imagery of the post-70 Apocalypses of Ezra and Baruch. And it is fleshed out in the long historical narrations of Josephus, which attempt both to justify the

---

[22]C. K. Barrett, *The Gospel According to St. John* (Philadelphia, 1978) p. 93, n. 1: "The best attempt to provide a specific *Sitz im Leben* for the Gospel is that of Martyn"; see pp. 137–38 and *passim*. Barrett has reservations only as to whether Martyn's thesis alone does justice to the range of John's background and intention. Culpepper, *Anatomy of the Fourth Gospel*, has a different agenda and perspective, but his literary analysis achieves results that are not at all incongruous with Martyn's.

dominance of Rome in Jewish eyes and to define and defend the essential character of Judaism as a monotheistic religion and a sane and sober ethical philosophy rather than a dangerous and subversive movement. The Judaism of the late first century was badly, if not mortally, wounded after the bloody and disastrous war of 66–70 C.E. It was to suffer further trauma within another half-century in the wake of the suppression of the Bar Kokhba rebellion. The sober sages who were conducting the retrenchment of Judaism, preserving the ancient traditions along Pharisaic lines, truly had no need of the spiritual enthusiasm, messianism, sectarianism, and apparent challenge to the Law and to traditional monotheism that the Johannine community represented.

The Johannine Christians, on the other hand, had the uncompromising zeal of new converts. They were not so much converts from Judaism to Christianity as converts to Jesus, filled with his spirit, born from above, filled with power and glory. (But their conversion to Jesus took them sharply away from the direction in which contemporary Judaism was heading; hence the continuing controversy with "the Pharisees.") They had received—and continued to receive—God's ultimate revelation of himself in the crucified Jesus, whom they believed to be the divine Son of God. If "the world," and particularly their Jewish confreres, insisted upon rejecting God's revelation, the only satisfying explanation was the darkness of their origin and their destiny of sin and death. On the other hand, God not only assured believers of eternal fellowship with himself, but granted them life and joy in this world. Thus the lines were fully and finally drawn; or so it seemed.

Historical circumstances have changed, and continue to change. The setting of modern Judaism is in many respects both more diverse and more hopeful than that of its late first-century counterpart. Yet the continued threat to the existence of modern Israel is almost universally viewed by Jews as a threat to Jewish survival. The Holocaust, of recent and bitter memory, represented a more dire threat to Judaism than the Roman war. After all, the Romans only wanted the Jews to be reasonable—by Roman standards, of course; they did not want to destroy the Jewish people or their religion. The Nazis wanted to destroy both.

There is something in the Johannine blacklisting of the Jews, the consigning of them to this world and to Satan, that in Jewish eyes foreshadows the Holocaust or the annihilation of Judaism. Such a dire, negative view of Jews and of the whole world is undeniably present in *John*. But, paradoxically, it is precisely John's Gospel that presents the motivation, meaning, and effect of God's revelation in Jesus as love. Furthermore, the love of God finds its true response in reciprocal human love that will lead to the unity of the community of love. It is a concept of revelation and response that is in principle universal. In the course of the vagaries and vicissitudes of history, the universal goal was jeopardized, and the dualistic division between truth and falsehood, light and darkness, seemed to be the last word.

Johannine Christianity and Pharisaic Judaism represent opposite poles and possibilities arising out of a common religious tradition. In its need to retrench and conserve the heritage the past had bequeathed to it, this Judaism appears in the *Gospel of John* as remarkably conservative, which in a sense it certainly was. If Johannine Christianity would scarcely qualify as "liberal," it nevertheless enshrines and places a high premium upon elements of spontaneity, novelty, and uniqueness, which are, however, indigenous to—and derived from—the same parent tradition. Within that tradition it is in the nature of the new to take a critical stance towards the old, and of the old to look askance at the new. The potential polarities arising out of a common tradition could not be better illustrated. They stand over against each other as making mutually exclusive claims for allegiance and loyalty (e.g., Jn 9:28; 14:6). The resolution of those claims seems impossible apart from the dissolution of one side or the other. It belongs to the honesty and the integrity of the discussion to honor the reality of the opposing claims. It belongs to the necessity of our mutuality and coexistence, however, not to terminate the conversation but, despite the Pharisees and the Johannine Christians, to continue that dialogue for the sake of the revelation and tradition out of which we both live.

One final observation: it would be wrong to conclude from the tension between Pharisaic Judaism and Johannine Christianity that the one simply represents a conservative and defensive posture toward the inherited tradition while the other represents spontaneity and the claim to new revelations and insights. Within the former, the impetus to preserve the tradition precisely by correlating it with, or making it applicable to, new and emerging problems and situations is a mark of Pharisaism's distinctiveness and originality. Moreover, within Johannine Christianity the need to hold on to what through revelation or experience has established itself soon became urgent, as Raymond Brown has recently shown.[23] The Johannine Epistles are "Johannine Pastorals" (Conzelmann); that is, their goal is to assert and defend the revelation already given. Thus they lay heavy stress on what was "from the beginning" (of the tradition); they speak of the love command as the "old commandment" (1 Jn 2:7) rather than the new (Jn 13:34). This point is important to bear in mind, for it shows that the tensions between Pharisaic Judaism and Johannine Christianity are, phenomenologically speaking, not tensions proper to Judaism and Christianity as separate religions, but tensions that arise almost inevitably *within* a religion, particularly within religions such as Christianity and Judaism, whose essence consists both of the claim that God has spoken and of the claim, however refined or attenuated by qualification or concepts of inference or mediation, that God continues to speak in ways that are—or should be—determinative of human existence.[24]

---

[23]*The Community of the Beloved Disciple*, pp. 93–144. This view becomes basic to his magisterial commentary, *The Epistles of John* (Anchor Bible 30; Garden City, N.Y., 1982), where he sets it out and defends it exegetically.

[24]Only after having completed this paper did I become aware of the careful study and proposals put forward by N. A. Beck, *Mature Christianity: The Recognition and Repudiation of the Anti-Jewish Polemic of the New Testament* (London and Toronto, 1985) esp. pp. 248–74. Beck is thoroughly cognizant of historical-critical issues and literature, and should be consulted for the latter. He makes the noteworthy point that John's polemic operates at different levels (see R. E. Brown) and is not simply directed against Jews in an undifferentiated way (pp. 268–70). Whether one should drop "the Jews" in translating *Ioudaioi* and replace it with "the religious authorities" or the like, as Beck suggests, is an important and debatable question. Exactly the same issue arises from the standpoint of feminist hermeneutic in dealing with and translating allegedly sexist or paternalistic language in the Bible. My own conviction is that we cannot resolve these issues by removing offensive aspects of Scripture occasioned by the concrete circumstances of historical origin. Those who want to read "Jews" will continue to do so, no matter what others say or think!

DISCUSSION

FENN: I am fascinated by the intensity that you describe in these texts. It seems to be a higher level of intensity and emotion than we perhaps find in other texts. But I'm also fascinated by the tendency to explain this in terms of religious cultures or antagonisms within the fold. And, frankly, I can't quite add it all up. And that's just a reflection of my training as a sociologist. How many of the variants have you explained? How much of the intensity can you explain given the methods you adopt? That is, wouldn't you have to look outside of the text if you were trying to explain all the variants of the increase of the intensity of the time? Then, if you do that, it seems to me, you might have to entertain questions like, Was this a pathological response to a crippling disaster? And I do want to ask such questions.

SMITH: Well, let me make one or two rejoinders. I think the intensity is so charged and so important that it explains and justifies the effort that J. L. Martyn made to find a desirable setting for it—whether he's right or wrong. I think that it's the right instinct to do that and he himself has backed away from linking his thesis to the establishment of the Twelfth Benediction in the ninth decade and so forth. It may be a local phenomenon, but it seems to be something very real. Whether it's pathological or not, I don't know. But I think there is a danger of that kind of pathology there; when love is rejected, the reaction is very strong. It's very much like the attitude of military people that peace is the greatest thing, but when somebody violates peace, then that justifies dropping the bomb.

CHARLESWORTH: This is very helpful, Dr. Smith. Could you say a few words on the *aposynagōgos* and the malediction against the *Notzrim* or *Minim*?

SMITH: To me, Kimelman's arguments that the *Notzrim* are latecomers to the text are convincing, but that doesn't mean that the *Minim* are not Jewish Christians. And from what I can see, they may well be. It's one thing to say that the Twelfth Benediction made it impossible for Christians wherever it was used to remain in the synagogue. It's another thing to say that the Twelfth Benediction, as Martyn suggests, was promulgated throughout Judaism by the Council of Jamnia between 80 and 90. And as Kimelman points out, if it was, it's very strange that we don't have any evidence for its use in that way.

BEKER: But that's the *aposynagōgos* reference. Does it have to be tied to the Twelfth Benediction?

SMITH: I don't know if it has to be tied to the benediction. I think that Martyn's effort to tie it to that was a brilliant ploy. In a way Martyn relies on Davies, who describes what might have happened in *The Setting of the Sermon on the Mount.* I think that Martyn is taking up Davies' suggestion and applying it to *John,* where it is more appropriate than with reference to *Matthew.*

CHARLESWORTH: That's very helpful. What I really find lacking in what Christian scholars do when they refer to Jamnia (Yavneh), is that they tend to assume we know what happened at Jamnia. We have nothing like a copy of the proceedings of the council at Jamnia.

PRIEST: But there's a point, though. I was brought up with the same understanding of the malediction as Martyn espoused. Even though there is no direct evidence about certain things, we're still dealing with a period in which there is very direct evidence about certain other things—the most important things. It seems to me that a calculated inference is legitimate—not to say with absolute certainty, This is what happened; but when dealing with historical texts, we are forced to use creative historical imagination from time to time. And it may be dead wrong, but at least it's a starting point from which we can operate.

SMITH: Yes. In that respect, I think Martyn's proposal is a brilliant stroke.

CHARLESWORTH: I find two things very fascinating. The first is that John is the one evangelist who constantly rewrites and recasts his traditions more than anyone else and, at the same time, *John* is the one gospel in which we can see clear strata and redactional activity. For example, in 3:22, 3:26, and 4:1 Jesus is baptizing. But later editors do not want Jesus to be a baptizer. This step is clearly very important because it reflects a process of abstracting Jesus from the context in which he lived, of sapping the Jewishness out of Jesus. And this leads us to my second point, that in *John* we find a harsh anti-Judaism: the Jews are the cosmic forces militantly organized against Jesus, and he in turn is struggling not against demons but against "the Jews."

BEKER: Dr. Smith, don't you think, apart from hostility to the Jews, that once you say "before Abraham was, I am," you have lost everything in the Jewish-Christian dialogue?

SMITH: I'm not so sure of that. I think it depends on what kind of discussion we're talking about. I think that the evangelist John in his explicit statements seems to allow no rapprochement between Christians and Jews. But I also think that *John* gives us an agenda that we've got to talk about.

CHAPTER FIVE

History and Interpretation: "Hebrew Truth," Judaism, and the Victorine Exegetical Tradition

Grover A. Zinn

Introduction

Examining the relationship between the religious cultures of Judaism and Christianity in the Middle Ages is a task fraught with various difficulties.[1] In the first place, the documentation available to scholars tends to be limited to official documents that reflect the respective public attitudes of the Church, royal governments, local officials, Jewish communities, and Jewish leaders. Details of the daily interaction of Jews and Christians are much harder to recover, but the glimpses we do have are illuminating. Second, one must keep in mind from the outset that situations varied greatly from location to location and from time to time. Conditions in the Rhineland differed from those of northern France, and the climate of the twelfth century differed from that of the thirteenth. Making generalizations is a difficult task at best and at worst is dangerously misleading. Finally, one has to be certain that the medieval period is being understood on its own terms, within the limits of its own presuppositions and possibilities. This requires clearing away the intervening layers of historical experience that can color our perception of the past, whether dealing with Jewish or Christian traditions. Examples of such layers are the experiences gained in the Italian Renaissance, the Protestant and Catholic Reformations of the sixteenth century, and the Enlightenment; the shaping of cultures by the enforced creation of Jewish ghettos and the subsequent liberation of Jewish communities in

Europe; and the deeply felt influences of the nineteenth-century transformations of Jewish traditions in Europe and in America. In addition there is the present-day situation influenced by possibilities and realities of Jewish-Christian cooperation and communication as well as by the shadow forever cast by the Holocaust.

In short, we need to grasp the twelfth century as it was, without automatically expecting it to give us either positive or negative answers to modern sorts of questions. Yet, without being anachronistic, the twelfth century may indeed suggest some interesting approaches to Jewish-Christian relationships. It may also give us at least a glimpse of some paths that were possible alternatives to the roads that became so well worn in the course of the thirteenth and fourteenth centuries. Certainly it behooves us to keep in mind that Friedrich Heer called the twelfth century the "open century" in contrast to the thirteenth, when diversity was diminished and orthodoxy became increasingly an overriding concern.[2]

The twelfth century was a time when the Western Christian theological tradition began to take a new shape. Indeed, it was the time in which, for better or for worse, "theology" as we think of it today was becoming a systematic discipline.[3] Schools associated with major cathedrals flourished vigorously in cities of northern France, thus giving birth to a new scholarly culture that was almost totally clerical in composition. In these schools,

---

[1] For Jewish-Christian relations in northern France in the medieval period, see R. Chazan, *Medieval Jewry in Northern France: A Political and Social History* (Baltimore, 1973). For the period of Rashi, see C. Roth, ed., *The Dark Ages: Jews in Christian Europe 711–1096* (World History of the Jewish People, 2d ser., vol. 2; Rutgers, 1966). A. Grabois, "The *Hebraica Veritas* and Jewish-Christian Intellectual Relations in the Twelfth Century," *Speculum* 50 (1975) 613-34, focuses on France and Parisian schools in particular. See also: J. Katz, *Exclusiveness and Tolerance: Studies in Jewish-Gentile Relations in Medieval and Modern Times* (London, 1961); B. Blumenkranz, *Juifs et Chretiens dans le monde occidental, 430–1096* (Paris, 1960); idem, *Les auteurs chretiens latins du moyen age sur les Juifs et le Judaisme* (Paris, 1963); and J. Cohen, *The Friars and the Jews: The Evolution of Medieval Anti-Semitism* (Ithaca, 1982).

[2] F. Heer, *The Medieval World: Europe, 1100–1350* (Cleveland, 1962).

[3] For the development of Christian theology in the twelfth century two works remain classic: J. de Ghellinck, *Le mouvement théologique de XIIe siècle* (2nd ed. aug. Museum Lessianum, Sect. hist. 10; Bruges, 1948); and M.-D. Chenu, *La théologie au douzième siècle.* (Études de philosophie médiévale 33; Paris, 1957). There are useful essays by R. W. Southern, J. W. Baldwin, N. Häring, and R. and M. Rouse in R. L. Benson and G. Constable, with C. D. Lanham, eds., *Renaissance and Renewal in the Twelfth Century* (Cambridge, Mass., 1982). See also G. R. Evans, *Old Arts and New Theology* (Cambridge, 1980).

biblical exegesis enjoyed a remarkable new efflorescence and systematization, following the ninth-century effort of the monastic scholars of the Carolingian Empire[4] to gather the thoughts of the church Fathers. In this renewal—and, as we shall see, reformulation—of biblical exegesis, schools located in Paris played an especially important role.

Along with the emergence of new centers of thought there was also a great groundswell for reform and innovation in religious life during the twelfth century in western Europe.[5] Benedictine monasticism was reformed and invigorated by the foundation of the monastery of Cîteaux and the development of the Cistercian order. The emergence of new forms of religious community can be seen in the forming of houses of Praemonstratensian and Victorine regular canons. These regular canons were clerics who were conscious of being different from monks and having a distinctive conception of ministry, summarized in the phrase "to teach by word and example." They understood themselves to be following the shared communal life of the early Christians in Jerusalem and that of the group of priests who lived a fully communal life in the episcopal household of Augustine of Hippo. Moreover, the hermetic or semihermetic life was reaffirmed in places like Le Grande Chartreuse in France and Valambrosa in Italy. All of these developments in city and countryside, in schools and monasteries, in social life and religious sensibilities, indicate the ferment and the creativity so evident during the period deservedly called the "Renaissance of the twelfth century."

My own work has focused on the thought of several regular canons who were associated with the Abbey of St.-Victor in Paris during the twelfth century. These men were bold innovators in the fields of biblical exegesis, theology, and mysticism, while also being shaped profoundly by the inherited riches of patristic thought, particularly the Augustinian tradition. They combined commitment to a new form of disciplined religious life (that of regular canons) with an equally strong commitment to scholarship and the formation of a school in

---

[4]The fundamental study is by B. Smalley, *The Study of the Bible in the Middle Ages* 2d ed. (Oxford, 1952).

[5]For twelfth-century religious life, see G. Constable, "Renewal and Reform in Religious Life," in Benson and Constable, eds., *Renaissance and Renewal*, pp. 37-67, with extensive notes and bibliography.

the two-fold sense of an institution for instruction and a tradition of thought. The founder of the intellectual tradition of the
Victorine school was Hugh of St.-Victor, who died in 1141.[6]
His successor at St.-Victor in the field of literal biblical exegesis
was Andrew of St.-Victor, who died in 1175,[7] while Richard of
St.-Victor followed Hugh's distinctive presentation of a Victorine mystical tradition as well as contributing to exegesis.[8]

In her magisterial treatment of the Victorine biblical exegesis,
Beryl Smalley emphasized the significance of the Victorine
combination of scholarship with a highly disciplined religious
life. She summed up the importance of this by noting that in
the early twelfth century, "a gulf had opened between monks
and scholars. Contemporaries constantly stressed their difference in function: the scholar learns and teaches, the monk
prays and 'mourns'. The canons regular courageously refused
to admit the dilemma."[9] They pursued scholarship in its latest
form while also living the life of a religious order committed to
the Augustinian Rule.

What I present in this paper is twofold: (1) some of the
harvest of my own research, particularly as related to the
thought of Hugh of St.-Victor; (2) some gleanings from fields
tended well by others who have spent much more time that I
assessing the use of Jewish exegesis by Christian interpreters
either trained at or influenced by the school of St.-Victor.

The Synagogue Window in the Abbey of St.-Denis

Before turning to the school of St.-Victor and its founder,
Hugh, let us examine several twelfth- and thirteenth-century

---

[6]On Hugh, see R. Baron, *Science et sagesse chez Hugues de Saint-Victor* (Paris, 1957); J.
Ehlers, *Hugo von St. Viktor: Studien zum Geschichtsdenken und zur Geschichtsschreibung des
12. Jahrhunderts* (Wiesbaden, 1973); Smalley, *Study*, pp. 83-106; G. A. Zinn, Jr., "De
gradibus ascensionum: The Stages of Contemplative Ascent in Two Treatises on Noah's
Ark by Hugh of St. Victor," *Studies in Medieval Culture* 5 (1975) 61-79, and "Mandala
Use and Symbolism in the Mysticism of Hugh of St. Victor," *History of Religions* 12
(1972-1973) 317-41. On the Victorine school in general see the excellent survey by J.
Chatillon, "De Guillaume de Champeaux à Thomas Gallus: chronique d'histoire lit-
téraire et doctrinale de l'École de Saint-Victor," *Revue du moyen age latin* 8 (1952) 139-62,
247-73.

[7]The basic work remains Smalley, *Study*, pp. 112-85.

[8]See G. A. Zinn, trans. and intro., Richard of St. Victor, *The Mystical Ark, The Twelve
Patriarchs, and Book Three on the Trinity* (Classics of Western Spirituality; New York,
1979).

[9]Smalley, *Study*, p. 83.

images found sculpted on cathedral facades, displayed in
stained glass, or drawn on the pages of manuscripts (see illus.
1-9). All deal with personifications of Church and Synagogue.[10]
The first set of figures is found on the facade of Reims Cathedral (illus. 1) and shows a crowned figure of *Ecclesia* (Church)
on one side of the facade and a dispirited, blindfolded figure
of *Synagoga* (Synagogue) on the other. This thirteenth-century
example shows the dominant way in which the paired representations of Church and Synagogue were depicted in the
medieval period. There is a more famous treatment of this
theme, namely the figures on the facade of the Cathedral of
Strassbourg (again, a thirteenth-century construction), the orig-
inals of which can now be seen in that city's Cathedral museum
(illus. 2, 3). *Ecclesia* appears crowned, with head proudly erect
and gaze directed firmly ahead while she holds a chalice and
a cross-shaped staff with a furled banner. Everything suggests
regality, awareness, and dominion. The depiction of *Synagoga*
is just the opposite. Her head hangs listlessly, her eyes are
blindfolded, the staff she holds is broken, the pennant hangs
limply, and her head and body are turned away from the
viewer. The depiction is one of despair and defeat.

An earlier, less expressive but equally typical example of this
kind of negative juxtaposition of Synagogue and Church is
found in an eleventh-century manuscript drawing that shows
yet again the contrast between the erect, aware, dominant
figure of the Church and the defeated, downward-directed,
despised figure of *Synagoga*. Such contrasting images were to
dominate this iconographic "topos" in the medieval period.

A quite different presentation of the figure of *Synagoga* is
found in a twelfth-century stained glass window in the Church
of the Abbey of St.-Denis near Paris (illus. 4).[11] Therein Christ

[10]For the representations of Church and Synagogue, see B. Blumenkranz, *Le Juif
médiéval au miroir de l'art chrétien* (Paris, 1960), and W. S. Seiferth, *Synagogue and Church
in the Middle Ages: Two Symbols in Art and Literature*, trans. L. Chadeayne and P.
Gottwald (New York, 1970). [See also the important and impressively illustrated
following publication: B. Blumenkranz, "La représentation de *synagoga* dans les bibles
moralisées françaises du xiiie au xve siecle," in *Proceedings of the Israel Academy of Sciences
and Humanities* 5 (1976) 70-91. J.H.C.]

[11]For the Abbey church, see E. Panofsky, *Abbot Suger. On the Abbey Church of
St.-Denis and Its Art Treasures* (2d ed. Princeton, 1979), with introduction and extensive
notes. For an important collection of recent studies, see P. L. Gerson, ed., *Abbot Suger
and Saint-Denis: A Symposium* (New York, 1986). For the windows at St.-Denis, see L.
Grodecki, *Les vitraux de Saint-Denis*, I (Corpus vitrearum Medii Aevi; Paris, 1976).

is depicted standing between figures representing *Synagoga* and *Ecclesia*, as he crowns the figure of Church and lifts a veil from the face of Synagogue.[12] This window was part of a major architectural and iconographic program instituted when Abbot Suger of St.-Denis rebuilt the west front and choir of the monastic church in the first half of the twelfth century. Architecturally the new construction presented the basic elements of what would later be called gothic architecture. Suger had distinctive ideas about the role of the new and (for his day) large windows newly installed in the choir of the church. Suger emphasized that the windows were meant to illumine the mind by means of the deeper symbolism conveyed by the gloriously colored figures (formed by pieces of colored and painted glass) and skillfully arranged scenes depicting biblical events or theological concepts. In a window that modern scholars have labeled the "anagogical window" because of Suger's idea that the material images would raise the mind to grasp immaterial spiritual truths, the Abbot had his artisans depict a number of scenes of typological or allegorical significance. The roundel depicting Christ, *Synagoga*, and *Ecclesia* was one element in this "anagogical window."

When compared with the other examples just described, this window in the Church of the Abbey of St.-Denis (illus. 4) has several striking characteristics. As in the other examples, *Ecclesia* appears with a crown and holds a staff (admittedly of strange shape here) and a chalice. The figure of *Synagoga*, however, differs greatly from the personifications previously noted. She holds the tablets of the Law cradled firmly in her left hand, and the staff in her right hand is held upright. The staff is not broken, nor are the tablets of the Law held listlessly as they are by the Strassbourg figure. The contrast with the depiction of the Synagogue in Notre Dame, Paris, is even more striking (illus. 7).

The Synagogue, according to the designers of the Church of the Abbey of St.-Denis, is not a defeated Synagogue; she stands

---

[12]On this window, see Grodecki, *Les vitraux*, pp. 100-101, and "Vitraux allegoriques de Saint-Denis," *Art de France* 1 (1961) 32-35; also K. Hoffmann, "Sugers 'Anagogisches Fenster'" in *St.-Denis, Wallraf-Richartz Jahrbuch* 30 (1968) 57-88, and the brief remarks of B. Blumenkranz, "Géographie historique d'un thème de l'iconographie religieuse: les representations de 'Synagoga' en France," *Melanges René Crozet* (Poitiers, 1966) vol. 2, pp. 1141-57, see esp. p. 1147.

equally with Church. Of great importance are Christ's gestures. He stands between the figures and has on his chest a circular device that probably represents the seven gifts of the Holy Spirit. With his right hand Christ crowns *Ecclesia*; with his left hand he unveils *Synagoga*. *Synagoga's* gaze is clear, not blinded; she stands erect, not bowed down in defeat. We have here a complex stained glass image that represents a different perception of Synagogue and, presumably, a different perception of Hebrew and Jewish history than that which is suggested by the above-mentioned cathedral facades and manuscript illumination. It hints openly at an equal appreciation of both Church and Synagogue. This is the positive side. On the negative side, in terms of appreciating the Jewish tradition, it suggests that the Synagogue is unveiled and given full awareness by Christ. While not ignoring the Christocentricity of the imagery of the window, it is possible nonetheless to appreciate the equality suggested and to emphasize the absence of characteristics of defeat, destruction, and blindness.[13]

Hugh of St.-Victor

If one seeks a possible background to the positive ideas embodied in the St.-Denis window—as opposed to the images of negation found at Reims and Strassbourg—a good place to begin would be the Abbey of St.-Victor at Paris. Elsewhere I have suggested that certain ideas set forth by Hugh of St.-Victor may well have been instrumental in shaping Abbot Suger's

---

[13]Two other representations of Church and Synagogue that seem to show Synagogue being unveiled are examined in detail by Grodecki in "Vitraux allegoriques." One of these is a tree of Jesse illumination in the Lambeth Bible (London, Lambeth Palace Library, Ms. 3, fol. 198). There Mary is flanked by figures of Church (crowned and gazing at Mary) and Synagogue (gaze turned downward and away from Mary), while above Mary's head there is a bust of Christ surrounded by seven doves representing the seven gifts of the Holy Spirit. An unattached hand reaches down to hold a veil that is being either raised or lowered over Synagogue's face. The general interpretation holds that this is an "unveiling"; see Grodecki and also W. Cahn, *Romanesque Bible Illumination* (Ithaca, 1982) p. 191 and pl. 151. Cahn refers to Synagogue as "'unveiled' and yet confounded in her spiritual blindness." Given Synagogue's posture, her open eyes, and the ambiguous way the veil is held, it is not impossible that this represents the act of veiling Synagogue. I hope to address this important question on another occasion. The association of the seven doves with Christ in both the Lambeth Bible illumination and the St.-Denis window is a tantalizing similarity. For a recent treatment of Christ, and also Mary, shown with the seven doves, see H. Rademacher-Chorus, "Maria mit den Sieben Gaben des Heiligen Geistes," *Zeitschrift des Deutschen Vereins für Kunstwissenschaft*, Bd. 32, heft 1/4 (Berlin, 1978) pp. 30-45.

conception of symbols and the symbolic role of the central doors of the west front of the Abbey Church of St.-Denis.[14] Perhaps Hugh's positive attitude toward the Hebrew tradition and his use of contemporary Jewish exegesis in his own biblical interpretaton played a role in shaping the attitudes embodied in the St.-Denis window. The present state of research allows no firm conclusions to be drawn. But the window is a suggestive "pointer," as it were, to attitudes and relationships that deserve to be examined and explored in detail.

The Abbey of St.-Victor was founded in 1108 by William of Champeaux.[15] William had been, until then, chancellor of the cathedral of Notre Dame in Paris and master of the cathedral school. In 1108 he retired from teaching in the cathedral school and established a small community of regular canons at a site dedicated to St.-Victor just outside the walls of Paris on the left bank. The community quicky grew to become one of the most important religious houses at Paris and in the north of France during the twelfth century. Scarcely twenty-five years after its foundation, the Abbey was not only a Royal Abbey under the patronage of King Louis VI (an honor it shared with the ancient Benedictine Abbey of St.-Denis); it also had an internationally known school attended by students from all across Europe and from the British Isles. The Victorines are a prime example of the vigorous growth of houses of regular canons in the twelfth century, and typify the combination of devotion, discipline, and scholarship noted by Beryl Smalley in the previously cited passage.

The distinctive intellectual and spiritual traditions of St.-Victor were formed in large part by Hugh of St.-Victor. Hugh stands out in the early twelfth century as a person with a broad range of abilities and interests. He worked to restore the fundamental importance of the literal and historical meaning of the biblical text in the face of earlier medieval tendencies to ignore the letter in favor of symbolic allegorical interpretation. He also stands out for the fact that he turned to Jewish exegetes—and

---

[14]G. A. Zinn, Jr., "Suger, Theology, and the Pseudo-Dionysian Tradition," in Gerson, ed., *Abbot Suger and Saint-Denis*, pp. 33-40.

[15]The best study of the early years of St.-Victor is now J. Chatillon, *Theologie, spiritualité et metaphysique dans l'oeuvre oratoire d'Achard de Saint-Victor* (Paris, 1969) pp. 53-85. The earliest years of the Abbey are looked at in some detail by J.-P. Willesme, "Saint-Victor au temps d'Abelard," in *Abelard et son temps* (Paris, 1981) pp. 95-105.

encouraged his students to do the same—for assistance in clarifying the literal sense of the Hebrew scriptures. In the realm of what we today call theology, Hugh produced the first systematic medieval theological *summa*, thus standing at the head of a long line of thinkers from the Middle Ages to the present who have engaged in comprehensive and systematic theological writing. In the area of mysticism, Hugh wrote some of the earliest treatises that systematize Christian teaching about the mystic path and the mystic experience. In the generation that followed Hugh, Andrew of St.-Victor developed Hugh's emphasis on literal exegesis with unusual fervor, while Richard of St.-Victor paid particular attention to the contemplative life. Thus at St.-Victor we encounter a recently-founded religious community in which new ideas and new ideals of scholarship were being explored in many areas.

To understand Hugh of St.-Victor's attitude toward Hebrew and Jewish traditions, it will help to look at two aspects of his thought. The first involves Hugh's sense of history and the "shape" that he gave to history in his massive *Chronicon*. The second is his use of the Hebrew language and Jewish exegesis in interpreting the literal and historical sense of scripture.

One important factor that distinguishes Hugh's theology from that of other twelfth-century thinkers, especially Abelard, is his emphasis upon history.[16] Hugh insisted that the literal and historical sense of scripture formed the systematic foundation of all exegesis and thus was the foundation of all theological reflection. Moreover, he stressed that the "foundation of the foundation" (as he termed it), was historical narrative, the sequence of events in time from the creation to the present day and on to the culmination of history in the Last Judgment.[17] When in his *Didascalicon* Hugh described the course of biblical studies at the school of St.-Victor, he made it quite clear that the three traditional senses of scripture (history, allegory, and tropology) were now to be understood as distinct scholarly

---

[16] A point made forcefully by Chenu, *La theologié*, pp. 62-89.

[17] See Hugh's emphasis on the "foundation of the foundation" in "De tribus maximis circumstantiis gestorum," the preface to his *Chronicon*. The preface is edited by W. M. Green, "Hugo of St. Victor: *De tribus maximis circumstantiis gestorum*," *Speculum* 18 (1943) 484-93; see esp. p. 491, lines 10-33. For the role of history in Hugh's thought, see G. A. Zinn, Jr., "Historia fundamentum est: The Role of History in the Contemplative Life according to Hugh of St. Victor," *Contemporary Reflections on the Medieval Christian Tradition: Essays in Honor of Ray C. Petry* (Durham, N.C., 1974) pp. 135-158.

disciplines to be mastered in an organized sequence of studies.[18] This understanding differed from the common patristic and medieval conception of the senses of scripture as levels of meaning in individual passages of scripture. To convey his new idea of this sequence of studies Hugh adopted, and in adopting transformed, the image of a building, which Gregory the Great had used to describe the relation between the three senses in interpreting individual passages of scripture. Hugh used it to describe the building of a curriculum, as it were, not just a set of multiple meanings. History, said Hugh, is the foundation in the study of the Bible. Next comes allegory, which erects the superstructure of the walls and roof. Finally, the tropological, or moral sense, covers the building with beautiful color. Hugh's words put it succinctly:

> First of all, the student of Sacred Scripture ought to look among history, allegory, and tropology for that order sought in the disciplines—that is, he should ask which of these three precedes the others in the order of study.
>
> In this question it is not without value to call to mind what we see happen in the construction of buildings, where first the foundation is laid, then the structure is raised on it, and finally, when the work is all finished, the house is decorated by the laying on of color.[19]

Hugh goes on in the following chapters of the *Didascalicon* to outline a course of study in which each "sense" is presented as a distinct discipline with its own purpose, methodology, and reading list of biblical books. Moreover, in the case of the first two senses or disciplines Hugh composed special handbooks to assist the student. For the historical sense Hugh composed his *Chronicon*.[20] For the student of allegory, who must be thoroughly versed in theological as well as textual knowledge and sensitivity, Hugh wrote his justly famous *summa* of

---

[18]Smalley, *Study*, pp. 87-88, speaks of Hugh modifying the form of biblical study by "introducing a special course of studies as a preliminary to the investigation of each sense."

[19]*Didascalicon*, 6.2; trans., J. Taylor, *The "Didascalicon" of Hugh of St. Victor: A Medieval Guide to the Arts* (Records of Civilization: Sources and Studies 64; New York, 1961) p. 135. Based on Gregory the Great, Moralia in Job, Epist. missoria, 3, *Patrologia Latina* 75.513C, ed. M. Adriaen, CC, Ser. Lat., 143.4.

[20]See Green, "Hugo of St. Victor," for an edition of the preface and description of the tables in this work.

theology, *De sacramentis christianae fidei* (On the Sacraments of the Christian Faith).[21]

The reading lists of biblical books established for the disciplines are revealing. For history the student should read *Genesis, Exodus, Joshua, Judges, Kings, Chronicles*, the four gospels, and the *Acts of the Apostles*, in that order, which is the order of historical narrative.[22] As Hugh says, "These eleven seem to me to have more to do with history than do the others." The exegetical tradition was full of exhortations not to neglect the letter or the historical sense. But here in a systematic introduction to biblical study we have a new and distinctive emphasis on the practical application of a firmer grasp of the significance of history as narrative for the study of Scripture and for the foundation of theological reflection. The list for allegorical reading reflects a different goal and purpose.[23] The order is no longer historical, for the New Testament is to be read before the Old. The selected books are two gospels (*Matthew* and *John*), the epistles of Paul, the canonical epistles, the *Apocalypse*, the beginning of *Genesis* on the works of the six days, the three last books of Moses on the mysteries of the Law, *Isaiah*, the beginning and end of *Ezekiel*, *Job*, the *Psalms*, and the *Song of Songs*. Noteworthy in this list are the inclusion of only two gospels and the highly selective list of Old Testament books. The latter are all important for their allegorical/typological significance. In some cases (e.g., for *Genesis* and *Ezekiel*) Hugh has even selected the portions of the books that are most important in this connection.

Our Victorine exegete makes it quite clear that by the historical sense of Scripture he means the narrative structure of the text in historical context, not merely the literal sense of the words.[24] In the *Didascalicon* Hugh uses *Isaiah* 4:1 as an example of the need to seek the narrative sense of the biblical text and to understand links between narrative units. The verse reads: "In that day seven women shall take hold of one man, saying, We will eat our own bread and wear our own apparel: only let us be called by thy name, to take away our reproach" (AV). Hugh

---

[21]Trans. R. J. Deferrari, *On the Sacraments of the Christian Faith* (De sacramentis). Publications of the Mediaeval Society of America 58; Cambridge, Mass., 1951.

[22]*Didascalicon*, 6.3, Taylor, p. 137.

[23]*Ibid.*, 6.4, p. 144.

[24]*Ibid.*, 6.10, p. 149.

shows that careful analysis yields a clear literal sense, even though some contemporaries seem to have been perplexed by the passage. In this verse, declares Hugh, individual words and phrases are easily understood, but there are interpreters who can make no literal sense of the verse taken as a whole. These persons interpret it only symbolically and refer it to the seven gifts of the Holy Spirit given to Christ. Hugh goes on to point out that the historical sense is discerned easily enough if narrative context is taken into account. Hugh explains that earlier the prophet had spoken of war and a great slaughter. With the male population now radically diminished, the situation has become so desperate that seven women seek one man to be husband of all so that they will not die without children. To overcome the man's hesitation at supporting them, they declare that they will furnish their own food and clothing. With this appeal to common sense interpretation and an appreciation of historical context, Hugh urges a stronger sense of the narrative context of Scripture. As Michael Signer has pointed out in an unpublished paper on Christian and Jewish exegesis in the twelfth century, a concern with narrative units of text in historical interpretation was a distinctive element of not only Victorine exegesis but of the practice of Jewish exegetes in northern France as well.[25]

To assist the student in literal and historical exegesis Hugh compiled a handbook that bore the title *Chronicon*. This was essentially a collection of historical tables with brief narrative introductions. It covered not only biblical history but the history of the ancient Greek and Roman empires, and Christian rulers in Europe to Hugh's day. However, even chronological tables can be "shaped" in a decisive way by selective inclusion or exclusion of material and through the use of headings.[26] This was the case with Hugh's opening chronology extending from the six days of creation to the fall of the Jerusalem Temple in 70 C.E. It bears the title, "The restoration according to Hebrew truth." Hugh follows the basic chronological information

---

[25]M. Signer, "Peshat, Sensus Litteralis, and Sequential Narrative: Jewish and Christian Exegesis in the Twelfth Century." (Unpublished article.) I am indebted to M. Signer for use of this material.

[26]Much of the following discussion of Eusebius is drawn from my article, "The Influence of Hugh of St. Victor's Chronicon on the Abbreviationes chronicorum by Ralph of Diceto," *Speculum* 52 (1977) 38-61.

as compiled from the Hebrew Bible (as opposed to a chronology compiled from the Septuagint text that appears in the second table of the *Chronicon*) by earlier chroniclers such as Eusebius and Bede. However, he differed from Eusebius and Bede in crucial particulars.

In the Middle Ages the scheme of the six ages of history tended to dominate chronicles and historical writings. There were five pre-Incarnation periods (Adam to Noah; Noah to Abraham; Abraham to Moses; Moses to David; David to the Exile; the Exile to Christ). The sixth age stretched from the Incarnation to the end of time. Augustine formulated the division, and he was followed by Isidore, Bede, and the chroniclers of the eleventh and twelfth centuries. Hugh included the six ages in his chronology, but he chose a different pattern for the primary framework. That primary pattern was one of "four successions": the patriarchs from Adam to Moses; the judges from Moses to David; the kings from David to the Babylonian Exile; the Jewish high priests from the Exile to Christ. By emphasizing the four successions rather than the six ages, Hugh was able to give something of a new "shape" to the past and to root it in certain forms of community found in biblical history and Hebrew life. With this new shape for historical recollection Hugh called attention to a portion of the past that had been overlooked, slighted, or totally neglected in the chronicle tradition that began with Eusebius of Caesarea and continued through the works of Bede, Isidore, and others. In chronicling Hebrew history from the Babylonian Exile to the time of the Incarnation, Eusebius had shifted attention away from the Hebrew people and their history. Postexilic history (which begins at the same point that Hugh's fourth succession begins) had been traced by Eusebius through the rulers of the kingdoms of the Persians, Greeks, Egyptians, and Romans, with only passing mention of the Maccabees and their successors among the Jews.[27]

Two reasons seem to explain why Eusebius ignored the succession of high priests among the Jewish people. First, there is his obvious preoccupation with classical culture and the confluence of the classical and Christian traditions in his day. Second, as D. S. Wallace-Hadrill has pointed out in his study of

---

[27]See Jerome's translation of Eusebius' *Chronicorum* in *Patrologia Latina* 27.84-91.

Eusebius, the Greek historian had an ingrained negative attitude toward the Jewish tradition as it existed in the immediately pre-Christian centuries, especially in the Hellenistic period.[28]

Hugh's use of the four successions and his consequent emphasis on the high priests directly opposed the slighting of the postexilic Jewish tradition by Eusebius and his successors down to Hugh's day. The high priests, shoved off the stage of history in Eusebius' chronology, now returned in Hugh's work to share equal footing—indeed, equal billing—with patriarchs, judges, and kings in the history of the Hebrew people. For Hugh the process of salvation (to which he gave the technical term "works of restoration," *opera restaurationis*) has been carried out in a temporal process, manifest first in the history of the Hebrew people, then the Christian.[29] To neglect any part of that history is to overlook an aspect of God's work. The history of the world's kingdoms was, in the imagery of one of Hugh's other works, the confusion that existed in the flood of the world outside the safety of the Ark of salvation, which was stabilized by the keel of salvation history.[30] What Hugh did in the *Chronicon* was to refocus the past to produce a different meaning with a present purpose. Hebrew truth became a significant theme in Victorine thought. Hugh emphasized it in conceptualizing history, in working out his theology (which affirmed the efficacy of Hebrew sacraments in the time of the Law and was systematized according to historical development, not logical structure), and in exegesis.

To judge from the distribution of manuscripts, Hugh's *Chronicon* enjoyed a fairly wide use. I know of only one writer, however, who incorporated Hugh's chronology in his own work. He was Ralph of Diceto (d. ca. 1202), an English cleric

[28]D. S. Wallace-Hadrill, *Eusebius of Caesarea* (London, 1960) chs. 8 and 9; see esp. pp. 168-72.

[29]In addition to the *Chronicon*, the sheme of the four successions appears in *De scripturis et scriptoribus sacris*, 17, *Patrologia Latina* 175. 24 AD. On the *opus restorationis* see Hugh's remarks in *De sacramentis christianae fidei*, 1, prol. 2, *Patrologia Latina* 176. 183A-184A, trans. Deferrari, pp. 3-4. For history and the *opus restorationis*, see Zinn, "Historia fundamentum est," pp. 141-43, and R. W. Southern, "Aspects of the European Tradition of Historical Writing: 2. Hugh of St.-Victor and the Idea of Historical Development," *Transactions of the Royal Historical Society*, fifth series, vol. 21 (1971) 159-79.

[30]*De vanitate mundi*, 2, *Patrologia Latina* 176.720A-720D, trans. by a Religious of C.S.M.V., *Hugh of St. Victor: Selected Spiritual Writings* (London, 1962) pp. 181-82.

and historian who was dean of St. Paul's, London.[31] Ralph copied Hugh's tables with their special structure directly into his chronicle. However, Ralph had a secondary interest in classical history, which he reveals by interrupting the third and fourth sections of the chronology with extracts from works bearing on the history of Greece and Rome. It is possible that the use of Hugh's schema in other chronicles, published or unpublished, remains to be noted.

If Hugh's chronology and exegetical theory emphasized history and the literal sense, then his actual literal interpretation of scripture opened a new avenue of approach, namely a practical openness to and use of Jewish exegesis. Among Hugh's earliest works are his notes on the literal sense of the Pentateuch and other books from the Hebrew scriptures.[32] These have been studied closely by Beryl Smalley, whose work forms the cornerstone of all further explorations of this material.[33] She notes that Hugh compared the Vulgate text with a literal Latin translation of the Hebrew text in order to clarify difficult passages. This was, to be sure, not unlike earlier efforts by Alcuin and Stephen Harding, who consulted Jewish rabbis concerning the Hebrew text in the course of correcting the Latin Vulgate text.[34] Hugh did not simply perpetuate their practice, however. He went further. He consulted contemporary Jewish exegetes in order to determine Jewish interpretations of particular passages, and he gives these in his commentary. Some of the opinions that Hugh mentions can be traced to the school of Rashi. One explanation is found in Rashi, and three are found in the works of Rashbam, Rashi's grandson. The extent and depth of Hugh's own use of the Hebrew language and Jewish exegesis are not great; his knowledge of Jewish exegesis comes from oral communications, it would seem, rather than from consultation of Jewish texts. But he did indicate a necessary task for others to undertake if they meant to recover the exact meaning of the words and the precise sense of the historical narrative in the Hebrew scriptures, the Christian Old Testament. It remained for one of Hugh's stu-

---

[31] Zinn, "The Influence."
[32] Printed in *Patrologia Latina* 175.
[33] Smalley, *Study*, 97-106.
[34] See Grabois, "The *Hebraica Veritas*," 615-19.

dents, Andrew of St.-Victor, to develop Hugh's program with serious intent, while Herbert of Bosham, who was deeply influenced by Andrew, was to show what a more complete mastery of languages and texts could yield.

Andrew of St.-Victor

As is the case with all early Victorines, we know very little about Andrew's early life and background.[35] Smalley calculates that he produced his first major work, a commentary on the literal sense of the Octateuch, by about 1147. This means that he probably studied directly under Hugh, who died in 1141. Andrew was absent from St.-Victor for two periods in his life, both times as prior of the house of regular canons at Wigmore, in England. Andrew died in 1175, leaving behind a rich collection of literal commmentaries on the Hebrew scriptures. He adopted Hugh's emphasis on the fundamental role of literal exegesis, but he went much much further than Hugh in seeking to understand the Hebrew text and Jewish exegesis. For a medieval exegete, Andrew's work is striking. He limited himself to the literal sense of scripture. In doing this, he was conscious of engaging in something new with his single-minded dedication to the literal sense. He was defensive, but he was also convinced of the rightness of his chosen undertaking. He reminded his readers in the prologue to his commentary on the Prophets that truth is deep and has many secrets. Each generation must seek out more, he explained, and yet much more remains to be discovered. Andrew wanted to do what he could to set before his readers the harvest that he had gathered from scripture with the aid of the patristic commentaries (Origen, Augustine, Jerome, and others), the medieval Gloss, Josephus, and contemporary Jewish exegetes. Andrew also turned to the Hebrew text and measured the Latin Vulgate against it.

---

[35]For Andrew's life and works, see Smalley, *Study*, 112-85; see also her "Andrew of St. Victor, Abbot of Wigmore: A Twelfth-Century Hebraist," *Recherches de theologie ancienne et medievale* 10 (1938) 358-73, which is the basis for the chapter in *Study*. The influence of Rashi on Andrew and other medieval Christian exegetes is set out in H. Hailperin, *Rashi and the Christian Scholars* (Pittsburgh, 1963), following Smalley's work. See also Grabois, "The *Hebraica Veritas*," pp. 619-34, for the influence of Jewish exegesis.

Smalley's careful and detailed consideration of Andrew's exegesis yields many insights concerning his use of Jewish exegesis and the ways in which he incorporated it in his work. Early in Andrew's work Jewish materials are present, but not scrutinized. By the time Andrew examined the prophetic books, however, he had devised a very revealing format for his work. He presented the Vulgate text with the Christian literal sense and the Hebrew text with the Jewish literal interpretation. On one especially notable occasion, in dealing with passages in *Isaiah* that refer to the suffering servant, Andrew gave only the Jewish literal exegesis, referring the passages on the servant to the Jews in captivity and their expiatory function, or (according to another Jewish exegetical tradition) to Isaiah himself. A Christian literal sense is absent. Smalley remarks of Andrew's exegesis of *Isaiah*, "It is extraordinary to think that this was written at St.-Victor, by a pupil of Hugh, that he was begged to continue his work, was begged to resume his abbacy, and finally buried 'with great honour'. The twelfth century is full of surprises."[36]

There are more surprises in Andrew's exegesis of the pasage, "Behold a virgin shall conceive . . ." (Isa 7:14ff.). Andrew insisted that the literal fulfillment of the prophecy belonged to the Jewish people; the Christian fulfillment in Christ was to be found only in the spiritual, allegorical interpretation.[37] This was too much for Richard of St. Victor, who took up his pen to write a treatise sharply critical of Andrew's interpretation. Interestingly, as Michael Signer has pointed out, a good part of this intramural argument between two Victorine canons turns on the way in which one reads and divides the narrative units of the text.[38] Andrew took *Isaiah* 7 and 8 as a connected narrative, and he thus produced an interpretation that connected the virgin of chapter 7 with the prophetess of chapter 8. Richard's response offered theological criticism of Andrew's exegesis, but he also divided the narrative in a different way by insisting that chapters 7 and 8 formed distinct narrative units. Here, within the twelfth-century Victorine community,

---

[36]Smalley, *Study*, pp. 165-66.

[37]*Ibid.*, pp. 110-11, 163.

[38]M. Signer, "Peshat, Sensus Litteralis," and also "Between Exegesis and Polemic: Peter the Venerable and Richard of St. Victor." (Unpublished article.)

we have a foretaste of the kind of conflict that can emerge with differing conceptions of literal exegesis and with varying perceptions of the vitally important idea of the narrative text.

Herbert of Bosham

The remaining inheritor of the Victorine tradition of literal exegesis to be discussed in this paper is Herbert of Bosham.[39] Herbert is a fascinating figure for many reasons. Raphael Loewe has praised him as possibly the best Christian Hebraist between Jerome and Pico della Mirandola and Reuchlin. In addition, Herbert knew some Greek, and he may have been able to read Aramaic and Arabic, all achievements of no small merit.[40] Apart from his prominence as an exegete who pursued the literal sense of Scripture and drew upon Jewish resources to do so, Herbert had an interesting and significant career.[41] He was born about 1120 in Bosham, Sussex, England. He went to Paris to study under the renowned master Peter Lombard, probably around 1150, and then returned to England to enter the service of King Henry II. Herbert is mentioned with the title "master" in a royal letter of 1157. He must have been one of the clerks who served Becket when he was Chancellor, for Herbert went with Becket when the latter became archbishop of Canterbury. Herbert was in the inner circle of Becket's entourage, and he served the archbishop faithfully in England, during exile on the continent, and after Becket's murder as one of the promoters of the martyr's cause. It was Herbert who gave Becket instruction in scripture and theology; and this occurred daily, if we accept Herbert's account of a typical day in the archbishop's life.[42] While sharing Becket's exile in France, Herbert visited the Abbey of St.-Victor with Becket in 1169. At that moment Andrew of St.-Victor was at Wigmore in England for his second time as Abbot, but Andrew's works

---

[39]Smalley, *Study*, pp. 186-95. A more lengthy treatment of Herbert will be found in Smalley's *The Becket Conflict and the Schools* (Oxford, 1973) pp. 59-86. See also the *Dictionary of National Biography*, "Herbert of Bosham."

[40]See R. Loewe, "Herbert of Bosham's Commentary on Jerome's Hebrew Psalter," *Biblica* 34 (1953) 44-77, 159-92, 275-98; here, pp. 52-58.

[41]Details in Smalley, *Becket Conflict*, see esp. pp. 59-74. Herbert's relationship to Becket is also portrayed at numerous junctures in F. Barlow, *Thomas Becket* (Berkeley, 1986).

[42]Barlow, *Becket*, p. 80.

would have been available at St.-Victor. Moreover, Herbert may have come into contact with Andrew's work, or may even have heard Andrew lecture, in Paris before 1147 or after 1154–1155. We know unfortunately far too little of Herbert's contacts and of the personal influences that were decisive in his life.

Tantalizing possibilities leave one dangling: a papal commendation to the office of provost at Troyes in 1165 raises the exciting possibility of contact with the Jewish community there, but the actual outcome of the commendation is unknown. However, the fact that a busy man who spent years in the entourage of a beleaguered archbishop took up the study of Jewish exegesis is of more than passing interest. It is even more significant when we note that he devoted himself to the acquisition of substantial linguistic skills and also to the direct study of the writings of Rashi and other more ancient authorities. He was not content merely to interview Jewish scholars for their opinions.

In fact, as one considers Herbert of Bosham a question takes shape: Was there a wider network of persons interested in the Victorine emphasis and in Jewish exegesis? There were of course the three parisian masters who are identified by Smalley as the major continuators of the "Victorine tradition" in literal exegesis, which means including Jewish materials.[43] These three, Peter Comestor, Peter the Chanter, and Stephen Langton, all drew Jewish materials directly from Andrew's commentaries. Langton and the Chanter seem to have utilized fresh interpretations obtained from conversations with rabbis; Peter Comestor's time as dean of the chapter in Troyes, the home of Rashi and a center of Jewish scholarship, raises interesting unanswered questions about the possibility of his direct contact with Jewish scholarship. Moving beyond this "parisian" circle, in this connection it is interesting to note the history of the only extant manuscript of Herbert of Bosham's literal commentary on the Psalms. It is in the library of St. Paul's, London, having been given to the church by Henry of

---

[43]On the three masters, see Smalley, *Study*, ch. 5; most recently, see D. Luscombe, "Peter Comester," and Gilbert Dahan, "Les interpretations juives dans les commentaires du pentateuque de Pierre le Chantre," in K. Walsh and D. Wood, eds., *The Bible in the Medieval World: Essays in Memory of Beryl Smalley* (Studies in Church History, Subsidia 4; Oxford, 1985) pp. 109-29 and 131-55.

Cornhil, Dean of St. Paul's, who died in 1254.[44] It will be recalled that Ralph of Diceto, who died as dean of St. Paul's about 1202, is the one person known to have made direct use of Hugh's *Chronicon* with its emphasis on "Hebrew truth" in the opening chronology. The existence of two deans interested in "Hebrew truth" provides interesting fuel for speculation.

Without going into great detail, several things can be said about Herbert's work. First, he did not limit himself in his biblical studies to the literal sense. He edited the *Magna Glosatura* of Peter Lombard, who had been his master in Paris. As Smalley pointed out, Becket ordered Herbert to carry out this rather complicated editorial task, which was only completed sometime between Becket's murder (1170) and 1176.[45] The edition, in four volumes, was given to the monks of Christchurch, Canterbury. Second, however conversant he was with the allegorical interpretation of Scripture, in his own commentary on the *Psalms* Herbert followed the Victorine example and used the results of Andrew of St.-Victor's singleminded devotion to literal exposition. Moreover, Herbert commented on the *Hebraica*, the text of the *Psalms* which is a Latin translation made from the Hebrew by Jerome and considered to be more accurate than the text then commonly found in the Vulgate Bible. Herbert collated several versions of the *Hebraica* in order to improve the text and also offered his own improvements in the Latin when he thought the Hebrew warranted such.[46] According to Loewe, Herbert had at hand a text of Rashi's commentary and also used other commentators, both contemporary and ancient.[47] The Jewish materials and influences in his commentary were thus not only due to conversations, as they apparently were with Hugh. We have now entered a new world that extends beyond oral communication to the independent use of textual material. Now a Christian scholar was using Jewish texts to extend the boundaries of his own knowledge. The threat that such studies posed in the eyes of some can be seen in prohibitions against the study of Hebrew with rabbis

[44]On the manuscript see B. Smalley, "A Commentary on the Hebraica by Herbert of Bosham," *Recherches de theologie ancienne et medievale* 18 (1951) 29-65.
[45]Smalley, *Becket Conflict*, p. 82.
[46]Loewe, "Herbert of Bosham's Commentary," pp. 48-51.
[47]*Ibid.*, pp. 59-70.

and the increasingly negative theological judgments against Judaism in the last half of the twelfth century and in the thirteenth.

With Herbert, one has the sense of being in the presence of a person who was exploring with subtlety, skill, and deep interest a wide range of Jewish scholarship in order to further the literal exposition of the Hebrew scriptures within Christian circles. He went to great lengths to determine which psalms were messianic in intent, and distinguished between Jewish and Christian interpretations on this topic. He disagreed with Rashi's nonmessianic interpretations of certain psalms, but in some cases he was willing to accept a nonmessianic interpretation of a psalm. Herbert was even willing to entertain rather speculative questions of the "what if" type concerning religion. Herbert describes a time when he wondered, as Smalley puts it, "whether, if the Christian faith were unfounded, in that the Messias had not come, but must still be awaited, as the Jews say, God would impute a faith in Christ to righteousness."[48] Clearly this well-trained parisian master of theology was willing for a moment to hear the other side and reflect, at least for one brief time in his life, about the possibility of its truth.

Implications for Today

One could follow Herbert further. For our purposes we have probably gone far enough. He shows the depth to which a dedicated exegete could probe in seeking to complement Christian exegesis with the insights of the Jewish interpreters and to enrich the understanding of the text by careful consideration of the Hebrew. The broader confluence of the two streams of Jewish and Christian biblical interpretation was yet to come in Nicholas of Lyra and those who followed him.[49] But with the foundation laid by Hugh, the practical application by Andrew, and the more complete probing by Herbert we gain some sense of the scholarly interchange on scriptural topics that could occur in that "open century," the twelfth.

If the study of these things suggests anything today, it should urge two things. First, we should do what Andrew and

---

[48]Smalley, *Study*, p. 192.
[49]See Hailperin, *Rashi*.

Herbert did—sit down with interpreters of other traditions and explore their tradition-centered understanding of texts, both historically and in light of present scholarship. We will then learn more of our common past, our shared problems, and our possible convergences. Second, as historians, our conversations on common topics may well lead to a more perceptive interpretation of individual traditions. Certainly the cooperative study of medieval exegesis, an endeavor scarcely begun with the work of Smalley, Loewe, and others, is a rich field.

In closing, let me present an observation that first occurred to me while reading some of I. A. Agus' remarks on Rashi and the transition in Rashi's own studies from a tradition that emphasized oral teaching and memorization to one that with Rashi began to move toward a greater dependence upon written texts.[50] Perhaps this shift was a very individual step, grounded in Rashi's own peculiar circumstances as a student with limited time and resources. Perhaps it was a part of the need to have a written text as a basis for teaching activity. But in either case, it reflects the kind of profound shift in "mentality" that Brian Stock has examined in his book, *The Implications of Literacy*.[51] Stock is concerned with the movement from oral cultures to textually based cultures in the eleventh and twelfth centuries, with more than a little emphasis on northern France. In this shift he finds many of the roots of central characteristics of medieval and modern cultures. Perhaps the closer study of such a shift in the Jewish tradition will lead to a clearer understanding of twelfth-century developments generally. Certainly the twelfth-century development of schools, of collections of theological sentences, of an organized literate "elite," and of a distinctive theology in the schools had a profound impact on Christian culture. Likewise the rich intellectual culture, focused on biblical interpretation and Talmudic tradition in the Jewish communities of northern France, exerted a lasting influence on Judaism. It may well be that examining Jewish culture in northern France in the twelfth century from the perspective of an emerging shift to textuality will yield new insights as well. In

---

[50]I. A. Agus, "Rashi and His School," in Roth, *Jews in Christian Europe 711-1096*, pp. 210-48, esp. 220-22.
[51]B. Stock, *The Implications of Literacy* (Princeton, 1983).

any case, to explore further the interaction of Jewish and Christian exegetes in the medieval period can do nothing less than furnish a clearer perspective on what is shared in our common—yet too often divided—past as Jews and Christians. Moreover, as suggested above, it may also lead to a renewed dialogue in the present situation.

DISCUSSION

CHARLESWORTH: Professor Zinn has emphasized four dimensions that are exceedingly important to me. First, he reveals the clear evidence of the study and knowledge of Hebrew by Christians, especially Herbert of Bosham, Thomas Becket's tutor. Second, he demonstrates that Christians were taking Jewish exegesis seriously, were in dialogue with Jews, and were trying to learn how to apply Jewish exegesis to their own tradition and text. Third, he has shown us that there is some very important art that we really do not know anything about—one such piece clearly depicts Jesus unveiling the synagogue, and this depiction clearly clashes with the ones on the facades of many cathedrals in Europe. And finally, he has pointed out that exegesis need not be limited to one point but can have many points, which is precisely the Jewish dimension, and which pervades the work of Andrew of St.-Victor, so that we find in Christianity in the twelfth century an incredible interpretation of *Isaiah* 7, 9, and 11 coming from the Victorines.

BEKER: Let me ask Dr. Zinn a question. Isn't it interesting that this open century, with its attention to the Hebrew, is also the century of the Crusades?

ZINN: Yes, but let's make the distinction. Rheinland Jewry suffered in the Crusades in the twelfth century. In the late twelfth century northern French-Jewish communities were not as threatened.

BEKER: I'm interested in a larger landscape. These twelfth-century Christian writers interested in invoking the Jewish exegetes—what was their reaction to the Crusades?

ZINN: There is not much reaction to the Crusades in Victorine literature, but Hugh does use one interesting image that depicts Christ in a battle with the devil. He stands in the midst of an army, made up of the Hebrew people *and* the Christian people. He leads them through history banishing the enemy.

BEKER: Along with the Hebrew people?

ZINN: Yes. The Hebrew and the Christian people always cling together in his understanding. This is why Hugh's sense of the historical holds the narrative to be so important: the Hebrew tradition is always there.

BEKER: It is that these people were so interested in the continuity of the Hebrew tradition. This went along with the Crusade policy. These centuries were among the worst of Jewish persecution. Now what exactly is going on? Is this the ivory tower syndrome?

ZINN: This is what we don't know in the case of St.-Victor because all we have are these texts. We don't have any statements about who they saw or the context in which they carried out their discussions with Jewish scholars.

BEKER: No contingency, right?

ZINN: Right. No contingency. But it is also interesting that the church of St.-Denis is the place where the king deposited the royal banner that he took into battle. There is a connection with the Crusades and St.-Denis. And here we have a more complex question. What you have to ask is whether these people were living on two levels. What does this say about the study of the tradition of Jewish exegesis? How does it relate to the relationship between Christians and Jews? We don't have a full answer to that. People have tried to explain the window at St.-Denis by saying that apparently there was a very positive relationship between a Jewish community near St. Denis and the Abbey. But I do not think that is adequate at all.

HILLERBRAND: But, Dr. Zinn, can you turn it around the other way? Start with empirical reality, as Dr. Beker has said; this is the time of the most severe suppression of Jews until our own day and age. You know that. Now turn to the texts. Does it surprise you that the texts contain no theological analogue to the empirical situation?

ZINN: That's an interesting way to put it. And in one instance we do have something of an analogue, because St.-Victor was also a place where very important liturgical sequences were written by a man named Adam. Adam was first at the cathedral and then went to St.-Victor, although it is a problem working out what sequences he wrote and when. But if you go to the sequences, a rejection of the Jewish tradition is present. That represents a different attitude. And in some of these liturgical sequences you get the traditional depiction of the synagogue as blind. We need to understand one Victorine attitude along with the other.

HILLERBRAND: Are there sermons that are anti-Judaic or anti-Semitic?

ZINN: Not that I know of at St.-Victor. Of course, there were certainly others elsewhere, such as Peter the Venerable and the Abbot of Cluny.

HILLERBRAND: Were they pointed and ruthless?

ZINN: Not ruthless. And then we have records of dialogue—some actual, some artificial—between Christians and Jews. That just takes us back to ambiguity, I think. But I would still come back to the fact that it's clear the twelfth century was a time of terrible repression and fearful, fearful times for certain Jewish communities. But it is necessary to make geographical distinctions in certain time periods between the situation, say in the north of France and what was going on in the Rheinland. And this is where historians have to look more closely at the texts. There may also be some significant differences in *theological* attitudes or judgments and *practical* exegetical conversations.

BEKER: When they mentioned Rashi and others, would they simply talk about *Isaiah* and not about what was going on in the Jewish community?

ZINN: This is what I wish we knew. Did they just sit down and talk about the text or did they sit down and also talk about the Jewish community? There are comments about Jewish festivals and some observations about Jewish life. They are aware of Jewish culture. They discuss these things because they see the Jewish community surviving and carrying on their own tradition, and thus capable of throwing light on the meaning of the text.

SMITH: Are there Christian scholars consulting rabbis, and making inferences from patterns of Jewish exegesis? Are there explicit statements about this kind of thing?

ZINN: There are explicit statements that will refer to them as

"Hebrew truth," meaning contemporary Jewish interpretation. Herbert constantly refers to his Jewish interlocutors. There are some marginal inscriptions in the manuscript of Herbert's commentary that say this is from Rashi and this is from somewhere else. But the key phrase that they use is, "The Jews say this."

SMITH: Well, is there explicit evidence that shows they were getting some of their material not simply from reading Jewish commentaries but from face-to-face consultation with their Jewish contemporaries?

ZINN: The inference made by Beryl Smalley and others is that in the beginning they went to the local Jewish community and asked the Jews how they interpreted these things.

PRIEST: In the early period, though, they could not have consulted commentaries because they didn't know Hebrew well enough to do this.

ZINN: Correct. They had to use Latin or French, probably French because Andrew used French phrases to explain words. With Herbert of Bosham, however, you have a man who knew Hebrew well enough to use the written tradition. As I mentioned in the paper, the movement from oral traditions to written traditions is an interesting aspect of Christian culture in this period, and it seems to have been significant in Jewish culture as well, at least with Rashi.

1. Reims Cathedral. Juxtaposition of the Church and the Synagogue. Note how the Church (at left) stands triumphant, with crown in place, staff erect, chalice raised, and eyes open to the future. In sheer contrast, the Synagogue (at right) is bent, with fallen crown, probably a broken staff (now lost; see illus. 3, 7), a fallen hand (which once may have held a book, probably depicting the Old Testament; see illus. 3, 7, 8), and eyes blindfolded. The sculptures graphically depict the centuries-long Christian belief that God's covenant with the Jews had been broken and was now replaced by a "new covenant" exclusively with the church. *Courtesy of Kunstgeschichtlichen Institut der Philipps-Universitaet, Marburg, West Germany.*

2. Strassbourg Cathedral. The Church as portrayed in the facade of the famous thirteenth-century structure. Note the erect posture, crown securely placed, erect staff depicted as a cross, caressed chalice, and triumphant gaze. *Courtesy of Kunstgeschichtlichen Institut der Philipps-Universitaet, Marburg, West Germany.*

3. Strassbourg Cathedral. The Synagogue as conceived by the architects and builders. Note the bent posture, bare head, splintered staff, fallen hand with fallen book (?), and downcast blindfolded eyes. *Courtesy of Kunstgeschichtlichen Institut der Philipps-Universitaet, Marburg, West Germany.*

4. Church of the Abbey of St.-Denis near Paris. Christ with the Church and the Synagogue. See the discussion by Professor Grover Zinn in this volume. *Courtesy of William W. Clark.*

5. Notre Dame de Paris, north entrance. The depictions of the Church and the Synagogue (see illus. 6, 7) are opposite the central door. *Courtesy of James H. Charlesworth.*

6. Notre Dame de Paris, main doors, flanked by depictions of the Church (left) and the Synagogue (right). *Courtesy of James H. Charlesworth.*

7. Notre Dame de Paris, sculpture of fallen Synagogue. Observe the typical portrayal of the Jews: the bent torso, crown fallen to the ground, shattered staff, fallen hand with the five books of the Torah, and severely blindfolded eyes. This is surely one of the most shocking portrayals of Judaism in European cathedrals. It is horrifyingly anti-Jewish. *Courtesy of James H. Charlesworth.*

8. Freiburg Cathedral, carving of disheveled Synagogue. Note the erect posture, and crown in place; but also observe the raised but broken staff (?),
fallen hand with a book (the Torah?), and constricting blindfold. This
depiction of the Synagogue is impressively less harsh than the one at the
entrance of Notre Dame de Paris (illus. 7). *Courtesy of the Directors of the
Cathedral, Freiburg im Breisgau, West Germany.*

F.X.BLISARD

9. Medieval drawing of the Church and the Synagogue flanking the crucified Christ. From a composite manuscript of the early eleventh century. *Re-drawn from Vos. Cod. Oct. 15, f. 3v.; by permission of the Bibliotheek der Rijksuniversiteit te Leiden.*

CHAPTER SIX

Martin Luther and the Jews

Hans J. Hillerbrand

Introduction

The topic "Martin Luther and the Jews" is by no means new.[1] The topic has been explored extensively over the years, especially since World War II, recently with particular intensity in conjunction with the Luther anniversary of 1983. Understandably, the foremost contributors to the discussion have been Lutheran and Jewish scholars. In fact, there has been an official consultation between the Jewish Committee for Interreligious Consultations and the Lutheran World Federation on the topic of Luther's legacy.[2] There are those for whom Martin Luther is a singularly insightful interpreter of the Christian faith, and they are profoundly perturbed by his strident and obscene anti-Semitic pronouncements, even as there are, among those who—indirectly or directly—suffered the consequences of Nazi anti-Semitism, some who are similarly sincerely searching for explanations.

The real topic is certainly not so much "Martin Luther and the Jews" as "Germany and the Jews." We are primarily jolted by the haunting question of whether Luther helped mold German thinking so that the way was prepared for the Nazi ideology that prevailed between 1933 and 1945.[3] Thus, at issue is not antiquarian scholarly interest but a most relevant contemporary question.

The connection between Martin Luther and Nazi totalitarianism was quickly made. Karl Barth asserted in 1939 that Luther's mistaken political ethics helped cause the rise of

Hitler; this view was popularized in William Shirer's best seller *The Rise and Fall of the Third Reich*.[4] One of the first major statements connecting Luther's anti-Semitism with Nazi totalitarianism came at the end of World War II with the publication of Peter F. Wiener's *Martin Luther: Hitler's Spiritual Ancestor*.[5] The charges were broad and comprehensive and went beyond the strident anti-Semitic remarks of Luther's later years. Luther's treatment of the Anabaptists, his pronouncements on sexual morality, and his coarse language came under severe attack as a demonstration of the adverse impact of the German reformer on German mentality and history.

In my opinion, the broader context of Luther's historical image cannot be ignored. Martin Luther has always had—but particularly in the late nineteenth century—a "bad press." This has had to do not only with the notion of liberal Protestants that the reformer was medieval in his outlook, but also with the vitriolic attacks of late nineteenth-century papalistic Catholics, notably Denifle and Grisar, who argued the depravity of Luther as person and theologian. In a similar vein, Paul J. Reiter, a Danish psychiatrist, concluded that Luther was a textbook case of a manic depressive, who might have even suffered from an advanced case of epilepsy.[6] Erich Fromm, in turn, viewed Luther as a classic authoritarian personality.[7]

---

[1]Two recent monographs have extensive and useful bibliographies: H. A. Oberman, *The Roots of Anti-Semitism in the Age of Renaissance and Reformation* (Philadelphia, 1984), and E. W. Gritsch, *Martin—God's Court Jester: Luther in Retrospect* (Philadelphia, 1983). Other recent studies are J. Brosseder, *Luthers Stellung zu den Juden im Spiegel seiner Interpretation* (Munich, 1972); B. C. Sucher, *Luthers Stellung zu den Juden: Eine Interpretation aus germanistischer Sicht* (Niewkoop, 1977); H. Kremers, ed., *Die Juden und Martin Luther—Martin Luther und die Juden* (Neukirchen-Vluyn, 1985); H. Lindner, *Martin Luther und die Juden* (Wuppertal, 1984). See also L. Siegele-Wenschkewitz, "Der Beitrag der Kirchengeschichte zu einer Theologie nach dem Holocaust: Christlicher Antijudaismus als Wurzel des Antisemitismus," *Concilium* 20 (1984) 413–16; E. L. Ehrlich, "Luther und die Juden," in H. Strauss and N. Kampe, eds., *Antisemitismus: von der Judenfeindschaft zum Holocaust* (Frankfurt am Main, 1985) pp. 47-65; A. Baumann et al., eds., *Luthers Erben und die Juden: Das Verhältnis lutherischer Kirchen Europas zu den Juden* (Hanover, 1984). The Yearbook of the Leo Baeck Institute may be used for a comprehensive annual bibliography.

[2]J. Halperin and A. Sovik, eds., *Luther, Lutheranism, and the Jews* (Geneva, 1984), with papers by E. L. Ehrlich and M. Edwards.

[3]See Kremers, *Die Juden und Martin Luther*, esp. pp. 301ff.

[4]W. L. Shirer, *The Rise and Fall of the Third Reich* (New York, 1960) p. 236, "The great founder of Protestantism was both a passionate anti-Semite and a fervent believer in political authority."

[5]There was a vehement response from the pen of G. Rupp, *Martin Luther: Hitler's Cause or Cure?* (London, 1945). Recently, Rupp has summarized his point of view again: "Martin Luther and the Jews," *Nederlands Teologisk Tidsskrift* 31 (1977) 121–35.

Our topic can best be delineated by (1) summarizing Luther's writings on the Jews, (2) reflecting on their meaning, and (3) speaking about their historical impact.

The Historical Record

There is scholarly agreement that the early Luther spoke thoughtfully and positively about Jews. He supported the humanist Johannes Reuchlin and his advocacy of the study of Hebrew, the deep concern being the advocacy of open discussion.[8] Luther's lectures on the *Book of Psalms* contain repeated references to the Jewish people, who were seen as a paradigm for human estrangement from God.[9] Luther hoped for their conversion to Christianity, prayed for "Jews, heretics, and all people in error,"[10] and counseled that "we should not treat the Jews in an unfriendly manner, for future Christians might be among them."[11] Only they, and not the Gentiles, have the promise that they will be forever "in Abraham's seed." In his tract *Concerning Married Life*, Luther wrote that "I may well eat, drink, sleep, walk, ride, buy, talk, and act with a pagan or Jew or Turk or heretic, even marry one."[12]

In his 1523 tract *That Jesus Christ was Born a Jew* Luther expressed optimism about the possibility of Jewish conversion to Christianity; but his main point was to stress that love must be foremost in all relationships, including Christian relations with Jews.[13] On the common attitude of Christians towards Jews, he commented, "They have treated the Jews as if they were dogs and not human beings."[14] Or again: "We must receive them cordially, and permit them to trade and work with us. . . . If some are stiff-necked, so what? After all, we are ourselves not such good Christians either."[15] Luther's attitude was un-

---

[6]P. J. Reiter, *Martin Luthers Umwelt, Charakter und Psychose* (Copenhagen, 1941).

[7]E. Fromm, *Escape from Freedom* (New York, 1941) p. 95.

[8]W. Maurer, *Kirche und Synagogue* (WA Br. 1,7; Stuttgart, 1953) p. 89.

[9]WA 56, 46; 56, 199. See also the *Operationes in Psalmos* (1519–21), for example, WA 5, 427: "Therefore we must condemn the fury of certain Christians who think that they please God by persecuting the Jews with fierce hatred."

[10]WA 7, 226.

[11]WA 7, 600.

[12]WA 10, II, 283.

[13]WA 11, 307ff.

[14]WA 11, 315.

[15]WA 11, 336.

doubtedly influenced by his optimism about the persuasiveness of the newly restored gospel. Accordingly, in his *Short Form of the Ten Commandments*, he urged his readers to pray for the Jews who might be converted and who should not be unnecessarily offended by Christian quarreling or harshness.[16] For Luther the basic issue in Christian-Jewish relations was simple, and very much what it had been all along: Jews should convert to Christianity. In so doing, they would appropriate their own scripture in its authentic fashion.[17] To be sure, Luther's tracts were an invitation to dialogue, but with a rather fixed notion of its outcome—namely, acceptance of the point of view presented, which was in general the standard stance of sixteenth-century religious colloquies.

Luther's major pronouncement on societal issues of 1520—his *Open Letter to the Christian Nobility*—included no references to Jews or the "Jewish question." It would seem that for Luther the legal and social situation of the Jews in Germany and the Holy Roman Empire was not an important and ongoing concern. This attitude seems evident for the 1520s.

From the end of the 1530s onward, however, a different tone can be discerned in Luther's writings. There is less optimism about the possibility of Jewish conversion; and there is greater concern about evidence of Jewish religious vitality. Luther's most strident remarks about Jews come from the years immediately preceding his death, a fact that prompted Roland H. Bainton to remark that "it would have been better had Luther died before taking to the pen with these tracts."[18] The most infamous pronouncement was the 1543 tract *Concerning the Jews and Their Lies*, though it is important to keep in mind that this was not an isolated publication.[19] There was, in fact, a string of such writings—the tracts *Concerning Schem Hemphoras and the Genealogy of Christ* and *Concerning the Last Words of David*, as well as Luther's very last sermon, preached a few days before his death.[20]

Concerning the Jews and Their Lies was, like many of Luther's

---

[16]WA 7, 226.

[17]WA 11, 315.

[18]R. H. Bainton, *Here I Stand* (New York, 1955) p. 297.

[19]WA 53, 412ff.

[20]The writings are found in WA 53, 579ff.; WA 54, 28ff.; and WA 51, 187ff. Luther's sermon has an apprendix entitled "An Admonition against the Jews."

tracts, a polemical retort. A rabbi had written a forcefully argued tract against Luther's *Against the Sabbatarians*; he challenged Christians to convert to Judaism. Luther's response did not intend to be a "dialogue," but summarized for Christians the main tenets of the faith, as they pertain to the relationship with Judaism. Accordingly, Luther discussed such topics as circumcision, the Mosaic Law, the possession of Canaan, Jerusalem, and the Temple. The tract was a restatement of Christian tenets, foremostly delineated in terms of a christocentric interpretation of the Old Testament. This meant the repudiation of the Jewish claim to be the sole chosen people and their rejection of Jesus' messianic claim. Luther's language was shocking, if not obscene. One example suffices: "Now, what ought we Christians do with this rejected and damned people, the Jews? . . . We have to practice a fierce mercy in hopes that we can at least save a few of them from the glowing flames. Vengeance is out of the question. Revenge already hangs on their necks, a thousand times worse than we could wish on them."[21] As to particulars, Luther proposed such ruthless measures as the burning of Jewish books and of synagogues, and manual labor for all Jews.

The theological themes of the tract had been stated before. What was new was the sharpness of tone as well as the appeal to the political authorities to suppress the Jews. These years of Luther's life were characterized by outbursts of anger and vitriolic pronouncements on his part. His remarks about Anabaptists or the pope were every bit as vitriolic—and obscene—as those against the Jews. The Jews were not a separate category in Luther's polemic; they were an integral part of those who misinterpreted or falsified the true gospel. And that included the Catholics, the pope, the Anabaptists, even the Turks.[22] Quite consistently, Luther's anti-Catholic tract *Concerning the Papacy in Rome Which Was Founded by the Devil*, of 1545, vies with the anti-Jewish pronouncements for abusiveness of style and content, even as his less formal remarks about the Anabaptists—less formal, I believe, because he did not view them as

---

[21]WA 53, 522.
[22]On Luther and the Anabaptists, see J. S. Oyer, *Lutheran Reformers against the Anabaptists* (The Hague, 1964). On Luther's later anti-Catholic polemic, see E. Gritsch, "Luther and the Jews: Toward a Judgment of History," *Luther and the Jews* (New York, 1983) p. 7.

a real threat—expressed the same substantive unwillingness to tolerate them. The differences were minor. Luther did not call for the involvement of governmental authority to deal with Catholics, as he did with the Anabaptists and the Jews. His basic explanation was that Catholics affirmed the fundamental tenets of the faith even as they were law abiding and not revolutionaries. By the same token, one might suggest that Catholics enjoyed political power at least in some places, thus raising the specter of retribution.

The Interpretation

The explanations for Luther's attitude toward the Jews have varied, his harshness eliciting universal condemnation and expressions of regret. In a thoughtful summary, Eric Gritsch has noted four lines of interpretation:[23]

1. *The basic difference between the young Luther and the old Luther.* This point of view, which has echoes in other areas of Luther's thought (puzzling since the "young" Luther of the 1520s was almost forty years of age), holds that initially Luther was a friend of the Jews, but, under the impact of sundry influences, turned into a fierce opponent in later years.[24] Explanations vary. Political strategy may have played a role. Luther's early declarations of tolerance had been strategic moves, made when he himself was very much in need of political support. By the late 1530s Luther and his cause had become somewhat politically secure. Luther could afford to be candid, outspoken, and show his true feelings. And he did.

2. *Luther's apocalyptic world view coupled with his conviction of the imminent end of the world.* Since the end of the world was in sight, the time had also come for the conversion of the Jews.[25]

3. *Luther's precarious health.* From the 1530s onward, Luther was subjected to chronic physical pain, severe problems with kidney stones, gallstones, and depressions. Not only was he rendered incapable of sound judgment, his whole personality may well have changed.[26]

---

[23]Gritsch, *Luther and the Jews*, p. 7.

[24]The initial statement of this view was by R. Lewin, *Luthers Stellung zu den Juden* (Berlin, 1911).

[25]This argument is forcefully presented by H. A. Oberman, *The Roots of Anti-Semitism*, see esp. pp. 117ff.

4. The essential theological consistency of the young Luther and the mature Luther. Reading human history as sacred history, Luther saw the Jews as the chosen people who had rejected the Messiah, whose hearts God had hardened, and who were a pernicious influence on Christendom. They epitomized works righteousness, which meant that they were not reading their own scriptures authentically.

We may note yet another possibility explaining the change from the early 1520s to the early 1540s. Martin Luther was overpowered by his conviction that the gospel had been restored in his time and that it was within the reach of anybody, no matter how unlearned, to appropriate and understand it. No external authority, such as Church, council, or pope, was necessary, because the meaning of Scripture was simple and clear. Accordingly, Luther asserted in his famous declaration in Worms in 1521 that "his conscience was *captured* by the Word of God." That also was the meaning of his objection to the comment that Emperor Charles V suppressed the reform movement because he followed his conscience: Luther insisted that this was impossible, because someone in error did not follow his conscience.[27] It is assuredly a "poor excuse" if "someone has heard God's word for fifteen hundred years and always says 'I do not want to know it'." He will certainly "pay for his guilt seven times."[28] Clearly, if the simple and self-evident gospel message was not accepted, something pernicious was at work.

Luther must be seen in the context of traditional Christian views of the Jews as well as sixteenth-century practice. Thus, Luther's statements have antecedents in the sordid tradition of medieval anti-Semitism. It has been pointed out that there was nothing new in Luther's statements, and, therefore, that tradition more so than Luther should be seen as the fateful legacy.[29] If anything, then, Luther should be faulted for not breaking

---

[26]See on this point H. G. Haile, *Martin Luther: An Experiment in Biography* (New York, 1980).

[27]See W. Köhler, *Dogmengeschichte als Geschichte des christlichen Selbstbewusstseins* (Zürich, 1951) p. 55.

[28]WA 53, 526.

[29]See the remarks by Maurer, *Kirche und Synagogue*, pp. 103-04. In *The Roots of Anti-Semitism* Oberman makes the point that Luther was, in fact, more positive in his views than either Reuchlin or Erasmus. On Erasmus see G. Kisch, *Erasmus' Stellung zu den Juden* (Tübingen, 1969).

away more from the traditional legacy. However, Luther no longer gave credence to such traditional allegations as Jewish ritualistic murder, well poisoning, or the desecration of the host.[30] He called such allegations "fool's work." But he was not beyond gossiping—some of it quite vile—as, for example, in his *Admonition against the Jews*, where he observed that "if they could kill us all, they would truly do it, and, in fact, they do it quite often, especially those who pretend to be physicians."[31]

Provocatively, Heiko A. Oberman has recently suggested that the Jewish question was a central theme in Luther's theology.[32] On one level, it clearly was not. In terms of the sheer quantity of Luther's writings, the Jews do not rank prominently at all. Yet, on another level, it undoubtedly was. Luther was consumed with the dualism between God and Antichrist, between grace and law, faith and works, and in that setting the Jews epitomized what stood at the very heart of Luther's thought: what is God—and how can we know him? In this light, Luther's theological observations about the Jews may be subsumed under four headings.

1. The theological affirmation. No equality exists between Judaism and Christianity. The former has been superseded by the latter. Jesus is the Messiah, the end of the Law, and this means the centrality of gospel and grace. The Hebrew Scriptures must be interpreted christologically. As people of the Law, the Jews epitomize an erroneous understanding of God, namely, that of works righteousness. Scripture has been fulfilled; the prophecies of the Old Testament have occurred; the Jewish religion has no longer any reason to exist.

Since the repudiation of all forms of works righteousness formed the pivotal core of Luther's theology, his repudiation of the Jews—as a theological entity—was categorical. The Jews were exemplars of false religion, as were Catholics, Turks, and Anabaptists. However, if a Jew converted to Christianity, he or she was fully a Christian, and no longer a Jew. Luther acknowledged kinship between a baptized Jew and a baptized Gentile, even as there was kinship between an unbaptized Jew and an unbaptized Gentile.[33]

---

[30]W. Bienert, *Martin Luther und die Juden* (Frankfurt am Main, 1982) p. 177.
[31]WA 51, 195.
[32]H. A. Oberman, *Luther: Man Between God and Devil* (Philadelphia, 1985).

By the same token, one must be cautious not to overstate the point. The Jews were not only a people adhering to a certain religion, but also a people. Or, to put it differently, to be a Jew meant to be a Semite. Thus, the attack on the one was an attack on the other. If, moreover, as was the case in Spain, the sincerity of the Jewish conversions to Christianity was doubted, it was easy to be anti-Semitic, even though the real issue was anti-Judaism.

2. *The missionary impulse.* Especially in his early writings Luther stressed the obligation to preach the gospel to the Gentiles and the Jews, arguing the solidarity of guilt, judgment, and grace, of all people, Jew and Gentile. Some scholars have argued that Luther's call for conversion of the Jews in later years had, in light of his overtowering sense of the imminence of the end of the world, no real practical significance.[34] Still, the mandate "to preach the gospel," which had been recently restored, was thereby prominently expressed. Luther's strategy was to be friendly toward Jews and to accept them, so as to remove any barrier to the Jewish acceptance of Jesus. Luther also advised that Jesus should first be presented as Messiah, as foretold in Scripture, and only afterward as true God.

3. *The view of history.* For Luther the course of history vindicated his theological judgment about the Jewish people who had been unwilling to accept the Messiah. How could one understand the peripatetic homelessness of the Jews, and their chronic persecutions? Surely, he reasoned, it is because God had removed himself from them. The tensions between synagogue and church were for Luther not only a manifestation of specific tension, but also part and parcel of a larger struggle against the world in which the Church is engaged.

Intriguingly, this view of history so expressed by Luther,

---

[33]Oberman, *The Roots of Anti Semitism*, p 102. J. Friedmann's recent article "Jewish Conversion, the Spanish Pure Blood Laws and Reformation: A Revisionist View of Racial and Religious Antisemitism," *Sixteenth Century Journal* 18 (1987) 25, demurs. See also J. Brosseder, "Luther und der Leidensweg der Juden" in Kremers, *Die Juden und Martin Luther*, p. 131.

[34]To have pointed out the difference between the early and the later Luther in this regard was Lewin's major contribution. The most thorough analysis of the issue is by M. Stöhr, "Luther und die Juden," *Evangelische Theologie* 20 (1960) 157-82. An insightful statement is "Martin Luther und die Juden," W. D. Marsch and K. Thieme, eds., *Christen und Juden* (Göttingen, 1961) pp. 115-40, recently reprinted in Kremers, *Die Juden und Martin Luther*, pp. 89-108; see esp. 98, "Zwanzig Jahre später hat sich sodann das Bild völlig gewandelt."

runs counter to the reformer's "theology of the cross," that is, to the affirmation that God's presence and work in history is always "in hiding," always contrary to appearance and experience. Thus, the seemingly simple lessons of history are not at all the authentic ones. The most obvious conclusion to be drawn from Luther's "theology of the cross" surely would be that *sub contrarie* the suffering and persecution of the Jews testify precisely to a diametrically different reality, namely to their eternal election.

Still, Martin Luther argued, in line with the Christian tradition, that Jesus, who came as the Messiah of Israel, was rejected by his people. Accordingly, God concluded a new covenant with a new "Israel," while the stubbornness of the old Israel perpetuated the Law which was fulfilled, in fact, through the fulfillment of the promise—the coming of the Messiah. Israel appears as the manifestation of God's judgment and grace, even as God's working in history manifests the stubbornness of the Jewish people and the synagogue. There is no more promise for Israel. God is silent. Israel experiences the silence of God, which is his wrath. Luther noted: "And thus the wrath of God has come over them, about which I do not like to think, even as I have not been happy writing this book. With anger and sarcasm I had to remove the terrible insight from my eyes as I wrote against the Jews."[35] In his later writings Luther appears to have abandoned the notion of the permanence of Israel's eternal election. No longer is theirs a promise, Luther writes, in which they can find comfort.[36]

4. *The charge of blasphemy.* Ironically, Luther shared with all Christian theologians of his time the notion that there could be no place for dissenters in Christendom. When Luther received word of alleged Jewish missionary efforts among Christians and about Christians who sympathized with Judaism, he concluded that the solidarity of the cohesive Christian society was challenged. Luther fully accepted the medieval concept of the "Corpus Christianum," the notion of the identity of the religious and civic community, the former imposing its will on the latter. Theological claims for truth were sustained by governmental authority. Therein lies Luther's medieval legacy,

---

[35]WA 53, 541.
[36]WA 53, 447.

which was of such fateful consequence for all dissenters, especially Anabaptists and Jews.

It is true enough that the Luther of the early years of the Reformation seemed willing to see society as a marketplace of ideas. In those years this was also an existential sentiment—after all, Luther's own cause was at stake—even as it grew out of his conviction that the clarity and simplicity of the Word of God, freely preached, would inevitably lead to its acceptance. The free exchange of ideas was thus bound to have only one possible outcome, the acceptance of the gospel by all. Luther's denunciation of civil liberties for the Jews paralleled his denunciation of religious and civil liberties for the Anabaptists, whom he preferred to be hanged or incarcerated, and for whom he conceded no place in a Christian society.

The discrepancy between the early and the later Luther is evident here. In his early pronouncements, Luther certainly viewed the Jews as enemies of the gospel. By 1543 he had declared the Jews to be enemies of society as well. The Jews were a mortal danger for the Corpus Christianum, no matter how much Luther eased the stridency of the worst of medieval anti-Semitism.

The Legacy

The legacy of Luther's thought in the centuries since the Reformation is every bit as important as that thought itself, if not in fact more so. Thus, a recent analyst of Jewish-Christian conversations has noted that "Hitler's program was but the crown and pinnacle of a long history of hatred toward the Jew, participated in (if not initiated by) those whose duty it was to teach their children the truths of Christianity."[37] Here is indeed the crux of the matter, which transcends the antiquarian interest in the theology of a historical sixteenth-century figure. The question is how Luther's influence can be traced through subsequent centuries.

One may argue that the line from the sixteenth to the twentieth century is not easily drawn, and that the roots of twentieth-century anti-Semitism lie in the nineteenth century. Luther's influence must be seen in a complex fashion.

---

[37]H. Singer, "The Rise and Fall of Interfaith Dialogue," *Commentary* (May 1987) 51.

To begin with, Martin Luther's institutional legacy—the Lutheran Church—was only one of several institutional embodiments of the Protestant Reformation; in fact, in the broader European context, it was by no means the most significant one, with Calvinism being able to lay claims to primacy of importance. Indeed, even in Germany Lutheranism never ruled supreme, since Catholicism continued to be, through political developments and vicissitudes, a vital force. Prussia, that growing reality in German affairs from the late seventeenth century onward, was considerably influenced by the Calvinist tradition. Moreover, until German unification under Bismarck, "Germany" was anything but a homogeneous entity. It was an artificial whole, politically no less than culturally, with strong elements of particularism, notably in Prussia, Bavaria, and Austria. None of these embodied a Lutheran ethos. Importantly, however, Lutheranism in nineteenth-century Germany participated in the surge of Germanic nationalism, which saw the Protestant Reformation as the epitome of the German spirit and Luther as the quintessential German.

The question of Luther's historical impact must also be related to the development in countries, other than Germany, where Lutheranism ruled supreme. Did Luther's anti-Judaism cast its shadow also over the Scandinavian countries and their political and cultural systems, instigating intense anti-Semitism in Northern Europe? One would be hard pressed to provide a positive answer. The seedbed of nineteenth-century anti-Semitism was Catholic Austria rather than Lutheran Scandinavia, a reality that suggests that more was involved in the late nineteenth century than Luther's theological influence.

What is more, the impact of the Christian religion on European society since the sixteenth century must be seen in the context of the dramatic theological and intellectual changes that occurred over the years, particularly since the eighteenth century. Christianity in 1600 differed dramatically from Christianity two hundred or three hundred years later. Two crucial developments influenced the change. Chronologically, one occurred in the seventeenth, the other in the eighteenth century. The former related to what is called the "Age of Confessionalism," that is, that period in European History in which emerging autocracy succeeded in combining even more political power (including that over the church) in the hands of the ruler.[38] Clearly, the legacy of Martin Luther and the Reformation was reinterpreted to sustain such enhancement of political power.

The second element, the Enlightenment, challenged—even though it did not completely remove—a great many of the traditional Christian dogmas on which the edifice of anti-Semitism had been built. The influence of the Enlightenment on the dissolution of traditional Christian dogma was, of course, truly revolutionary. To a considerable extent, theological orthodoxy vanished—and with it the most blatant traditional points of disagreement between Judaism and Christianity. The questioning of Jesus' divinity, the repudiation of his miracles, and his new role as a purveyor of universal religious truth, removed a great deal of the traditional *scandalon* that had hovered over Jewish-Christian relations, even though Enlightenment Christianity still included the foil of the superstitious religion of the Old Testament. Lessing's fable of the three rings, representing the three world religions, heralded the possibility of a new chapter in Jewish-Christian relations, for, according to the fable, the three rings were identical in appearance, even though one was genuine and the two others were not. No one could know, therefore, which of the three was authentic. The classic Christian claims of theological superiority were dismissed as empirically irrelevant.

At the same time there were other elements of importance for the relationship of synagogue and church. German Pietism offered a new approach to the relationship between Judaism and Christianity in that it bestowed little importance on theological doctrine or even on the role of Israel in salvation history. The individual's acceptance of Jesus as savior was the most importance point of the Christian religion. What mattered, in other words, were conversion and the individual's religious experience. To hate Jews was unchristian. The positive qualities of the Jewish religion were praised.[39]

In this context Lutheranism underwent change, as the staunchly theological Luther and his fierce pronouncements

---

[38]H. Schilling, "The Reformation and the Rise of the Early Modern State," in J. D. Tracy, ed., *Luther and the Modern State in Germany* (Kirksville, Mo., 1986) p. 21: "public opinion is wrong in blaming Luther and the Lutheran Reformation for the faults of German political life in the nineteenth and twentieth centuries."

[39]Maurer, *Kirche und Synagogue*, p. 56.

(including those against the Jews) were found in many ways an embarrassment. One preferred to see Luther as the discoverer of freedom of conscience against the tyranny of the Dark Ages, as the exponent of the enlightened conscience, of toleration, of a universal religion of moral precepts.

The opening of the ghettos in the eighteenth century had exposed the Jewish tradition to very much the same Enlightenment currents, even as in the seventeenth century Spinoza's biblical criticism had affected both Christian and Jewish theology. Thus, both religions underwent change and, in so doing, tended to become more alike. Enlightenment Christianity and Enlightenment Judaism became more alike and increasingly indistinguishable.

This process continued into the nineteenth century, despite the conservative anti-Enlightenment reaction during the early decades of that century. Reform Judaism emerged in Germany, prompting, for example, the synagogue in Augsburg to abolish the observation of the ceremonial law in 1875. Jewish conversions to Christianity could easily be seen as a move from one affirmation of ethical monotheism to another.[40]

By 1900 Christianity had been deeply modified for almost two centuries. Luther and the Protestant Reformation of the sixteenth century were seen through the eyes of the Enlightenment. This was the case even among those whose theological orientation was (in the language of the day) "positive," that is, conservative. Immanuel Kant and the ideals of the *Bildungsbürgertum* dominated the German scene.

At the same time, two new developments began to make themselves noticed. Although unrelated to each other, they converged to bear on our topic. One was the rise of modern anti-Semitism; the other the rise of modern Luther scholarship. The latter meant a rigorous analysis of primary sources and an appreciation of Luther's theological affirmations. At least initially the image of Luther as German liberator from foreign influences lingered on. Moreover, those facets of Luther's

---

[40] A more detailed account of the history of the Jews in Europe in the nineteenth century needs to point out the slowness of the process of legal equality for Jews; the persistence of pogroms not only in Russia but Germany. See, for example, H. G. Kirchhoff, "Judenhass und Judenschutz: das Progrom des Jahres 1834 in der Stadt Neuss," *Almanach für den Kreis Neuss* (1985) 15–28. There was a conservative Jewish reaction against modernism. Neither, however, significantly alter the picture.

thought that had been ignored because they did not harmonize with the Enlightenment perspective were given attention. Thus, Heinrich Graetz, author of a monumental *Geschichte der Juden*, took note of Luther's tirades against the Jews and condemned them vigorously.[41]

Among the complex causes for the surge of nineteenth-century anti-Semitism, one is relevant to our topic. Emancipated Jews tended to be liberal since the ideology of liberalism had profoundly affected them. Its ideals had opened the gates of the ghetto and provided steady assimilation of Jews into the larger society. These Jews stood on the other end of the spectrum from those who bewailed the shortcomings of modernity and took a decidedly conservative stance. Not surprisingly, most Protestant leaders in Germany were politically conservative.[42] Pointedly, the *Realenzyklopädie für Theologie und Kirche* noted around the turn of the century that "one felt the Jews' undue importance, sensed the racial difference, and resented their aggressiveness."[43]

Parenthetically we might note that the religious histories of both Germany and North America in the second half of the nineteenth century manifested a clash between "modernist" Christianity and a conservative reaction. In both places the attack upon Christian modernism was not confined to theology, but embraced an attack upon modern civilization as well. In North America the clash led to the emergence of Fundamentalism, with its affirmation of Americanism and America's manifest destiny as features relevant to our topic.[44] In Germany the clash led to a similar development through the affirmation of a German destiny and the denunciation of all those who were thought to be culprits of modern perversity. The political activities of the Prussian court chaplain (and rabid anti-Semite) Adolf Stöcker serve as telling illustration for the late nineteenth-century German situation. Interestingly enough, Stöcker's anti-Semitism had no recourse to Luther nor did he accuse labor

---

[41](2d and 4th eds. 1900–09). See also I. Schorsch, *Jewish Reactions to German Anti-Semitism 1870–1914* (New York, 1972) p. 70.

[42]D. R. Borg, "Volkskirche, 'Christian State,' and the Weimar Republic," *Church History* 35 (1966) 186.

[43]*Realenzyklopädie für Theologie und Kirche* 9:510.

[44]See G. M. Marsden's *Fundamentalism and American Culture: The Shaping of Twentieth Century Evangelicalism 1870–1925* (New York, 1980).

unions and socialism—the evils of the modern world—of being Jewish, even as the Jews were not denounced as the negative element in society.[45] There were probably few outright anti-Semitic clergy in Lutheran ranks, but many, being conservative as well as nationalist in orientation, made the easy identification of liberalism, democracy, labor unions, and socialism as essentially Jewish. In turn, Martin Luther became the progenitor of German values against foreign perversion, and his hostile pronouncements against things foreign were readily quoted.[46] The recent study of Robert P. Ericksen on the German theologians Gerhard Kittel, Paul Althaus, and Emmanuel Hirsch, all of whom embraced in one way or another Nazi notions, points out the import of this conservative mentality.[47] All the same, a comprehensive assessment of nineteenth-century German Protestantism, published by the eminent church historian Reinhold Seeberg in 1900, included a lengthy section on the emancipation of women and the challenges connected with it, but said nothing about Jewish-Christian relations, a telling indication that the author did not see this issue to be important.[48] On the other hand, there are also clear indications that in this context Luther was viewed as star witness for anti-Semitism, prompting a concerned Lutheran pastor, Eduard Lamparter, to identify Luther, together with Adolf Stöcker, as the foremost negative influence in this regard.[49] It is worth noting that Adolf von Harnack, the eminent figure in German Protestantism at the turn of the century, had no place for the semitic roots of Christianity and argued that the Old Testament should be removed from the Christian Bible, a theological rationale that could be easily turned into the general prejudice that Judaism was inferior.[50]

---

[45]See G. B. Ginzel, "Martin Luther: 'Kronzeuge des Antisemitismus,'" in Kremers, *Die Juden und Martin Luther*, p. 190.

[46]Two examples may suffice: K. O. v. d. Bach, *Luther als Judenfeind* (Berlin, 1931), and E. Vogelsang, *Luthers Kampf gegen die Juden* (Tübingen, 1933), the latter particularly important because Vogelsang was an insightful Luther scholar. E. Schaeffer, *Luther und die Juden* (Berlin, 1917), stressed Luther's positive views of Jews.

[47]R. P. Ericksen, *Theologians under Hitler* (New Haven, 1985).

[48]R. Seeberg, *Die Kirche Deutschlands im neunzehnten Jahrhundert* (Leipzig, 1903).

[49]E. Lamparter, *Evangelische Kirche und Judentum. Ein Beitrag zum christlichen Verständnis von Judentum und Antisemitismus* (Stuttgart, 1928) p. 17.

[50]H. J. Kraus, *Geschichte der historisch-kritischen Erforschung des Alten Testamentes* (Neunkirchen, 1956) p. 351.

Religion and Society

In recent years historians have paid increasing attention to the convergence of popular religion, superstition, and folklore in the creation of the *Zeitgeist* (spirit of the time). Thereby, historians focus on what in general parlance is called the "common man," in other words the reading habits, the value systems, the intellectual principles of the common people in a society. Such intellectual history "from below" deals with sources different from those relied upon in traditional intellectual history. It takes, for example, the enormous popularity of the novels of Karl May in late nineteenth-century Germany as an indication that those books shaped German society as much as did the official Christian religion, which the people had already begun to desert.

In this context it becomes clear that a popular anti-Semitism existed in late nineteenth-century Germany and that it was nurtured, both formally and informally, by a number of sources. Clearly, the Christian religion was one of those. That the "Jews" had murdered the savior could be heard from pulpits each Easter season, and certainly not from only Lutheran pulpits. Language contributed to reality. The Jewish neighbor living across the street had the same appelation as did the "Jews" of the New Testament. Thus, language provided kinship across the centuries and condoned the concept of collective guilt.

The topic "Luther and the Jews" thus takes us to the question of the influence of religion in the emergence of modern consciousness. Did the legacy of negative Christian—specifically Lutheran—attitudes toward the Jews contribute to the emergence of blatant anti-Semitism at the beginning of the twentieth century? Was there, despite the changed environment of four centuries, a tradition of theological anti-Judaism enunciated by Luther and the Lutheran tradition? Does the path from Wittenberg lead to Auschwitz?[51]

Lutheranism and the Lutheran church in Germany were unprepared for the challenge of Nazi racial ideology. Part of the explanation lies in the way nineteenth-century theological

---

[51]See U. Tal, *Christians and Jews in the Second Reich (1870–1914)* (Jerusalem, 1969 [in Hebrew]).

reflection reinterpreted Lutheranism and embraced an identification of Christianity and Germany that epitomized the former as profoundly in harmony with the German "spirit." The Christian church in Germany, both Lutheran and Catholic, did not have the resources to deal effectively with Nazi political and social ideology. The embarrassing declarations of German church leaders in support of Nazi racial statutes are too well known to require restatement here.[52]

Did the problem lie in the *understanding* of Luther, or in Luther *himself*? Luther's own failure is clear and evident. It lay both in his theological and his political perspectives. Theologically, Luther echoed the traditional Christian notions of the christocentric interpretation of the Hebrew Scriptures and the reading of salvation history through the eyes of the Apostle Paul. In particular, the convergence of Luther's understanding of salvation history and his eschatology deprived him of a full understanding that if the Hebrew Scriptures are the "Old Testament" the eternal election of Israel (in keeping with Rom 9–11) is even more clearcut. Luther was unable to understand society in any other way than as Christian society. In such a Christian society truth was orthodox Christian truth, alternate notions were labeled blasphemous and had to be suppressed. There was no place for religious dissenters in sixteenth-century society, be they Jews or Anabaptists. Luther also echoed a notion widespread (though by no means universal) in traditional Christian theology, namely, to state the key elements of Christian dogma against the backdrop of a blatantly negative repudiation of the religion of the Old Testament, rather than in positive terms (as done, for example, in the Apostles' Creed).

A caveat is in order. Considering the formidable bulk of Luther's writings, particularly those dealing with Jews and Judaism, the strident parts are not very prominent. Indeed, in comparison with the extremes of medieval Christian anti-Semitism, Luther's pronouncements were moderate. Luther dissociated himself from the medieval notion of the Jews as "murderers of God," even as we need to keep in mind that expulsion, recommended by Luther for the Jews, was the nor-

---

[52]See Kremers, *Die Juden und Martin Luther*, p. 317; a statement by German bishops of December, 1941, declared that "haben deshalb jegliche Gemeinschaft mit Juden-christen aufgehoben."

mative way of dealing with *any* religious dissenters at the time, as was embodied, for example, in the Peace of Augsburg of 1555.

When all is said about Luther and his flagrant anti-Judaic pronouncements, it remains that the real failure was not so much that of the reformer of the sixteenth century as that of his followers in the twentieth century. A genuine understanding of the Christian gospel should have opened the eyes of his followers to the realization that, throughout its history, the greatest failing of Christianity has been its surrender to prevailing political and intellectual structures. Yet that is precisely what happened both before 1933 and afterward. Once again, all religious persuasions—not only Lutheran—became handmaidens of political interests and goals, no matter how vigorous the voices of those who spoke up in protest. Once again, history was abused to provide rationalization for political ends. Luther's theology became a proof text for Nazi racism.

The irony is, of course, that Martin Luther had profoundly and repeatedly warned against such falsification of the gospel. His followers, who should have known best, listened least.

Much has happened since Luther's death in 1546. Even those who still share Luther's vision of the Christian gospel see many things differently than he did. They no longer believe that the earth is flat or hold the devil responsible for bad beer. The concept of truth has undergone change, and wise sages of both the Jewish and the Christian tradition have reminded us that the real threat in our time has come from those who deny that men and women have an eternal destiny.

Those who affirm such a destiny have become fewer in number. Some of those continue to affirm Christian superiority, but even they seek to delineate this without offense to those who believe differently. Others have found in the Bible that God may have made more than one covenant, and that those who affirm the one covenant, and those who affirm the other, share a common yearning for a creation that is healed of imperfection and graciously brought to perfection.

DISCUSSION

BEKER: Oberman's recent book links apocalyptic with anti-Semitism. But you seemed dubious about this, Dr. Hillerbrand. Could you explain how, for Oberman, Luther's apocalyptic world-view, coupled with the conviction of the end of the world, found expression in anti-Jewish sentiment?

HILLERBRAND: Oberman starts with the statement that Luther's attitude toward the Jews is a central problem or issue in his theology. Secondly, in comparison with the key group of Luther's contemporaries, most notably Reuchlin and Erasmus, Luther is more warmly disposed toward Jews than they are. By immediately focusing on Luther's "The Jews and their Lies" treatise, one does not appropriate what historically is important, namely, the larger matrix of Luther's contemporaries as well as the whole of Luther's observations. And then Oberman identifies the Calvinist tradition—a sort of urban reformation—as a key source for the emergence and formulation of principles of toleration which, by the eighteenth century, did significantly change the place of Jews in European society. The argument is that the Reformation in its totality was in fact a new and positive chapter in Jewish-Christian relations, even though Luther may not have been as forceful and lagged behind the Calvinist tradition. The eschatological part of Oberman's argument runs this way: Luther was convinced that the last days were at hand; the gospel had been fully restored; and the Jews remained—in these last days—stubborn about accepting this gospel. All this is related to his sense that salvation history was now at the sixth day, now about at the end.

BEKER: What does that mean, the sixth day?

HILLERBRAND: Luther's view of history saw all of history moving in 1,000-year stages, which, in allusion to the creation story, he called "days." There were to be six of these. And during the sixth sequence of 1,000 years will take place the second coming of Christ.

SIKER: You give the four standard reasons for explaining Luther's change. Do you think one is any more telling than the others?

HILLERBRAND: The first one. I do believe that there is a change over time in Luther. And the change has to do, first of all, with a clear diminishing of his interest in or optimism about Jewish conversion. The attitude is different. That 1542 tract on "The Jews and Their Lies" was not addressed to Jews; the "Jesus Christ was Born a Jew" treatise of 1523, however, was. The later tract was addressed to Christians and was to solidify their faith against counter-proselytizing.

SIKER: Is there much evidence that counter-proselytizing was a major problem in the beginning of the Reformation churches?

HILLERBRAND: I don't think so, and the scholarly consensus would agree with that. But Luther talks as if it was a major issue. There is an intriguing analogy to the Anabaptist threat, because the evidence is that in general the Anabaptists were a small, fringe group. And while Luther didn't want to pay as much attention to them as he paid to Catholics and to Jews, still he talked as if—certainly after Muenster in 1535—there were Anabaptist revolutionaries behind every bush and that political authorities had to guard themselves because otherwise there would be a revolutionary upheaval of society.

SIKER: Why do you think Luther exaggerated that so much?

BEKER: For political reasons.

HILLERBRAND: You might say that Luther always tended to exaggerate. But political reasons were crucial in as much as Luther felt that he had to rebutt all those who threatened the cause of reform and weakened it against the Catholics. Let me get back to my point, which I think is pivotal for understanding Luther. And that is that he was so convinced, so profoundly convinced, that his premise on the simplicity and clarity of Scripture was correct that anything he perceived as a challenge to that premise sent him into an emotional tailspin.

BEKER: That's very interesting. I was wondering, in a similar vein, when he heaps together Catholics, pope, Anabaptists, Turks, and Jews, whether they are all in the same pot. I was wondering to what extent the Peasant's War was really a terrific challenge to Luther's own standing—and to what extent the Peasant's War was befriended by the left-wingers? I would have thought that, perhaps for the sake of his immediate political security from the princes, he made not just a theological judgment but also a political judgment with respect to the Peasant War, which he perceived as a real threat to him personally. And then he threw all these other groups in the same pot. Wouldn't this hostility towards the right-wingers be deflected and spilled over against the Jews? Weren't they all part of the same waterfall, so to speak? So he lumps all these groups together—Catholics, pope, Anabaptists, Turks, and Jews. These vitriolic comments against the Jews, are they simply part of the generally vitriolic relationship that constituted a challenge to him, not so much the Jews themselves as perhaps the left-wingers?

HILLERBRAND: I think each one of them is in fact *pars pro toto*, and the common denominator is a form of religion that is law and not grace. And there was, therefore, in Luther's eyes, kinship between Jews and Anabaptists, between Anabaptists and Catholics, and even between Anabaptists and Turks. I think that's it. It's no coincidence that during the last years of Luther's life he made these terribly obscene pronouncements not merely against one group but against all of them. There is the tract concerning "the papacy founded by the devil," with its terribly obscene woodcuts. In fact, Luther was more ruthless with respect to the treatment of the Anabaptists, in saying they should be hanged because they were revolutionaries. When asked about similarly ruthless comments or suggestions to the authorities about what they should do with Jews, he went no farther than expulsion, which was the standard way of dealing with Jews at the time. It is all cut from the same cloth.

Getting back to some of the comments made earlier, I interpret Luther in the context of his sense of ultimate failure, not externally. Externally he had political support; the churches had been officially recognized which preached the gospel the way he had interpreted it. But in terms of what he had thought, namely, that once the gospel of grace were put on the table everybody would join ranks—that had not taken place. And I think Luther could not deal with it.

CHARLESWORTH: Dr. Hillerbrand, I have two questions. First, is it an irony of history that when Germany under Bismarck was unified, and when the focus on Luther became more clear, his anti-Jewish statements were then put in a wider context, and that these phenomena may have given rise to a growing anti-Judaism in Germany?

HILLERBRAND: I would put it a little differently. First of all, German anti-Semitism in the Bismarck period is relatively pale as compared to that in Austria and France, not to mention Poland late in the nineteenth century. That raises some rather interesting questions. In German anti-Semitism, Luther played a minor role. It was the Luther who was seen as the epitome of things German rather than the Luther who wrote some tracts against the Jews that was important. What happened was that there was greater scholarly preoccupation with Luther, in the course of which sources became available that had not been available before. And by the time of the outbreak of World War I, there was clear recognition of Luther's anti-Semitic frankness. So we don't have to wait until 1933 for this explicit recognition of Luther's role. In fact, there is, one might say, a type of latent progression from the turn of the century to 1933 in how Luther is viewed. There were some Lutheran clergy who in 1917 established a society for the understanding of Judaism, with very pro-Jewish concerns. Still, when, nurtured by quite different sources, anti-Semitism became a political reality for Germany, Lutheranism simply could not deal with it.

CHARLESWORTH: That touches on my second question. In light of the perception of Luther's revolting anti-Jewish statements, have Lutherans had more trouble coming to grips with the question of the Jew, or has that recognition been more of a catalyst? Do Lutherans in light of Luther have more difficulty than Methodists in light of Wesley in coming to grips with the ramifications and perplexities of being Christian?

HILLERBRAND: There is a dual legacy. Frankly, this question occurred to me in writing the paper: what do Swedish or Finnish Lutherans think and feel about this? The problem becomes intense when you talk about Germany because it involves a twofold burden, namely, a progenitor whose shadow falls so formidable on the religious side, but also the other shadow of being German, that is, being part of a society that allowed this awful thing to happen. So, the answer is that, beginning with a reinterpretation of *Romans* 8, Lutherans—

and certainly German Lutherans—have been in a state of re-
flective penance since 1945. But they assuredly were not between 1933 and 1945. You know that even the Confessing
Church had a great deal of negative legacy to work through.

BEKER: I think it's a mistake to look at Germany in a vacuum.
I think that the measures taken, of course, were horrendous.
But the soil for what happened in Germany was spread very
widely over western Europe. Although the Dutch were very
pro-Jewish, still the whole rise of the National Socialist Party
in Holland was preceded by a very heavily anti-Jewish climate.
I just want to ask, would it be correct to say in retrospect that
the Holocaust happened not simply in a German vacuum in an
otherwise pro-Jewish climate but in a general anti-Jewish climate moving through western Europe—France, Belgium, Holland, and so on?

HILLERBRAND: In my judgment, much water went over the
dam between 1540 and 1900. And, more basically, I am doubt-
ful about how influential theological ideas are in society, any-
how. But, be that as it may, it is clear that when disaster began
in Germany in the late 1920s, the Lutheran church had nothing
with which to meet the challenge.

PRIEST: I would agree with you that theological ideas don't
play much of a role, but they are, in my judgment, a powerful
force for legitimating conclusions arrived at on other grounds,
but then sanctified for those people who still take religion
seriously.

HILLERBRAND: I would say in that sense Luther, as "the
German" speaking against foreigners, is probably a greater
influence for our topic and a greater legitimizing force than
Luther the explicit "anti-Semite."

CHAPTER SEVEN

Salient Christian-Jewish Issues of Today: A Christian Exploration[1]

A. Roy Eckardt

Christian antisemitism did not arise by the importation of ideas foreign to Christianity through some historical accident. Christian antisemitism grew out of the Christian Bible, i.e., the New Testament, as it was understood and interpreted by Christians over centuries. The roots of Christian antisemitism need be traced no further than Christianity itself; Christians have been antisemitic because they have been Christians. They thought of themselves as the people of God, the true Israel, who had been faithful to the inheritance of ancient Israel. Judaism, in the Christian view, had no reason to exist once Christianity came on the scene. We must learn, I think, to live with the unpleasant fact that antisemitism is part of what it has meant historically to be a Christian, and is still part of what it means to be Christian.

—Robert L. Wilken[2]

The post-Rosenzweig Jewish "return into history" must be matched, on the Catholic side, with a Catholic return into history. . . . Any purely realized eschatology (including those informing purely incarnationist theologies) can maintain itself only at the price of ignoring two central realities: first, the clear presence of the eschatological "not yet" in the New Testament itself, and second, the stark negativity of the radical not yet in our age disclosed in all its horror by the Holocaust.

—David Tracy[3]

Introduction

I include, for purposes of orientation, the foregoing historical-moral observation of Robert L. Wilken and the historical-theological-moral counsel of David Tracy, together with a hermeneutical-theological judgment of James A. Sanders: "Christian antisemitism stems largely from a failure to monotheize."[4] I refer also to one event: Dietrich Bonhoeffer's role in the assassination attempt upon Adolf Hitler (July 20, 1944), an act symbolic and inspirational of the twentieth-century Christian return into the history of Israel.[5]

The following exposition has three components: (1) Introduction; (2) *Shoah* (Holocaust), State of Israel, and Christian ideology and action; and (3) implications of today's feminist movement for the Christian-Jewish relationship.

The Christian Return into the Ongoing History of Israel

From among many published points of departure we may attend to two statements, one from Dietrich Bonhoeffer and

---

[1]Parts of chap. 12 of the author's *For Righteousness' Sake: Contemporary Moral Philosophies* (Bloomington, Ind., 1987); of chaps. 5, 7, and 9 of his *Jews and Christians: The Contemporary Meeting* (Bloomington, 1986); of his article, "Is There a Way out of the Christian Crime? The Philosophic Question of the Holocaust," *Holocaust and Genocide Studies* 1 (1986) 122–26; and of his paper "Christians, Jews, and the Women's Movement," *Christian Jewish Relations* 19 (June 1986) 13–21, provide much of the substance of this essay and are in many places utilized verbatim yet often with revision. See also A. R. Eckardt, *Black–Woman–Jew: Three Wars for Human Liberation* (Bloomington, forthcoming). In *Christ and Culture* (New York, 1951) H. Richard Niebuhr supplements and corrects Ernst Troeltsch's church-sect typology by means of a fivefold schema: Christ against culture, the Christ of culture, Christ above culture, Christ and culture in paradox, and Christ the transformer of culture. The present writer's *For Righteousness' Sake* seeks to supplement and correct Niebuhr's schema by means of an eightfold typology. The type brought to bear in the present essay is the eighth one, "history transforming faith."

[2]R. L. Wilken, *The Myth of Christian Beginnings: History's Impact on Belief* (Garden City, N.Y., 1972) p. 197.

[3]D. Tracy, "Religious Values after the Holocaust: A Catholic View," in A. J. Peck, ed., *Jews and Christians after the Holocaust* (Philadelphia, 1982) p. 99. See also Tracy's foreword to A. A. Cohen, *The Tremendum: A Theological Interpretation of the Holocaust* (New York, 1981).

[4]J. A. Sanders, "The Bible as Canon," *The Christian Century* 98 (1981) 1255.

[5]Figures representative of this theological movement include, in Germany, Johann Baptist Metz, Peter von der Osten-Sacken, Rolf Rendtorff, Luise Schottroff, and Leonore Siegele-Wenschkewitz; in the United States, Alice L. Eckardt, Robert A. Everett, Elisabeth Schüssler Fiorenza, Franklin H. Littell, John T. Pawlikowski, David Tracy, and Paul M. van Buren.

one from a contemporary writer, Choan-Seng Song. In a prison letter Bonhoeffer wrote:

> Unlike the other oriental religions the faith of the Old Testament is not a religion of salvation. Christianity, it is true, has always been regarded as a religion of salvation. *But isn't this a cardinal error*, which divorces Christ from the Old Testament and interprets him in the light of the myths of salvation? Of course it could be urged that under Egyptian and later, Babylonian influence, the idea of salvation became just as prominent in the Old Testament—e.g., Deutero-Isaiah. The answer is, the Old Testament speaks of *historical* redemption, i.e., redemption on this side of death, whereas the myths of salvation are concerned to offer men deliverance from death. *Israel is redeemed out of Egypt in order to live with God on earth.*[6]

If the redemption of Israel (within which, Bonhoeffer implies, Christian faith finds its own meaning) entails Israel's life with God upon this earth, what may Christians be summoned to say and do when or if Israel is threatened with extinction?

Choan-Seng Song of Taiwan has an essay entitled "From Israel to Asia—A Theological Leap." An added question will prepare the way for our encounter with him: What is the ground for judging that for Christians the re-creation of Jewish sovereignty in the country of Israel in 1948 falls in a genre of happenings different from the coming of Communism to the country of China in 1949, even with all our remembrance of, as Song puts it, China's "resolute rejection of Christianity"?[7]

For Song, the "Western theologian" has no business invading a history other than his own. Where is found, then, the "world" to which Song bids us turn? His answer is striking:

> Western theologians must . . . address themselves to their own situations, and wrestle with the question of how Israel can be existentially related to suffering and hope in the West today.

---

[6]D. Bonhoeffer, *Letters and Papers from Prison*, ed. Eberhard Bethge, trans. Reginald H. Fuller (London, 2d ed., 1956) p. 153 (letter of June 27, 1944; italics added except for the word "historical"). It is recognized that Bonhoeffer did not overcome a certain anti-Jewishness; see his *No Rusty Swords* (London, 1970) p. 222; also E. L. Fackenheim, *The Jewish Return into History: Reflections in the Age of Auschwitz and a New Jerusalem* (New York, 1978) pp. 35–36, 74–75.

[7]Choan-Seng Song, "From Israel to Asia—A Theological Leap," in G. H. Anderson and T. F. Stransky, eds., *Mission Trends No. 3: Third World Theologies* (New York and Grand Rapids, 1976) p. 219.

Israel must become their existential experience. . . . Theology cannot deal with the question of what God *is*. Its task is to come to grips with what God *does—and we cannot know what God does apart from events and realities in which we are involved existentially. . . .* An ecumenical theological community must be built on the foundation of situational authenticity.[8]

In and through the contentions of Bonhoeffer and Song—at least when they are considered together—the following can be suggested: *The Christian return into the history of Israel may come to serve as a means of contravening Christian imperialism vis-à-vis Judaism and the Jewish people.* And yet, to return into a history that is not one's own property introduces a moral temptation. Can we ever be part of something without wanting to have a say in what that something is or ought to be? There is, indeed, the haunting thought that the very insistence upon Judaism and Jewishness as foundational to the Christian faith may only compound anti-Semitism—through, for example, the ambivalence that the Christian world has long since acquired with respect to things Jewish.

To come to a consideration directly related to, or corollary of, what has been said thus far—*a Christian historicism*[9] *that is joined to the history and life of Israel has as its foundation stone and incentive the Jew Jesus of Nazareth.*

In and through the event of Jesus is manifest the essential historicity that weds the Christian community to Israel, a flesh-and-blood authorization that historical Israel is the root that sustains the church (Rom 11:18). Those who have been "strangers to the covenants of promise, having no hope and without God in the world . . . are no longer strangers and sojourners, but . . . fellow citizens with the saints and members of the household of God" (Eph 2:12, 19). Here, for Christians, is the all-decisive meeting place, or convergence, of religious faith

---

[8]*Ibid.*, pp. 221, 222 (italics added except for the single words "is" and "does").

[9]E. L. Fackenheim asserts that philosophic historicism "fails to philosophize about itself: It asserts the historical relativity of all things, those philosophical included; yet it claims or implies that it is itself exempt" (*To Mend the World: Foundations of Future Jewish Thought* [New York, 1982] p. 158). The historicism that underlies the present essay is self-critical, or strives to be. "Its self-critical character is made possible and underwritten by its *theocentrism*" (Eckardt, *For Righteousness' Sake*, p. 247).

[10]I understand "ideology" in a rather Marxist way to mean recourse to certain ideas and idea systems in the service of self-interest, particularly collective self-interest. Accordingly, deideologization is the struggle against ideology.

and historical event. Once such confessions as these are deideologized[10]—i.e., monotheized—they may become the spiritual implementation of what might be called "Jesus-historicity." The primary Christian challenge in the shadow of the *Shoah* is not simply to demythologize the Christian tradition but to deideologize it—to overcome its supersessionist elitism.

A proclivity related to the unhappy practice of dehistoricizing Jesus for the sake of theologisms (theological ideas) is the effort to dehistoricize him for the sake of a reputed moral-spiritual "universality." Thus do we find Jesus fabricated into a white South African, a black African, a Mexican *campesino*, a saint of India, a Japanese fisherman, an American business man (remember Bruce Barton?), and so on. On the contrary, Jesus remains what he was—an itinerant Jewish man of first-century Galilee, Samaria, and Judea. To speak of Jesus as other than a Jew of that time and that place is no longer to speak *of him*. As Gerard S. Sloyan declares: "To be faithful to Jesus Christ as the New Testament speaks of him is to be in full continuity with him in his Jewishness."[11]

True, different references and tributes to Jesus today entail radically diverse reactions, meanings, and life decisions. But really to speak of Jesus of Nazareth is to say to everybody (not excluding skeptics, cynics, and detached observers) that Christianity is a historical faith, a way of historicalness. At the foundation of the church is an event—the birth, life, and fate of a particular human being. At this vital juncture the Christian historian replicates "the quest of the historical Jesus," since that quest's basic concern is, in Michael L. Cook's wording, "the decisive importance of the historical Jesus for Christian faith."[12]

The historical-existential sources of Christianity reach infinitely deeper than the life of a solitary figure, however. For what is the history of a human being apart from his life with his people? A house rests upon a foundation, but it in turn is supported by the earth beneath, as perhaps by bedrock. The foundation of the church is a certain historical collectivity with its enormously diverse social ways, politics, fortunes, and complex traditions. This foundation is Jewish.

---

[11]G. S. Sloyan, *Is Christ the End of the Law?* (Philadelphia, 1978) pp. 27–28.
[12]M. L. Cook, *The Jesus of Faith: A Study in Christology* (New York, 1981) p. 13.

The broad foundations of the Christian tale come to focus in the dialectic between Jesus of Nazareth and the people from whom he came and to whom he ministered. If the covenant between God and Israel remains unbroken,[13] then the church is called to pledge itself to that covenant's truth. For at stake is nothing less than the church's own relation to God as a hoped-for part of that covenant. Catholics and Protestants have been learning anew—so writes David Tracy—"how Jewish a religion Christianity finally is."[14]

Does the Christian reaffirmation of Israel and Jewishness mean a return into history?[15] The link is found within the reality of Jewishness itself, a reality that is forever breaking out of religiousness into the great world—today's preeminent case being the State of Israel. In this way the religion called Christianity may itself be, paradoxically, redeemed from "pure" religiosity. In and through a historical Israel, the Church is empowered to carry forward its worldly obligations and to be saved from falling into otherworldly spirituality. For the Jewish people is wholly "secular" in an all-decisive respect: a people wholly of the world (*saeculum*) is present among us. The Jewish phenomenon is epitomized in James Parkes' characterization of the Jewish people as a *natural community*.[16]

To conclude these remarks on a Christian historicism that traces itself to Jesus and the Jewish people as its foundation, I would cite Jürgen Moltmann's lament over the churchly pretension of attempting through the device of impartiality to realize a universalist potential. "Only in and through the dialectic of taking sides does the universalism of the Crucified become a reality in this world. The phony universalism of the Church is something very different. It is a premature and untimely anticipation of the *Kingdom* of God."[17] The "taking of sides" with Israel constitutes a discrete, historical application

---

[13]Cf. A. Roy Eckardt, "The Recantation of the Covenant?" in A. H. Rosenfeld and I. Greenberg, eds., *Confronting the Holocaust: The Impact of Elie Wiesel* (Bloomington, Ind., 1978) pp. 159–68.

[14]Tracy, "Religious Values After the Holocaust," p. 89.

[15]F. Rosenzweig affirms the transhistorical quality of Jewish existence. In this, he is not alone. But historicalness remains a foremost attestation within Jewish life, markedly since the *Shoah*.

[16]J. Parkes, *Prelude to Dialogue: Jewish-Christian Relationships* (London, 1969) p. 193.

[17]J. Moltmann, "Dieu dans la révolution," in *Discussion sur 'la théologie de la revolution'* (Paris, 1972) p. 72.

of a fundamental principle of the contemporary theology of liberation—as in the now-famous watchword, "a preferential option for the poor." However, this particular commitment means not alone self-transcendence but also self-fulfillment. Through love of the neighbor who is not a Christian neighbor, the ideological taint of Christian self-concentration is fought. But insofar as Christians are, through Israel, returning to their own ancestral home and family, they fulfill themselves. (Here is suggested the ultimate foundation of Christian unity.)

The (Potential) Impact of the *Shoah* and its Aftermath, Including the Re-Creation of the State of Israel, upon Christian Ideology and Life

The word "potential" is placed in parentheses because in our day we cannot know the measure of the possible or ultimate decisiveness of these twentieth-century events for authoritative or lasting Christian action and thought. The Hebrew term *Ha-Shoah* has come to identify the series of events that is called, in German Nazi language, *die Endlösung der Judenfrage*, the (reputedly) Final Solution (or Final Resolution) of the question of the Jews.

The Theodicean Question

The *Shoah* has had shattering effects within the Jewish community on the issue of God and human suffering. The infliction of suffering upon Jews as Jews was hardly originated by the Nazis; on the contrary, as Charlesworth, Smith, and Hiller-brand have already shown, the Nazis were following in the long train of Christian persecutors of Jews. But while the *Shoah* was the culmination of centuries of anti-Semitism, it also differed qualitatively from what had gone before—simply and solely because of the absoluteness of its intention. The intention of the *Shoah* was to ensure that no longer would there be a single Jew upon Planet Earth. In this respect, the *Shoah* remains an absolute event, and will always remain such. Does it not therefore have absolute, or unique, significance for faith?[18] This significance entails two questions. (1) May not

---

[18]See A. L. Eckardt, "Post-Holocaust Theology: A Journey out of the Kingdom of Night," *Holocaust and Genocide Studies* 1 (1986) 229.

God be forbidden from treating Israel as "the suffering servant of the Lord"? Whatever function or value the suffering of the people Israel may have had in the past—or could conceivably again have in, say, the year 5000—appears negated by the *Shoah*. (2) May not Israel now and henceforth refuse to regard itself as suffering servant, because within the *Shoah* that very role acts to commit—or is committed to—its own self-destruction and self-refutation? Tadeusz Borowski tells of a mother in Auschwitz who is forced into the horrible place of fleeing from and denying her own child.[19] Irving Greenberg supplies the only conclusion: "The Suffering Servant now breaks and betrays herself. Out of the Holocaust experience comes the demand for redistribution of power. . . . No one should ever be equipped with less power than is necessary to assure one's dignity. To argue dependence on law, or human goodness, or universal equality [or, we may add, on the ostensible commands of God] *is to join the ranks of those who would like to repeat the Holocaust.*"[20]

The lesson of the *Shoah* in the present, specific context is the end of (i.e., a final judgment upon) human suffering as a positive religious category and thereby the revolutionary effacement of much accepted theodicean reflection. In the *Shoah* the traditionally blessed deed of martyrdom is obliterated, it is rendered meaningless, before the absolutizing hell of gas chambers and crematoriums. In this frame of reference, all subsequent theodicy is succeeded by politics. And were *Christians* to retain the notion of Jews as suffering servant, this would mean that they were arraying themselves at the head of "the ranks of those who would like to repeat the Holocaust," since the Christian world is the ultimate culprit behind the *Shoah*. Many contemporary scholars "advance the finding that the Christian church's traditional anti-Jewish teaching conspired with the Christian world to help make inevitable the Holocaust of the Jews of Europe. The finding has even become something of a truism. Be it noted that many of these historiographers are themselves Christians."[21]

When Cardinal John O'Connor of New York recently

---

[19]T. Borowski, *This Way for the Gas, Ladies and Gentlemen* (New York, 1967) p. 87.
[20]I. Greenberg, "Cloud of Smoke, Pillar of Fire: Judaism, Christianity, and Modernity after the Holocaust," in E. Fleischner, ed., *Auschwitz: Beginning of A New Era? Reflections on the Holocaust* (New York, 1977) p. 54; italics added.

declared that the suffering of Jews in the Holocaust "may be an enormous gift that Judaism has given to the world,"[22] he was denying in effect the apodictic wisdom of the German Roman Catholic theologian Johann Baptist Metz, who today counsels his students: "Avoid any theology that could have been exactly the same before or after Auschwitz."[23] The Jewish community immediately and instinctively understood that O'Connor's words constituted a moral transgression. For Jews know only too well that the very opposite is the case: the "gift" of the *Shoah* is not from Jews to the world but *to* Jews *from* the world, not excepting the Christian world of Cardinal John O'Connor. And as such, the "gift" is to be repudiated and condemned absolutely. The cardinal responded to the criticism of his declaration by saying, "If this is considered demeaning to the Holocaust, then it demeans my entire theology because mine is a theology of suffering."[24] Unwittingly, O'Connor here gave away the entire ecclesiasticizing and Christian imperialist game. For he was granting, if unknowingly, the entire point: the *Shoah* does indeed demean the whole theology of suffering. It in fact annuls that theology.

The Political Question

The political dimension is already identified as decisive in and through the foregoing discussion on theodicy. A few cita-

---

[21]A. R. Eckardt, "The Christian World Goes to Bitburg," in G. H. Hartman, ed., *Bitburg in Moral and Political Perspective* (Bloomington, Ind., 1986) p. 80. Among Christian studies directed to anti-Semitism, consult D. A. Rausch, *A Legacy of Hatred: Why Christians Must Not Forget the Holocaust* (Chicago, 1984); Alan Davies, ed., *Antisemitism and the Foundations of Christianity* (New York, 1979); A. R. Eckardt, *Your People, My People: The Meeting of Jews and Christians* (New York, 1974), chap. 2; A. R. Eckardt and A. L. Eckardt, "Christentum und Judentum, die theologische und moralische Problematik der Vernichtung des europäischen Judentums," *Evangelische Theologie* 36 (1976) 406–26; idem, *Long Night's Journey into Day: Life and Faith after the Holocaust*, enlarged and rev. ed. (New York, 1987); E. S. Fiorenza and D. Tracy, eds., *The Holocaust as Interruption*, (Concilium 175; Edinburgh, 1984); C. Klein, *Theologie und Anti-Judaismus* (Munich, 1975); F. H. Littell, *The Crucifixion of the Jews* (New York, 1975); R. Rendtorff and E. Stegemann, eds., *Auschwitz—Krise der christlichen Theologie* (Munich, 1980); and R. R. Ruether, *Faith and Fratricide: The Theological Roots of Anti-Semitism* (New York, 1974).

[22]Cardinal John O'Connor, as cited in Nat Hentoff, "Profiles," *New Yorker* (March 30, 1987) 87.

[23]J. B. Metz, in G. B. Ginzel, ed., *Auschwitz als Herausforderung für Juden und Christen* (Heidelberg, 1980) p. 176.

[24]Hentoff, "Profiles," p. 88.

tions will help fill out the point. These are from an essay by Alice L. Eckardt titled "Power and Powerlessness: The Jewish Experience," which in turn makes reference to other scholars:

> [The prophet] Jeremiah gave us a foretaste of Emil Fackenheim's prophetic counsel today: to survive, to survive as Jews, to raise Jewish children, to "return to history" through the reborn national community, and to live in the *hope* that God is still—in spite of the Holocaust—a redeeming God. . . . If "neither God nor his people is intended to be powerless," argues Abba Lessing, "then the first concern of the Jewish people today must . . . be public power. . . . [Existence] precedes ethics and power is of the essence when we dare to exist." . . .
>
> [The] silence of Auschwitz underlines the fact that hope without power is not a hopeful position in a world where power dominates, in a world that has seen all too clearly the price of powerlessness. . . .
>
> Those conclusions that most Jews have reached, along with some Christians who have understood the absolute challenge that the Holocaust continues to represent, include: an insistence that the end of Jewish statelessness . . . is a responsible religious and political commitment; that forces of death and destruction— radical evil—must be resisted on behalf of life and a community's existence . . . ; that martyrdom can no longer be either the ideal religious or the responsible political method of responding to tyranny or other forms of evil; that peace and community must be the continual goal of our strivings, but not at the expense of a "sacrificial offering" of some one nation or people. It is time for the Jewish "return into history" with all the responsibilities and ambiguities—and mistakes—of power and decision-making that this entails, and all the courage that it requires.[25]

The political-moral judgment upon Christians today centers upon the question: Do you or do you not affirm Jewish power, Jewish national sovereignty? If you do not, how is it possible for you to escape enlistment in "the ranks of those who would like to repeat the Holocaust"?

---

[25]A. L. Eckardt, "Power and Powerlessness: The Jewish Experience," in I. W. Charny, ed., *Toward the Understanding and Prevention of Genocide* (Proceedings of the International Conference on the Holocaust and Genocide, Tel Aviv; Boulder-London, 1984) pp. 185, 189, 193 (slightly emended).

The Challenge to Christian Credibility

The theodicean question and the political question converge and are brought to a climax in the moral question: Is the Christian gospel any longer morally credible? In the post-*Shoah* world many Christian spokespersons have expressed a readiness to "rethink" Christian teaching, to avoid Christian supersessionism. Yet very often these expressions appear as no more than nice or pleasing sentiments lacking in any concreteness. When a demand is made for specifics, the reformer tends to back away. And when a critic from within the Christian community raises the moral question concerning *concrete* Christian teachings, that is, christological teachings, he or she is usually dismissed as a "radical" who is undermining the faith. It is as if the *critic* were on trial. But is it not rather the entire Christian message that is on trial?[26] If such dismissals are to be accepted, where is there any hope for the kind of Christian change that may help prevent future Holocausts?

A major reason why the *Shoah* and post-*Shoah* attack upon Christian teaching has been devastating for many Christians lies in the traditional indoctrination of the Christian community with an assurance that the Christian faith is morally superior to Judaism. In and through the *Shoah* an opposite truth presents itself: Christianity's "teaching of contempt" (Jules Isaac) for Judaism and Jews stands in contrast to the sublime norm of justice that prophetic and rabbinic Judaism represent and embody. The contrast is pointed up in a prophetic judgment upon the New Testament by Rabbi Eliezer Berkovits:

> Christianity's New Testament has been the most dangerous anti-semitic tract in history. Its hatred-charged diatribes against the "Pharisees" and the Jews have poisoned the hearts and minds of millions and millions of Christians for almost two millennia now. . . . No matter what the deeper theological meaning of the hate passages against Jews might be, in the history of the Jewish people the New Testament lent its inspiring support to oppression, persecution and mass murder of an intensity and duration that were unparalleled in the entire history of man's degradation.

---

[26] An illustration of this attempt to dismiss one or more Christian post-*Shoah* theologians for "going too far" or being "too radical" is M. B. McGarry's review of A. R. Eckardt, *Jews and Christians* in *America* (May 23, 1987) 428–29.

Without Christianity's New Testament, Hitler's *Mein Kampf* could never have been written.[27]

Christian anti-Semitism is here identified as wholly anterior to and hence independent of the *Shoah*. But the *Shoah* acted to bring to fulfillment a very long history; hence it cries out for ongoing existential and scholarly Christian attention. The history of some nineteen hundred years was suffused by Christian supersessionism vis-à-vis Judaism and the Jewish people. Such supersessionism had at its theological heart—implicitly if not explicitly—Jesus' resurrection, to which we now turn.

The resurrection of Jesus as a real historical event has been questioned within religious history, not excluding Christian history. However, in the aftermath of the *Shoah*, the issue of the resurrection assumes a moral urgency that it did not have before. It was Jesus' fate to be crucified by the occupying and persecuting Roman imperium. But the fullness of Jesus' history extends to and climaxes in his resurrection, an event that conflicts with Christian-Jewish historical and religious solidarity. The issue may be stated as follows: on the one hand, a consummated resurrection of Jesus constitutes the basic theological (christological) threat to or indictment of Judaism and the Jewish people; on the other hand, any denial of the resurrection of Jesus comprises a life-and-death threat to the Christian faith and the Christian community.

Is Jesus dead, or is he alive?[28] If he is dead, the supersessionism of Christianity is ruled out, objectively speaking. But what if he is alive as is preached every Eastertide and all the in-between times? How is it possible to construe and proclaim

---

[27]E. Berkovits, "Facing the Truth," *Judaism* 27(1978) 324–25. Of course, most of the New Testament writers were themselves Jewish Christians. This fact may itself be, and indeed has been, put to anti-Semitic use.

[28]This question, while indistinguishable in a noncrucial way from the issue of the empty tomb, is also indistinguishable in a highly crucial way from that issue. That is to say, on the one hand the alleged emptiness of the tomb is no proof of the resurrection: Jesus' body could have been stolen or moved; on the other hand, as R. E. Brown points out, "it is an essential question whether the faith of the first apostles would have been so shaken" by a later discovery of Jesus' skeleton that they would have construed their preaching to be in vain. The empty tomb does not tell us what happened. "It is as a negative check that the empty tomb functions in our perception of the resurrection of Jesus" (Review Symposium on Pheme Perkins' *Resurrection*, in *Horizons* 12 [Fall 1985] 366). In short, the empty tomb proves nothing, but the full tomb would disprove everything. The empty tomb is a necessary but not sufficient condition to belief in Jesus' resurrection.

the resurrection of Jesus other than in supersessionist and triumphalist ways? The resurrection is held to be, after all, strictly an act of God, not a human achievement or claim (in the Christian view). Human beings can hardly raise themselves from the dead. Within and through the resurrection of Jesus, the old, false Israel is (reputedly) superseded by the new, true Israel—and this in a wholly objective manner. For is it not God who through a special sacred-historical act vindicates the Christian faith in the face of its denial by Jews? The doctrine of Jesus' resurrection intends to put "the imprimatur of God's very self" (Alice L. Eckardt) upon *the* focal (i.e., *sine qua non*) Christian teaching, in contradistinction and opposition to Jewish denials.

In *Faith and Fratricide*, as elsewhere, Rosemary Ruether argues that the root of Christian antipathy to Jews and Judaism is the church's effort through its Christology to historicize eschatological reality, to bring the End Time into this world. But Jürgen Moltmann declares, in *The Trinity and the Kingdom*, that on the date of the resurrection of the crucified Jesus "the eschatological era begins."[29] By conjoining the Ruether argument and the Moltmann declaration, Robert A. Everett (who, with these other two scholars, speaks from the Christian side) identifies the resurrection dogma as providing the distinctive Christian ideology of Jewish victimization.[30]

Are we driven to conclude, then, that at its very center the Christian faith is deprived, or acts to deprive itself, of moral credibility?

Either or both of the judgments of Ruether and Moltmann may of course be rejected, or at least qualified. But once they are acceded to and linked together, the fateful causal relation between the Christian message and the death camps of Europe becomes manifest. The historicization of eschatological reality appears to guarantee Christian supersessionist triumphalism, or anti-Jewishness. More than this, a potential Christian ideological contribution to a future *Shoah* is implied, because traditional Christian supersessionism remains abidingly central to the church's message. Elsewhere I have ventured to deal with this condition under the rubric of "the Christian crime."[31]

---

[29] J. Moltmann, *The Trinity and the Kingdom: The Doctrine of God*, trans., M. Kohl (San Francisco, 1981) p. 122.

[30] R. A. Everett, conversations with me on January 16-17, 1985.

[31] Eckardt, "Is There a Way out of the Christian Crime?"

Whether or not that exact expression is felicitous, a poignant eventuality suggests itself: the forlornness of today's Christian. Is that where we must come out? The Christian would appear to be utterly ashamed, utterly bereft, utterly alone: Is this the lesson of the *Shoah* to the Christian world?

In Jesus' story the prodigal's return to his father's house was a trick. The son was without food and all he wanted really was something to eat. So he hit upon a stratagem. Upon his arrival he would say, "Father, I have sinned . . . I am no longer fit to be called your son." Yet the deceit became gratuitous. For he was accepted, tricks and all. Before hearing a single word, his father "ran to meet him, flung his arms round him, and kissed him. . . ." It was not that the son had all at once mastered his prodigality, and was to be rewarded as a changed human being. That is not the point of the consequent merrymaking or of the story, and it is not the point of the Christian gospel. No: "For this son of mine was dead and has come back to life; he was lost and is found. And the festivities began" (Lk 15:18–24). Grace is the act of accepting the unacceptable. Where sin abounds, grace abounds the more. Grace says, "You are accepted."[32]

Christian human beings are indeed forlorn, yet they are not forlorn. They are ashamed, yet not ashamed. They are bereft, yet not bereft; alone, yet not alone. Christians fall among those who have betrayed Israel, the originative people of God. Christians are nobodies who are condemned for, among other sins, the act of anti-Semitism. But they are also received by a voice that says "I accept you."

One way to address the question of Christian integrity is thus through the nature, the reality of Christian acceptance. Yet the moral dialectic remains unfinished. Indeed, the exposition to this point is beset by conflict, even by contradiction. On the one hand, the Christian crime abides (thesis). On the other hand, the Christian is said to be accepted (antithesis). But is it not morally reprehensible to assert these two things together? How can there be acceptance of those who may very well persevere in their transgressions? Worse, is not God a transgressor in accepting the evil ones, thereby condoning evil?

---

[32]P. Tillich, "You Are Accepted," in *The Shaking of the Foundations* (New York, 1948) pp. 153–63.

And within and behind this entire moral and spiritual plight looms, almost as a specter now, the word of Paul, "If Christ was not raised, then our gospel is null and void, and so is your faith" (1 Cor 15:14). (Several years ago the Jewish scholar Pinchas Lapide said that he found no objection to the Christian claim of the bodily resurrection of Jesus. Peter Levinson of Heidelberg replied to Lapide: "If I believed in Jesus' resurrection, I would be baptized tomorrow."[33] Those who contend that the question of the resurrection of Jesus was and remains a purely internecine Jewish matter would do well to ponder Rabbi Levinson's rejoinder.[34])

Is there any way beyond thesis (the Christian crime) and antithesis (acceptance of the Christian) into a bearable synthesis?

Emil L. Fackenheim writes, from the Jewish side: "After Auschwitz, it is a major question whether the Messianic faith is not *already* falsified—whether a Messiah who could come, and yet at Auschwitz did not come, has not become a religious impossibility."[35] The issue of whether Judaism is falsifiable by history is out of bounds for Christians; Jews alone may deal with it. However, Fackenheim's judgment may be adapted to the moral crisis of late twentieth-century Christianity as follows: after the *Shoah* it is a major question whether the Christian messianic faith is not falsified—whether Jesus as the Christ has not become a religious and moral impossibility. The authentication (if authentication is possible) that the resurrection of Jesus cannot in fact embody eschatological fulfillment, even a fragmentary realization, lies in that event's contribution to the deaths of millions of human beings, including great numbers of small children.

Is Christianity immune or is it not immune to world-historical events since Jesus? We are assailed by a life-and-death dilemma: If the traditional Christian faith is *not* falsifiable or falsified by history, how is supersessionist anti-Jewishness ever going to be vanquished? But if the Christian claim *is* falsifiable—or, indeed, falsified—by history, does this mean that

---

[33]*Time*, May 7, 1979.

[34]As Sloyan writes, "the significance attached to Jesus' resurrection cannot be found in [its] Jewish background" (Review Symposium on Perkins' *Resurrection*, p. 359).

[35]E. L. Fackenheim, *Encounters between Judaism and Modern Philosophy: A Preface to Future Jewish Thought* (New York, 1973) pp. 20–21.

the Christian assurance of God's acceptance of the unacceptable is obliterated? In a word, is it fatefully the case that the final choice—the final dichotomy—for the Gentile has to be either Christian anti-Jewishness or pagan forlornness?

Where is God in all this struggle?

A pillar of contemporary liberation thinking, as mentioned earlier, is the moral demand to "take sides," a mandate laid not only upon human beings but upon God's very self. William R. Jones asks, Is God a white racist?[36] In the same way, Is God an anti-Semite? Or is God somehow out there fighting anti-Semitism? From a historicist perspective—a biblical perspective—God acts in and through contemporaneous human (as perhaps "natural"?) *events*. And the other side of the reputed Christian triumph through the resurrection is the alleged defeat of the old Israel, as incarnate in "wandering Jews"[37] barred from their land because of their sin, most grievously their rejection and deicide of Jesus Christ. However, in 1948 there was constituted the Third Jewish Commonwealth. What is to be done with this event? It can scarcely be ignored (in any Christian theology of history). To apply one humorist's line, Did the devil make the Jews do it? Alternatively, in one place the Psalter says that "he who sits in the heavens laughs; the Lord has them (the gentiles) in derision" (Ps 2:4). Could it be that a divine, even retaliative comedy is being staged for the sake of, among others, the Christian world? True, the resolution of the aloneness, the hopelessness of those beyond the covenant is supposed to take place through the resurrection faith. But is this to insinuate that ensuing history inflicts defeat upon the God of Israel? Is this God of Israel barren of abiding or fresh resources? If so, Christian forlornness is surely matched by the forlornness of God's very self. And is not the end the end of hope?

As the hellish twentieth century draws near its close, an existential challenge to the Christian community is whether there is a historical word from God that at once saves the Christian church from forlornness and saves it too from the unabated victimizing of Jews. Is no sign given, or is there a

---

[36]W. R. Jones, *Is God a White Racist? A Preamble to Black Theology* (Garden City, N.Y., 1973).

[37]Consult G. Hasan-Rokem and A. Dundes, eds., *The Wandering Jew: Essays in the Interpretation of a Christian Legend* (Bloomington, Ind., 1986).

sign? Is there given a historical event that judges and redeems the historically victimizing resurrection? Does there transpire an event of God that, in the very moment some Christians must go through the dreadful trauma of necessarily casting away the resurrection in its historically victimizing aspects, will nevertheless bring a certain assurance, a certain peace, an event that will say "I accept you," an event that will say: "The people of God—and therefore you piteous, latecoming aliens—are not forsaken"? (The challenge to propound a noneschatological, nontriumphalist teaching of the resurrection is here opened, and with it the winsome possibility that the resurrection may still have a place in Christian teaching.) If there is such an accepting event, and if that event is constituted by the reemerging commonwealth of Israel, we are given a sign and a witness that God continues to accept human beings totally apart from the resurrection of Jesus.[38] In this regard Robert A. Everett suggests that *the Israel of today may be sacramental for Christians*. That is to say, Israel is urging upon Christians, if only obliquely, that their victimization of Jews and their rejection of Judaism are not necessary to their acceptance by God and hence are not necessary to their acceptance of themselves. Christians do not need any such "works righteousness" (or "works *un*righteousness"). They can live wholly by grace.

Thus may reconciliation perhaps be brought between the thesis of criminality and the antithesis of acceptance. For the new and strange synthesis is not a mere idea. It is made possible by a deed.

Some Implications of the Feminist Movement for the Christian-Jewish Relation

The possibility arises of whether in the long run the contemporary women's movement[39] may have as much—or greater—

---

[38]This is not to argue for a religious justification of the political State of Israel. I have always opposed "territorial fundamentalism" respecting the legitimacy of that State. In a political context the only justification for Israel's existence is political, moral, and historical. But the latter position in no way excludes a religious or theological *interpretation* of historical events, an interpretation instituted wholly *ex post facto*.

[39]Since the maltreatment of females hardly waits for them to become adults, the phrase "women's movement" is not the most felicitous. "Feminist movement" and "feminism" are more common. But the polemic of women's liberation involves the insistence that women, while female, are much more than feminine.

import for the Christian-Jewish meeting as the *Shoah* and the renascent state of Israel.

A most weighty handicap of the Jewish-Christian dialogue to date is its overwhelmingly patriarchal or androcentric character and thrust. A prevailing consequence has been the dialogue's domination by problems of exclusivity over testimonies to inclusivity.[40] Of course, the histories of the human world have always shared an ideology of the special treatment of females. Such special treatment ranges from idealization to calumniation, from virtual divinization to demonization. The common factor in all such diametrically opposed attributions is that males have fabricated them, and the labels are never assigned to males as males. In a word, the woman is "the other," the one who is ever put on trial.

The moral and social issues posed by the women's movement impinge upon today's encounter of Christians and Jews in many decisive ways. Three such ways are here singled out.

1. *The Jewish tradition and the Christian tradition share the evil of sexism.* Jews who are tempted into self-righteousness by Christian hostility and prejudice may be reminded that all is hardly well within the Jewish house. Out of disillusionment with their own faith or through happy encounters with Jews, Christians sometimes tend to idealize Judaism or the Jewish communtiy. Soon or late they must come hard against a still-prevalent sexism there. Rachel Adler writes that the "problem" of Jewish women is their identification as peripheral Jews within Jewish law and practice.

> The category in which we are generally placed includes women, children, and Canaanite slaves. . . . [Members] of this category have been "excused" from most of the positive symbols that, for the male Jew, hallow time, hallow his physical being, and inform both his myth and his philosophy. . . . Children, if male, are full Jews *in potentio*. Male Canaanite slaves, if freed, become full Jews, responsible for all the *mitzvot* [Jewish obligations] and able to count in a *minyan* [the number needed for a prayer service]. Even as slaves, they have the *b'rit mila*, the covenant of circumcision, that central Jewish symbol from which women are anatomically excluded. It is true that in Jewish law women are slightly more respected than slaves, but that advantage is out-

[40]D. McCauley and A. Daum, "Jewish-Christian Feminist Dialogue: A Wholistic Vision," *Union Seminary Quarterly Review* 38 (1983) 147–90.

weighed by the fact that only women can never grow up, or be freed, or otherwise leave the category.[41]

The presence of sexism within the Jewish tradition and Judaism helps offset substantively as well as psychologically a stress upon the general moral asymmetry of the Jewish-Christian relation, a stress ordinarily necessitated by the pervasiveness and power of Christian anti-Semitism and triumphalism. (In point of fact, is not sexism the only serious moral count to be entered against the Judaic tradition?)

2. *Because the Christian church with its supersessionism and hostility to Jews has always been a male-dominated community, the power of womanism may have positive implications in the struggle against anti-Semitism.* Would Christian contempt for Jews and Judaism have become as bad as it has were the church not male sexist? Any affirmative response would assume that males and females are equally adept at such a sin as anti-Semitism—a response that is a long way from being demonstrated or convincing. Many feminists rightly discern close links between Christian imperialist anti-Semitism and characteristically male chauvinist behavior. For the entire structure of Christian imperialism was reared by males. The *Shoah* itself, for all its unprecedented and unique character, and for all its ensnaring of female practitioners, is at one with the common and perennial infamy of male wars and male destructiveness. As Rabbi Leonard Aaronson once put it, "the human male is a killer and a rapist."

Letty Cottin Pogrebin reckons with the bond between anti-Semitism and anti-womanism: "If you are not an ally of women, you cannot be considered an ally of Jews." Pogrebin contrasts the two Christian clergymen, Jesse Jackson and Jerry Falwell. Jackson's anti-Israel "evenhandedness" and anti-Semitic slurs appear to lower him in comparison with Falwell's expressed support of Israel. However, as against Jackson,

> Falwell and his ilk have made no secret of their moral imperialism: they intend *by law*, not just public suasion, to "Chris-

---

[41] R. Adler, "The Jew Who Wasn't There," in M. M. Kellner, ed., *Contemporary Jewish Ethics* (New York, 1978) pp. 348–49. Adler's reference to slavery could seem anachronistic in light of that institution's abandonment by Jews long ago. Her response, I should imagine, would be to point out that the passage of time has not freed women. Hence, the comparative allusion to slavery is not unfitting.

tianize America," impose prayer in public schools, revitalize family patriarchy, outlaw reproductive freedom, and give the fetus more rights than the woman in whose body it exists.

They have proved their enmity by word and deed. In comparison, Jackson is at worst an indiscreet bigot, . . . and at best an unknown quantity, a man whose commitments on the Jewish question have yet to be tested. But on the woman question, Jackson has come a long way: he has moved from anti-choice to pro-choice on reproductive rights, and from the knee-jerk male supremacy of the old black power movement to a position of sensitivity on women's needs.[42]

In summation, there appears to be some hope for Jackson and little or no hope for Falwell. Attitudes to women are identified by Pogrebin as the litmus test for actual and potential Christian attitudes to Jews. The surmounting of Christian imperialism as such may carry promise for both the male acceptance of women as equals and the Christian acceptance of Jews as equals.

3. *Anti-Semitism is by no means absent from the women's movement.* This situation helps counteract, or ought to, any temptation to idealize either the feminist movement or women—or, perhaps more accurately, it points up the power of patriarchal destructiveness in contributing to the present psycho-intellectual condition of women. Historically speaking, the presence of anti-Semitism in the women's movement "is rooted in anti-Judaic male theology of the past and was incorporated into the movement for suffrage in nineteenth century America." An example of the latter is the influential and blatantly anti-Semitic work of Elizabeth Cady Stanton, *The Women's Bible.* Some of today's Christian feminists "have fallen prey to the ancient masculine trap of triumphalism." Judaism and Jewry have

> always been the primary "other" onto which Christianity has projected those parts of itself to which it will not lay claim. In this scenario, Judaism becomes the bad parent whom Christianity as the adult child blames and punishes for those parts of its personality it does not like and for which it refuses to accept responsibility. The phenomenon of patriarchal projection is made manifest in Christian and post-Christian feminist writings that either explicitly or implicitly blame Judaism for the initial

---

[42]L. C. Pogrebin, "Women as the Litmus Test," *Present Tense* 12 (1985) 46–47.

and formative development of the misogyny and sexism we experience in both Christianity and Western civilization.[43]

Feminist anti-Jewishness is exemplified in the misrepresentation found among some non-Jewish feminists concerning the binding of Isaac by his father, Abraham, wherein the "sacrifice" of the child is transmuted into a renunciation of matriarchal protection in the furtherance of a patriarchal system. The plain truth, of course, is that the story teaches the *rejection* of child sacrifice. Again, womanist anti-Semitism is brought to the surface and compounded via the claim that Jesus of Nazareth was a feminist. To date, the feminist claim for him is seldom utilized, as it very well ought to be, in order to show that Jesus' evident openness to and sympathy for women was typifying a moral impulse strictly within Judaism and Jewish circles. Most often the claim concerning Jesus is turned into a negativistic-ideological stress upon the faults of traditional Jewish action, as against the presumed virtues of the central figure in Christianity. One complicating factor, which probably does not help things, is that it is sometimes Christian males who put forward the (alleged) feminism of Jesus in (alleged) contrast to Jesus' peers. In any event, the so-called feminism of Jesus was soon to be buried by a church whose sexism exceeded, if anything, the continuing sexism of the Jewish world.

Finally, it is the height of irony that Barbara Brown Zikmund, a contemporary Christian feminist, should "on one level" find totally unacceptable "the trinitarian formula of God as Father, Son and Holy Spirit" because "the words are redolent of hierarchy and patriarchy," and then in the very next breath, yet not unexpectedly, assert that Christian trinitarian theology has served to prevent Jewish monotheism "from undermining the significance of Christ." Indeed, so we are advised, "the doctrine of Trinity erodes the monarchical and patriarchal power of monotheism."[44] Having condemned a sexist Trinity, Zikmund barefacedly tries to rescue the Trinity by proclaiming, among other things, its virtue as an anti-Jewish resource.

---

[43]McCauley and Daum, "Jewish-Christian Feminist Dialogue," p. 182.
[44]B. B. Zikmund, "The Trinity and Women's Experience," *The Christian Century* 104 (1987) 354–56.

Today, the alliance of Christian trinitarian feminism with the Christian anti-Jewish polemic is, if anything, a burgeoning trend, as typified in Patricia Wilson-Kastner's *Faith, Feminism and the Christ*, with its endeavor to link Jewish and other monotheism to patriarchy.[45]

Many promising revolutionary movements are unable, or do not wish, to keep themselves free of anti-Semitism (cf. the bond between the Sandinistas and the Palestine Liberation Organization). In our present, specific context the anti-Semitism of the women's movement in its Christian guise returns us to the moral asymmetry that obtains between Jewishness and Christian identity as a whole. However, in fairness it has to be remembered that some of the anti-Semitism in the women's movement comes from people who have abandoned Christianity.

With the above three factors in mind let us do some tying together, through (1) a constructive critical comment directed to the future of Judaism, and (2) a word upon the contribution of the women's movement to the future of the Jewish-Christian meeting.

As Jewish feminists again and again point out, no problem is more conspicuous, stubborn, or serious than the rite of circumcision, involving as it does, traditionally and contemporaneously, "*the* physical sign of being in covenant with God."[46] If, as the Mishnah states, Abraham was not called perfect, that is, a completed human being, until he was circumcised, does it not follow that women have no way to become completed human beings? (Christian baptism is free of the taint of sexism; here is a place where the moral asymmetry between Judaism and Christianity is reversed.)

However wholly unacceptable is the apostle Paul's Christian supersessionism vis-à-vis Judaism,[47] Paul's emphasis upon the ultimate irrelevance of circumcision may be interpreted as an oddly prevenient Christian judgment upon the Jewish tradition. This is said strictly in the context of the discrete problem of sexism and not at all with respect to Paul's negativism upon

---

[45]Consult P. Wilson-Kastner, *Faith, Feminism and the Christ* (Philadelphia, 1983) p. 122 and passim.

[46]McCauley and Daum, "Jewish-Christian Feminist Dialogue," p. 164.

[47]E. P. Sanders, *Paul and Palestinian Judaism: A Comparison of Patterns of Religion* (Philadelphia, 1977); *Paul, the Law, and the Jewish People* (Philadelphia, 1983).

the place of Torah as a whole. The apostle's emphasis allies him, in an astonishing way, with womanism. I say "astonishing" because Paul was anything but a feminist. What I have in mind is the apostle's allusion to Jews and Gentiles: "Neither circumcision counts for anything nor uncircumcision, but keeping the commandments of God" (1Cor 7:19). This passage may be applied to our present topic.

In a biblical frame of reference, Paul is on the face of it talking nonsense, since in the Torah circumcision *means* keeping God's commandments (Gen 17:10). But in the late twentieth century the apostle's contention, applied to a Jewish feminist hermeneutic, gains contemporary power and application. In *Romans* Paul declares:

> So, if a man who is uncircumcised keeps the precepts of the law, will not his uncircumcision be regarded as circumcision? . . . For he is not a real Jew who is one outwardly, nor is true circumcision something external and physical. He is a Jew who is one inwardly, and real circumcision is a matter of the heart, spiritual and not literal. His praise is not from men but from God. (Rom 2:26-29 [RSV])

The plain implication of the previously cited words of Rachel Adler is that the observance of Torah and the commandments is a right wholly inherent to Jewish women. Paying full heed to Adler's lament over the marginalizing of Jewish females, we may venture *to recast*, on her behalf and theirs, the Pauline affirmation of *Romans* 2:

> Clearly a woman of Israel remains uncircumcised. But through her honoring of the precepts of Torah, this uncircumcision is seen to have no consequence. Her uncircumcision is to be deemed the same as circumcision. . . . For she is not a real Jew who is one outwardly, nor is true circumcision something that only males can achieve. She is a Jew who is one inwardly, and real circumcision means being treated as a human being, with full dignity and rights. Her praise is not from men but from God.

In contemporary parlance, the one way that Jewish men and Jewish women are made equal adherents of Judaism is through equally keeping Torah. "Neither circumcision nor uncircumcision counts for anything." The answer to "uncircumcision" is found, and can only be found, in the unqualified opening of Torah-observance to women. (We are led to a bizarre conclusion, to be taken not literally yet with the seriousness of laughter: The apostle Paul never knew it but he was, preveniently—though only at this single place—an unwitting supporter of today's Jewish feminism.)

My second series of comments relates to a possibly creative and redeeming contribution from within the women's movement to the Jewish-Christian meeting, with special emphasis upon Jewish-Christian reconciliation. A large number of phenomena or variables all have substantive relevance here: the meaning of revolution; the disparity between Jewishness and Christianness; the problematic of male saviorhood; the moral encumbrance within Christian feminism; the consanguinity among anti-Semitic, christological, and sexist idolatries; and the final nemesis faced by anti-Semitism. Let us consider the way in which all these variables converge within the redeeming quality of Jewish womanism.

In what follows the androcentric tradition is repudiated; a revolution is directed against that evil. One complicating point requires mention first. The difference between radical feminists, who tend to have little use of hope for religious faith, and reforming feminists, who are more hopeful or less unsympathetic to faith, impinges upon the differences between Jewishness and Christianness: Are the people who are involved Jews or are they Christians? For as everyone knows, or ought to, whereas the rejection or loss or absence of faith does not exclude a Jew from Jewishness, Christian faith is requisite to Christianness. Accordingly, a radical Jewish feminist and a radical Christian feminist, as just characterized, are not in identical predicaments vis-à-vis their respective communities, nor, accordingly, do they have the same potential opportunities.

From the standpoint of the Christian women's movement in its revolutionary form, Pope John Paul II's argumentation upon why only males can be priests—namely, that it was in male form that God became incarnate—must be turned against itself. That argument is viewed as self-refuting and self-condemning. For, in the context of revolutionary feminism, is not the best evidence of the untruthfulness and immorality of the traditional Incarnation-claim its pretension to male saviorhood? Insofar as males are constitutively (meaning historically) exploitive of women, how could a male ever be their savior? A malignant disease does not cure itself. In the frame of reference of radical feminism, the question is not whether women are to be priests; it is instead whether *men* are capable of being priests.

There are resources within the women's movement for meliorating Christianity's intolerance of Judaism and Judaism's (much lesser) intolerance of Christianity. Female inclusivity is a winsome and powerful weapon against male exclusivity. Yet, as we have noted, Christian feminism is itself not free of the taint of anti-Semitism that befouls Christianity as such. Accordingly, our present subject requires a much more discrete, much more careful, and much more profound approach.

There is the radical Christian feminism that cuts through the chains of a "savior" who does not save, one in whom, and in whose maleness, women are in truth victimized. The avowedly Protestant Christian feminist Dorothee Sölle and the avowedly post-Christian feminist Mary Daly can embrace in their repugnance for what the latter has called "Christolatry," the "idolatrous worship of a supernatural, timeless divine being who has little in common with the Jewish Jesus of Nazareth."[48] (Ought not "little" here read "nothing"?)

The point is that within and through the very struggle of Christian women *and men* against the christological victimization of women, there is also carried forward the struggle against the victimization of Jews. The contemporary radical Christian womanist attack upon the idolatrous deification of a male human being as reputed savior constitutes a unique and unprecedented world-historical and potentially world-transforming event. Here is the ground of the proposition that elements within the women's movement may come to rival the *Shoah* and the re-created State of Israel in their significance for the Christian-Jewish relation. The foundation of this judgment is that this new development cuts not merely in one epochal moral direction but in two. On the one hand, it attacks the deification of not just any human being but the specific deification that produced anti-Jewish supersessionism; and, on the other hand, it attacks the world-destroying sexism that came to penetrate Christianity (because of its male "savior") in historical continuity with the sexism of Judaism. The inner bond between Christian anti-Semitism and Christian antiwomanism

---

[48]D. Sölle, "Christianity and the Jewish Request for Signs: A Reflection on I Corinthians 1:22," *Face to Face* 11 (1984) 20.

is disclosed. The single root cause of both these phenomena in the Christian world is the triumphalism of a male "savior" aided and abetted by all his male followers through the long centuries. The whole of Christian history exhibits a single affliction, with two faces. There is the idolatrous divinizing of a human being, which establishes anti-Jewishness at the heart of Christianity, and there is the idolatrous masculinizing of divinity, which establishes antiwomanism as equally central.

If anti-Judaism and anti-Semitism are, as Rosemary Ruether has said, the left hand of Christology, androcentric sexism stands at Christology's right hand. Thus does the radical women's revolution become a resource, if an unintended one, for vanquishing the historic Christian derogation of everything Jewish. This is not to imply that the women's movement is to be used as a means to an end. Were such the case, we would remain in the abyss of the exploitation of females. The contribution of the women's movement to overcoming Jewish-Christian moral asymmetry is an event of free grace, and is to be received and celebrated as such.

There remains what appears to be a fatal catch—we are still confronted by a considerably sexist Judaism. If that faith has always kept itself free from human divinization of the sort that has morally imperiled Christianity, it has hardly escaped the sin of sexism, a tacit divinizing of the male creature. A final tragedy for the church would be its deliverance from the christological idolatries that ensure anti-Semitism only to land in the idolatries of an abiding Jewish sexism. All this suggests that the real hope and the real future for Christianity are linked to the Jewish woman's revolution—just as the Jewish ideal of justice and the sanctification of life enables the present and future prosperity of the Jewish feminist movement. For only the empowering grace of Jewish womanism—which, unlike Christian womanism, is not hung up psychologically and spiritually upon the problematic of the saviorhood/nonsaviorhood of a male being—can overcome, at one and the same time, all three of the evils that assail us—the mortal sin of Jewish and Christian androcentrism; Christian supersessionist and exclusivist imperialism against Jews and Judaism; and the anti-Semitism of the women's movement. Therefore, the way that Christian feminism may free the church from traditional Christian anti-Jewish, patriarchal triumphalism is through becoming the liberated and liberating emissary and partner of Jewish womanism. The prodigal daughter returns to her mother's household.

Overall, it may be suggested that the hope of today's Christian-Jewish dialogue is contingent upon its transfiguration into a Christian-Jewish-womanist trialogue. And, of infinitely greater import, the human, moral, and theological hope of the church may be seen to lie in Jewish womanism. Potentially, Jewish womanism as a nascent-historic phenomenon joins the *Shoah* and political Israel in leading the church upon its return into the history of Israel, including a transformation of the church's Christology in harmony with a Christian historicism. The strictly historical Jewish Jesus and the equally historical Jewish woman compose a dialectic—a form of wedlock, so to speak—that may serve to reconcile the past and the present with the future.

DISCUSSION

CHARLESWORTH: One thought that keeps coming to my mind when I think about Jewish-Christian relations is one word that hasn't yet been discussed: the word *theodicy*. It seems to me the greatest obstacles in the Jewish-Christian dialogue are the exclusive claims by Jews that they *alone* are the *elect* of God and the contention by Christians that the gospel demands the concerted *conversion* of the Jews. Surely each of these veer from the search for truth and understanding and founder on the attempt to speak as the very voice of God. Each is then marred by the question of theodicy. Does not 3,000 years of history show that only God can declare who are the elect and that only he holds the key to being declared righteous before him? And I think this impinges upon the whole question of what really is going on in the world today, whether we focus upon the Palestinian question, the question of Zionism, or the question of what we're doing here today. Dr. Eckardt may or may not have something to say on the subject, but I think it's such a big issue that it ought to be put on the table along with all the other things he has forced us to struggle with and try to come to grips with.

ECKARDT: That raises the question of suffering. I think that one thing the *Shoah* should have taught us is the moral bankruptcy of the teaching of the suffering servant. And this is one place where Christian holocaust theologians and Jewish holocaust theologians are coming together (viz., Greenburg and Rubenstein). And this is one reason why I tend to put this theological movement in Judaism under the heading of liberation theology, because that's exactly what black liberation theologians told us a long time ago. And of course women's liberation people are saying that you cannot use the concepts of suffering servant, or the suffering of God, or the redemptive value of suffering after the *Shoah*. My second comment, which is in a sense autobiographical, is that the whole notion of questioning God didn't have any meaning to me until I got into the dialogue. It would be really blasphemous (in terms of the Christianity that I was brought up in) to question God's justice; but I learned from Elie Wiesel and from Hassidism that you do question God, that human dignity is standing up before God and saying, "What the hell are You doing? And where did You get the right to make up suffering?" So, I learned.

BEKER: Dr. Eckardt, I thought your paper was interesting and probing, but my main question is this: What actually is your chief complaint about the resurrection? Why do you think that the resurrection and Jewish victimization go together?

ECKARDT: The reason is that I tend to think of the resurrection of Jesus Christ as a completely divine act—not very profound because all that says really is that when you're dead, you're dead. None of us can do anything using human resources in order to bring ourselves back from the dead. It has to be a totally divine act. In other words, I think of the resurrection in objective terms: an objective event that would have occurred, I think according to the New Testament, apart from reaction to it. This is why I don't understand what people mean when they say that it doesn't matter if there were cameras there to photograph it. I don't understand that type of reasoning. That's how I tend to think of the resurrection. Now, because I think of the resurrection as a completely divine event, if it happened, I don't think that there's any way to get rid of Christian supersessionism insofar as one affirms the resurrection as other than some kind of spiritual experience for Jesus and the Lord.

BEKER: I'd like to understand that logic. Why is the resurrection necessarily tied to supersessionism?

ECKARDT: Because it's not a human act. It's a completely divine act.

BEKER: Well, what does that mean?

ECKARDT: Well, if it were a human act of some kind, a human historical act which for which human beings are responsible, we could get rid of it and thereby get rid of our supersessionism.

PRIEST: If one takes seriously the doctrine of the resurrection, then that means that at the very best, granting that there are saving acts of God found in the history of Israel, this is affirmed by the church to be the culminating act. And therefore culmination does not necessarily (i.e., theoretically) require supersessionism, but it does practically.

BEKER: But on biblical grounds, the resurrection could simply be interpreted as the first fruits of the promise of God to Israel, and not, as church traditions have falsely interpreted it, as the culmination point. It could be just the first beginning of the harvest which pertains to the promise of God to Israel. My question is, Why does the resurrection necessarily entail supersessionism?

ECKARDT: And I can only answer it the way I have answered it. It's an exclusively divine act.

PRIEST: Please clarify something on this, Dr. Beker. I said that the resurrection is not necessarily theoretically the culmination. And, in fact, the New Testament witness doesn't see it that way.

BEKER: Correct.

PRIEST: Yet, very shortly in the development of Christian thought it did in fact become the culmination and led to supersessionism. But, it doesn't have to be.

ECKARDT: What Paul says I take very seriously—that if Christ has not been raised then Christian faith is in vain. I take that very seriously.

SMITH: I think that to deny the resurrection would mean that we are no longer speaking as Christians or Christian theologians, unless we can accommodate that or interpret that in some way. We shall have stepped outside our tradition, just as, if I say I am a Jew and I no longer want to talk about the People, I shall have stepped outside the bounds of my tradition.

ECKARDT: Here I would again be a little autobiographical: I think it's harder for me to have faith in the future resurrection of Jesus Christ than it is for you to have faith in the past resurrection of Jesus Christ. See, this is my faith. I completely eschatologize the thing. I don't deny the resurrection of Jesus Christ, but I see myself as living, let's say, on the Saturday between Good Friday and Easter.

BEKER: My underlying point is this. It doesn't benefit any Jewish-Christian dialogue to give up on basic Christian confession. I think that's the wrong type of genuflection.

ECKARDT: My theology has nothing to do with the Jewish-Christian dialogue. I'm not very interested in the Jewish-Christian dialogue. What I'm interested in is the truth. And I believe that what I said here about the resurrection contributing to the death of countless children is true historically. So the question then is, Is Christianity morally credible? Is there a disjunction between truth in the Platonic sense and goodness, or must the two be brought together? Now for me, and here I've been influenced a lot by Judaism, but also by the Christian social gospel, there's no way to separate truth and goodness. The challenge to the teaching of the resurrection of Jesus Christ today as a result of the *Shoah* is a moral challenge. I don't know if we have to make it an intellectual challenge, or something like that. After all, Jesus wasn't the first to be raised from the dead. There were other people. In *Matthew* 27 all kinds of people get raised from the dead and nobody seems to be interested in them. They don't even have names. There's nothing unique about Jesus being raised from the dead, except if it were a completely divine act that had some kind of eschatological significance.

PRIEST: Even for all his demythologization, etc., etc., Bultmann in his article on the relation of the Old Testament to Christian faith makes it very clear that if we remove from the New Testament those things which are distinctively Christian, we end up with either a vapid humanism or a kind of purified Judaism. And that would not encourage genuine development of Jewish-Christian relations at all. I must affirm that I believe in the resurrection of the dead. If I didn't, then I would not continue in the Christian faith. At the same time, I'm open to discuss what that means to a group which does not share that particular belief.

BEKER: Just on logical grounds it seems to me that if, for any reason—which I can't see—the resurrection would really deny the validity of the legitimacy of Israel's faith, then the resurrection would be bankrupt. But the New Testament never proclaims it as such. What the later Christian tradition does is one thing. But resurrection is Jewish language, it's a Jewish category. We are not talking about pagan categories. We aren't talking about Plato. We're talking about the fundamental Jewish confession. I believe in the Shema as I believe in the resurrection of the dead. It is in that Jewish framework that the resurrection of Jesus has to fit, has to be explained. So we operate within the world of Jewish thought and language. Now that's primary, it seems to me.

CHARLESWORTH: I must agree with Dr. Beker's comment that the Christian's belief in the resurrection of Jesus is not an impediment to Jewish-Christian dialogue. One thing we must emphatically do if there is going to be fruitful and honest dialogue between Jews and Christians is to be honest about where we differ. The belief in the resurrection of the body is a Jewish idea. It comes into the Bible through early Jewish thought. The early texts used the Greek term *ēgerthē* (Mk 16:6), which is a passive; I take it literally as a divine passive—*God* raised him up. Also, in the kerygma of the early Christian community, we find statements that God raised up Jesus from the dead. So I think "Jesus' resurrection" should be understood as a God-centered act performed on Jesus, a Jew. My next point is that all the people who, according to the New Testament, claimed to have seen the resurrected Jesus were Jews—Mary Magdalene, Peter, Cleopas, James, Paul, and so forth. So we're not moving away from a Jewish milieu, but we are pulled into a very difficult issue that encourages us as Christians to reflect on what are the real ramifications of the Jesus who was "bodily" resurrected.

HILLERBRAND: As I interpret the discussion, I hear Dr. Eckardt saying in his paper that there is only one way to interpret what Dr. Charlesworth just summarized, and that is in a triumphalist way. I hear Dr. Beker and others—and I count myself among them—saying, That is *one* way to interpret the resurrection, but there are also other ways to interpret it.

ECKARDT: I would put it differently. I would say that it is not a question of how we interpret the resurrection. I would say that—and again, I must be somewhat autobiographical—until ten years ago, this question never occurred to me. Even in one book I wrote in 1973, I still put a lot of emphasis on the resurrection as being a unique thing about Christianity, the usual stuff. But, you see, then I encountered—or was encountered by—the Holocaust. I think that those who say that we can go on and affirm the resurrection as we did before the Holocaust are essentially pre-Holocaust people. I'm a post-Holocaust Christian. I am trying to live with the fact that the moral credibility of my faith is under attack by this event. And the question is, How can I live with it? I know that some theologians simply don't think that this is a problem. But all I can do is confess that I didn't either until about 1973, and now my experience has been shattered by the *Shoah*.

BEKER: It seems to me that the issue of the resurrection is all the more important for its Jewish roots, because the real threat to the resurrection, and therefore to the authenticity of Judaism, was when, in early Patristic times, it was taken by Gnosticism out of the Jewish framework and the confession of the resurrection of the dead became the celebration of the immortality of the spirit. That's when the resurrection becomes supersessionist—as soon as it's taken out of this Jewish framework. So it seems to me that the materiality of the resurrected body is crucial to the Christian confession, because it confesses thereby that the Kingdom of God and the resurrection of the dead is a this-earthly event. I would suggest that you have the components wrong.

ECKARDT: What you say is absolutely right. But you see if I agree with exactly what you just said, if I said Roy Eckardt agrees exactly with what Chris Beker has said, then I would say I would have to be a missionary, too.

SIKER: Why? I don't understand that.

ECKARDT: Why? Because I would have to share this wonderful good news. Why should others be deprived of it?

HILLERBRAND: Let me ask a question as a church historian. I heard you say that as you look and view Christian history since the crucifixion, it is the Holocaust that constitutes that singular event that, as it were, disrupts everything. In other words, there are no prior events that happened—say, what happened in seventeenth-century South America, what happened in the Middle Ages—that raised the theological question about the suffering servant?

ECKARDT: Not in the same way, because I feel that my interpretation of the Holocaust shows the final logic here of Christian anti-Semitism as the ultimate event. And it is a unique event, even historically, because it stands for the destruction of every last Jew. It says, "There must be no more Jews."

SIKER: But is it merely the magnitude of the event that does that?

ECKARDT: No, the quality of the event, because it's not a numbers game.

BEKER: Dr. Eckardt, if you would have said that the Holocaust puts into question the moral credibility of the Christian faith, I could understand.

ECKARDT: Didn't I say that?

BEKER: No, because you fasten on the resurrection.

ECKARDT: To me the resurrection is the Christian faith. Without the resurrection, we have nothing.

CHAPTER EIGHT

Holocaust as a Pathological Act of Secularization

Richard K. Fenn

Introduction

It is striking to find Gaalya Cornfeld using the term "holocaust" to describe the destruction of Jerusalem in 70 C.E.;[1] the term could apply as well to the devastating campaign in the countryside that had massacred the residents of cities that had given refuge to the partisans. There is horror compounded by horror in these accounts by Josephus. Cornfeld uses the term well, since the Palestinian "holocaust" of 66–70 C.E. was as genocidal, although not as systematic and complete, as the holocaust of the twentieth century. In both holocausts the community life of a people in a particular time and place was reduced to ashes.

In the first century, authority was sacred, whether it was exercised by charismatic kings and emperors, generals and guerilla leaders, or priests and prophets. Authority in modern societies is largely secularized, that is, based on the prescriptions of reason and the law. Only its underlying, latent supports may be sacred.

It might therefore seem somewhat strained to call these two different events by the same term. Richard Rubenstein, for instance, attributes the twentieth-century holocaust to the apogee of a secularized society, to secularization that has reached an absurd peak.[2] Of course, there have been vainglorious and brutal princes before in history; however, Rubenstein argues that it was the Nazis' command of an extraordinarily rational, bureaucratic, and therefore efficient and systematic state apparatus that made the twentieth-century slaughter possible—not the engines of war but the offices of the state. Contrast patriarchal authority in the first century. In spurring his troops to fight against the partisans, Vespasian appealed to their loyalty to him and to his son Titus. Contrast the administration of the German Reich, which was based on decrees that were entirely legal in their origins—not the word of the charismatic general on horseback but the statutes divesting Jews of property, civil rights, and finally of citizenship itself. These differences are just what one would expect, however, and do not in themselves make a comparison between the two holocausts impossible.

In applying the term "holocaust" to both the twentieth-century and first-century destruction of Jewish communities, Cornfeld therefore prompts me to ask what it is that distinguishes these events from other tragedies and massacres. By *holocaust*, then, I mean to refer to *the destruction of one part of a social system by the social system to which that part once belonged*. It would be a misuse of the term to refer to the bombings of Nagasaki and Hiroshima as a nuclear holocaust, unspeakable as those acts were. But it would be entirely appropriate to speak of the destruction of American communities in a nuclear war initiated by the United States as a holocaust. In such a case, of course, it is probable that the nation itself would be destroyed along with its parts. Germany no longer exists as a single nation: it too was destroyed as a single social system. Defined in this way, it is clear that a holocaust requires that one part of a society or system be treated as if it were external: a part of the environment, perhaps, or beyond the horizon altogether, where it can be slated for destruction.

In this paper I will suggest that secularization is a useful concept for understanding the process by which one part of a society is treated as outside the system. Conceived as a process of secularization, the events leading up to the destruction of Jerusalem in 66–70 C.E. can indeed be compared with the holocaust of the twentieth century. The two systems being so very different, the process of secularization will follow a very

---

[1]G. Cornfeld, B. Mazar, and P. L. Maier, eds., *Josephus. The Jewish War* (Grand Rapids, 1982). All citations are from this edition.
[2]R. Rubenstein, *The Cunning of History* (New York, 1978).

different course in modern Germany than in Palestine of the first century. Nonetheless, the use of the same concept will help us to grasp not only what is different about the two events but also what they have in common.

The notion of secularization has somewhat different meanings according to whether one is speaking about a social process or a social act. As a social act, to secularize something or someone is to deprive them of any sacred meaning, significance, or entitlement. Church buildings and properties can thus be secularized. In a more general sense the church has secularized the beliefs and practices of indigenous communities by refusing to regard them as sacred. Popular cults have been relegated to the world of utilitarian or magical practice, for instance, or considered merely local or communal rather than larger in scope and significance. Intellectuals tend to secularize Christianity in Western societies by regarding it as a phenomenon of primarily private, individual, local, communal, or ethnic significance. Indeed, many sociologists argue that religion, and specifically Christianity in the West, *is* secularized precisely to the extent that it becomes extraneous to the primary institutions and values of modern, complex social systems. To secularize, then, is to define something or someone, an institution or a community, as marginal to some larger social system; that entity thus becomes peripheral, vestigial, on the way out. Such usage derives from the theological notion of the secular world as indeed passing away: part of the aeon that is heading irreversibly toward extinction and death.

The process of secularization does not necessarily lead to destruction and holocaust; the process can be benign. For instance, society secularizes nature by placing it outside the social system. The spirits of animals therefore no longer inhabit the human, and the rhythms of social life no longer follow the rhythms of nature and the seasons. A society secularizes time as well as nature by putting the past—and to some extent the future—out of its social life. The spirits of the dead therefore no longer inform the minds of the living, and the society no longer patterns itself after sacred precedents. Old debts, once paid, are canceled, and the society begins to live for the time being in an extended present. A society similarly can secularize the future by putting it beyond the framework of the present. Promises are then made without having to be fulfilled among the generation of those to whom the promise was made (e.g., social security benefits). The future, however much it may be at hand, never quite begins. Later generations, like earlier ones, become an environment that a society must take into account, but neither the dead nor the unborn are themselves members of the society. To secularize nature, time, and space thus gives a society time to develop its own plans, strategies, techniques, rules, and institutions without being haunted by the past or pressed into precipitate action by the arrival of the future.

Secularization can also lead to destruction when the process is pathological. In this paper I will therefore develop the argument that the Palestinian holocaust was due to a pathological process of secularization. I will trace that process to the repeated attempt to remove any traces of the sacred from symbols and practices that linked Jerusalem to Rome. The process was rendered pathological, furthermore, by the intensification of conflict until every crucial boundary collapsed: not only the boundaries separating Jerusalem from the Roman Empire, but the boundary separating the present from the past and from the future, and even the boundaries separating society from nature.

Step 1: Breaking Liturgical Ties

In the Palestinian holocaust the process begins with the attempt to break the symbolic and liturgical ties binding the Temple to Rome. Certainly the dissidents who pulled down the eagle over the Temple door, placed there by Herod, were severing the symbolic connection; it was a radical act of desecration against the symbol of empire. Similarly, a large crowd of protesters impressed Petronius that a statue of Caligula, to be placed in the precincts of the Temple, would desecrate the Temple and initiate bloody reprisals. In his *The Jewish War* Josephus makes it clear that the last liturgical ties between the Temple and Rome were broken on the eve of the civil war, 66–70.

Capture of Masada (summer of 66); cessation of the sacrifices for Rome.

(408) Meanwhile, some of the most ardent promoters of war banded together and made an assault on a stronghold called

> Masada . . . and, having captured it by stealth, slew the Roman guards and put a garrison of their own in their place. (409) At the same time another incident occurred in the Temple; Eleazar, son of Ananias the high priest, and a very rash young man then holding the position of captain . . . , persuaded those who officiated at the Temple to accept no gift or sacrifice from a foreigner. This action laid the foundation of the war with Rome; for they renounced in consequence the sacrifices offered for Rome and the emperor. . . . (410) The chief priests and the prominent citizens earnestly appealed to them not to abandon the customary offerings for their rulers, but the priests would not give in. Their numbers gave them great confidence, backed as they were by the stalwarts of the revolutionary party; but they pinned their faith above all on the authority of the captain, Eleazar. (*War* 2.17.408-10)

Virtually every rite not only blesses a tie that binds the members together into a sacred community; each rite also separates the participants from those outside. That is one axiom that seems to hold particularly true of rites of initiation or sacramental communion. Even at death, the survivors intensify their ties to the local community while separating themselves from the departed, who are encouraged to go on their way. The converse of this axiom is also true, however: that there is a second order of obligation, a symbolic relation that ties the insiders to the outsiders, the initiate to the uninitiated, the sanctified to the unsanctified, and even the living to the dead. As Freud noted of the rituals of his patients, they had to be repeated because the acts of symbolic separation were never completed in a final break with the past. No rejection was ever sufficient to make it unnecessary to repeat the rituals of separation. Even the dead seem to come back to haunt those who have dismissed them in the last rites. Even in Jerusalem, the very rites that sanctified the gathered community and dramatized their separation from the Gentile world included prayers for the emperor of Rome: prayers, of course, and not sacrifices, but the prayers kept alive the relationship that was being otherwise placed beyond the liturgical pale. To cease praying for the emperor was therefore a drastic cut of ties with the larger society of which Israel was a part.

It would be difficult to find in the modern world a functional equivalent of such *a disastrous liturgical act.* The holocaust would have occurred in Nazi Germany despite the symbolic ties of Jews to all of Europe; conversely, such a liturgical act would hardly have precipitated Nazi oppression. That is precisely the point: that the process of secularization in the modern world is carried out more by social routine than by dramatic liturgical acts. Neither prophecy nor liturgy can sever the ties created by modern bureaucracies. Those bureaucracies in turn have other means of binding individuals and communities to the political center. Can a liturgy bind together those who are separated by the nation-state into sovereign communities? I will return to this question at the end of this paper.

A second difference between the first and twentieth century is also immediately apparent from this account by Josephus. The relation between the Roman center and the Palestinian periphery was hardly rational, continuous, and efficient. It took time, vast expenditure, exceptional effort, and an enormous waste of resources for the imperial center to visit its wrath on the provincial periphery. Those visitations, furthermore, were discrete rather than continuous, violent rather than bureaucratic, and military rather than administrative. Contrast the Nazi repression of the Jews; it was relatively continuous, smooth, and exceedingly efficient. As Rubenstein reminds us, the Nazis even counted the number of potatoes that were necessary to feed the Jews in the coal mines of Auschwitz, who were working to produce the very coal that eventually, turned into gas, would be used to exterminate them. The presence of the German center on the Jewish periphery was continuous, administrative, legal, and lethal.

In comparing the onset of the holocaust in Germany with that in Palestine, it is therefore useful to look for the rupture of the symbolic rather than liturgical ties between the political center and the Jewish community. The progressive breaking of economic, civic, political, and legal relationships made it impossible for Jews to own property, hold office, and eventually even to offer the symbolic sacrifice of the citizen, i.e., taxes and votes. When the Jew, deprived of citizenship, could no longer engage in these symbolic transactions with the center, the process of secularizing the Jewish community was virtually complete. Placed outside the pale of the social system, and yet fully within its administrative control, the community could be exterminated.

I am arguing that for one society or community to pronounce a sentence of death over its relationship to another community or society is a radical act of secularization. The Nazis were pathologically literal in their understanding of what it meant to secularize a community, to mark it for eventual death. Indeed, it is literally pathological to secularize someone or something by marking it with the stigma of death or even to let the shadow of death transfigure it, as if magical gestures or actions could end a relationship. The secular is that which is destined to pass away. Whether that destiny is sealed by a liturgical or administrative act depends on whether the society engaging in the action is modern or antique. In either case, the presence of pathology depends on the type of desperate magical thinking that strives for a final solution. Whether the center and the periphery place each other beyond the pale in dramatic and violent conflict or in the slow and inexorable processes of political administration simply depends on the type of social system in question; either type of action may rest on unconscious magical thinking. In the next section of this discussion I will describe a second stage in the process that leads toward holocaust; the encirclement or encapsulation of the "secularized" other. Enough has perhaps already been said, however, to point to the importance of *liturgical ties* that can link communities that may be separated by ecological and political barriers, a point that I shall return to in my concluding comments.

Step 2: Encircling the "Secularized" Other

In the seige of Jerusalem, both the Romans and the Jews were undertaking a battle in which God would vindicate either the one side or the other; it was an "all or nothing" situation, in which only a total victory or total defeat could provide the judgment. The walls of Jerusalem would therefore be either preserved or breached, and in being breached the final judgment on Israel would be at hand. The Romans were undertaking a work in which their reputation and their glory were at stake, a combination of concerns that clusters in a single term, *doxa*. As Josephus puts it:

. . . the Romans were braced by respect for their honor and their arms, especially with Caesar in the forefront of the danger. (*War* 5.11.488)

The Romans' concern with their reputation was heightened by their dismay over the behavior of the "auxiliary troops,"— namely the Arabians and Syrians whose barbarous hatred and atrocities included disemboweling Jewish refugees in the hope of finding gold pieces in their victim's bellies, a symbolic expression of power over life and death not only in slaying the helpless but in seizing their money, which was in itself an emblem of life. The Roman leader Titus, according to Josephus, was concerned not only about the violation of orders prohibiting such savagery but about the reputation of the Romans, lest the auxiliaries involve the Romans (Josephus, *War* 5.13.556). The leaders' concern for their immortal fame also helped to maintain discipline, order, and fighting courage. At times discouraged by the fierceness and effectiveness of the Zealots' resistance at the walls of Jerusalem, the Roman soldiers were revived by their desire for reputation and glory; Josephus again—through a speech attributed to Titus—points directly to the desire to transcend death through *doxa* (glory):

> (479) The Jews are led by reckless audacity and desperation, emotions which are bracing while things go well, but are damped by the smallest setback. We who are inspired by discipline, courage and heroism, which are at their peak under the best conditions, are also sustained by them in adversity to the end. (480) Furthermore, you will be fighting for a greater cause than the Jews; for though they face the dangers of war to preserve their liberty and country, what greater prize could you win than glory and the assurance that after having dominated the world, we do not let the Jews be regarded as rivals? (*War* 3.10.479-80)

Indeed, the concern for glory and reputation were so fundamental to the Romans that Titus undertook a project that beggars the imagination, namely, to build a wall around the city of Jerusalem, whose own wall had already withstood several attacks by the Romans with all their imperial engines and ingenuity. The purpose of the new wall was partly strategic, enabling the Romans to build a rallying point from which to launch further attacks rather than to engage in attacks from exposed positions in the countryside. But Josephus, typically, points to the symbolic aspects of the project. In considering a longer seige, Josephus notes, Titus was concerned about the length of time that a strategy of attrition would require.

> (498) He feared, moreover, that the luster of success would be dimmed by the delay, for, given time, anything could be accomplished, but haste was essential to win renown. (499) If they wanted to combine speed with safety, they must throw a dyke . . . around the whole city. . . . (*War* 5.12.498-99)

The building of a wall was tantamount to the building of a cultic circle. It signified that the Romans as well as the Jews could construct a space dividing life from death. That is, the new wall fortified the boundary between the sacred and the profane. The walls of the Temple provided for the Jews a space that was sacred, pure, and beyond the pollution caused by sin and death. Outside the walls of Jerusalem was a world that, as Lifton might suggest, [3] was the world of foreigners and death. There were no more prayers to be offered that could transcend that barrier.

For the Romans to build their own wall created yet another space, a space reserved for foreigners and for death. In between the two walls was a valley, in which the corpses of those slain in battle would soon lie and putrefy. To them were added the bodies of those killed by famine or by the Zealots' own hand within their walls. The pile of bodies mounted until it impeded the progress of those still strong enough to flee the city or to emerge in sallies against the Romans (Josephus, *War* 6.1.1-8).

This polarization between the two peoples therefore served the collective desires of each side to achieve real and symbolic victories over death at the expense of the other. Such a polarity intensifies the perceptions of the enemy as extraordinarily potent both in sex and in combat; otherwise such a victory would not enhance the potency of the victor in life and over death. [4] Each seeks a glory associated with their own god and fights with a passion that alternates between frenzy and despair. Each engages in a slaughter that, in its symbolic aspects and atrocities, at times resembles sacrifice-without-ceremonial

---

[3] R. J. Lifton, *The Broken Connection: On Death and the Continuity of Life* (New York, 1979) p. 304.
[4] *Ibid.*, p. 307.

rather than combat. Each relies on the leadership of big men with their own powerful gifts of physical appearance or military prowess. Both fight with a hatred that is the inverse of envy.

A more complex society may find other ways to encapsulate a population that, once part of the larger society, is earmarked for death. One technique is simply ecological: to confine the population to certain residential areas. Water and food can easily be shut off from a ghetto, and escape from a ghetto can be made virtually impossible. A concentration camp simply reinforces the ecological restrictions on the movement of people and supplies. Exile within the perimeters of the nation-state (e.g., native American "reservations"; South African bantustans) is a third possibility, especially when it is reinforced by prohibitions (or impediments) against emigration. A fourth possibility extends to the nation-state itself: a nation, once excommunicated from symbolic or other exchanges from the nations surrounding it, can be encircled and crushed. In this latter respect alone, encirclement of Jerusalem seems distinctly modern. In the concluding section of this paper, I therefore stress the importance of dual citizenships, unrestricted rights to immigration and emigration, and international guarantees of free passage.

Nonetheless there is a crucial difference between the concentration camp and the seige of Jerusalem. In the Palestinian case, the community slated for destruction is placed outside the Roman system of administration. The offices of the state are no longer present within the enclosed city of Jerusalem. The garrison, the courts, the governor all have gone. In the case of the concentration camp, however, the state is present on the scene along with the encapsulated population. Placed outside the system by legal and administrative action, the Jews are still working within the framework of the state itself. The energies of the inmates strong enough to work at hard labor go into building ovens and mining coal for the production of the lethal gas that will kill them. The modern state constructs a situation in which individuals must still contribute to the very state that intends to kill them through their own contributions. In the Palestinian case, the Romans no longer received tribute money, prayer, or forced labor from the population encapsulated in Jerusalem, whereas the Nazis continued their administration of the state apparatus within the concentration camps themselves.

As the preceding passages, quoted from Josephus, make clear, however, there was nothing secular about Titus' claims to glory. The stakes were not merely military victory; the battlefield was essentially the scene in which claims not only to life but to immortality were being tested. In the conclusion, I therefore stress the importance of ridding Christian theology of delusions about the Christians' unique transcendence of death.

Step 3: Demanding a Final Test

The speeches of Titus are fine examples of the charismatic foundations even of patriarchal authority. Titus does not hesitate to refer to his father Vespasian; he is quick to involve all subordinate soldiers and their officers in a chain of loyalty and command that emanates from the father and the son. From the father and the son, indeed, proceeds a spirit that fills the soldiery with enthusiasm, as though possessed by a god. The supernatural aspects of charisma indeed come into play in the notion of glory. More than mere fame or reputation, it is the claim to an extraordinary source of vitality that is displayed in victories over death. Life, indeed, and immortality are the signs and consequences of such charismatic endorsements.

In speaking of charisma as the source of *pathological* developments in the process of secularization, I may seem somewhat unfair. Since Weber,[5] charisma has been a somewhat privileged term—privileged in lying beyond the criticism of religion, in a neutral zone where reductionism and debunking cannot deprive it of the semblance of reality. Let me be quite candid, then, in saying that charisma is simply an attribute, a characteristic attributed to the self by others who *wish* to believe that the individual in question is supernaturally endowed. The same person may, of course, attribute such endowments to himself or herself. Delusions can be shared, but they are still delusions.

Social change over several centuries does not itself change

---

[5]See the following hardy edition of Weber's work: H. H. Gerth and C. W. Mills, trans. and eds., *From Max Weber: Essays in Sociology* (New York, 1946).

the human potential for indulging in such delusions of grandeur. The grandiosity of the Nazis is simply an obvious and extended form of deluded claims to extraordinary endowments. The notion of a superior race or of a millennial Reich is the outward and visible sign of an inward and spiritual pathology that actually believes in an entire society's unique and supernatural powers. I will return to these claims of superiority in a moment, in discussing the tendency of charisma, when acted out, to destroy boundaries. Here it is important simply to make the point that has been underscored by several students of irrationality in modern societies, namely, that magical thinking seems to go "underground" as a latent aspect of apparently rational social organization. It is all the more pervasive and potentially destructive precisely because it *is* latent in modern societies.

Delusions of charismatic endowment are not entirely convincing, no matter how widely shared they are or how deeply held. That is why Weber finds charisma constantly subject to testing. The tests may be on the battlefield or in trials that are more highly ritualized. The tests may be sporadic or continuous, occasional or routine. The rationale for the test of charisma may be customary or rational, and the test may require the holder to be more or less customary or effective. Weber's point is that authority based on charisma is exceedingly unstable, whereas charisma, once it is institutionalized in routines or more rational procedures, becomes somewhat more stable. *My point is that charisma, precisely because it is delusional, will always be subject to the demand for proof in one form or another: miracles, victories, wealth, oracular utterance, extraordinary self-discipline, contact with the sources of original inspiration, and vindication in the court of history.* There is literally no end to the testing of charisma. That may be why demands increase, in bad times, for a final test of supernatural endowments. That is why, in the conclusion, I stress the claims to supernatural endowments or charismatic victories.

The demand for a final test of charisma is another sign of its pathological basis: that is, the belief that there is no limit to its powers. Magical thinking characteristically ignores limitations; in principle, there is no limit to magical powers. The individual or society that conceives of itself as charismatically endowed will typically acknowledge no limit to its sovereignty. That is what it means to be the recipient of charisma: heaven meets earth, and the limits of this world's horizon are obscured by the presence of the eternal. Nazis believed that the Reich would indeed inaugurate a millennium; the boundary separating the present from the future would be dissolved.

Indeed, the Nazis also believed that the boundary separating society from nature would also be overcome as a new race, genetically superior, would constitute itself as a purified society. The genius of the past would also be enjoyed in the present, as the spirit of prior generations would add to the charismatic endowment of the new society. These grandiose delusions are signs of the perennial—and pathological—predisposition to magical thinking that, under certain conditions even in modern societies, emerges from latency to the surface of social institutions. Josephus was right: the enthusiasms of generals and Zealots for a final test were both "madness"; they were the logical conclusion of belief in charisma. In the conclusion, therefore, I will argue for a development of Jewish-Christian theology that guarantees protection against reactionary or millennialist desires for a consummation or final test of a nation's charismatic powers.

In the end, charismatic claims are contemptuous of all social boundaries. The lines separating status groups and classes are broken down. The line separating the sacred from the profane is transgressed with apparent impunity. In the next section of this paper I will argue that the contemptuous treatment of all boundaries by those who see themselves as charismatically endowed is, in the end, a violent reaction against those who themselves have claimed to have extraordinary spiritual endowments. Especially when those who make such claims are among the privileged classes, the revenge of the newly endowed, the new claimants to supernatural authority, becomes especially vicious.

Step 4: Destroying the Boundaries

In the end, the last days of Jerusalem witnessed an assault on the boundary between the sacred and the profane. Take the more gruesome facts as a starting point, for instance. The auxiliaries (and perhaps some of the Roman soldiers) were disemboweling the Jews who were seeking refuge at the

Roman lines; it was a primitive custom of seeking in the bodies of the enemy the sources of life. Similar stories came out of the forced march of citizens from Pnompenh into the Cambodian countryside—stories of evisceration, cannibalism, and the seizure of money, glasses, and indeed any tokens of life in a desperate grab at the vitality of the victims, at symbolic immortality. Within the city of Jerusalem, however, the Zealots were seizing food and property from those among their fellow citizens who still had enough resources to have survived the famine. The Zealots speared them to death while sparing those who begged for an end to their suffering. Josephus's description leaves no doubt that there was something more in these brutal proceedings than a last-ditch effort by the rebels to survive a famine in a city under seige. Here was a final turning of the tables, a pernicious reversal, that destroys the last vestiges of the sacred:

> Deep silence blanketed the city, and night laden with death was in the grip of a yet fiercer foe—the brigands. (516) They broke as tomb-plunderers into the houses, rifled the deceased and stripped the coverings from their bodies, then departed laughing; they tried the points of their swords on the corpses, even transfixed some of the wretches who lay prostate but still living, to test the steel, and any who implored them to employ their hand and sword-thrust to end their misery, they disdainfully left to perish of hunger. (517) And each victim breathed his last with his eyes transfixed on the Temple, turning his gaze from the rebels he was leaving alive. (*War* 5.12.515-17)

It was such a scene that led Josephus, at a later point, to lament "a generation whose frenzy brought about the ruin of the whole nation" (*War* 5.13.566). It was indeed a disease, but it had progressed far beyond collective hysteria with suicidal propensities. Here collective madness prevails, and mass suicide is no longer merely a propensity. When the sacred is destroyed, the term "sacrifice" becomes meaningless. Pathological acts of secularization preempt the possibility of making anything sacred.

The Roman and Jewish camps were mirror images of each other. Whereas the Romans maintained their hierarchies of status or command and distributed authority and social honor in a direct line from top to bottom, in Jerusalem the notables were the first to die, and they died at the hands of those with the least status. The Roman order linked the most common foot soldier with Caesar in a continuous, however attenuated, association between those with the most glory or reputation and those with the least. The Zealots severed those ties between the notable and "no account." Now, as Lifton makes very clear, in every social order those closest to the bottom have the least claim on immortality.[6] Distinctions in status serve to reinforce the claims of higher castes or orders to greater shares of immortality; consider the caste system in India. In Jerusalem, however, the groups whom Josephus called "seditious" had systematically murdered and robbed the "eminent" citizens. It was a display of the same turning of the tables as their victimization of the starving. The implicit judgment is that no one shall live who has cast a shadow on the dignity of anyone else, because that shadow is the image or symbol of death.[7] The sacred postpones the final judgment and deprives death of its immediate sting. Once destroyed, the sacred cannot hold death at bay.

Both the Romans and the Zealots were using the sword and famine to slay Jews. Indeed, like the Romans, the Zealots were committing genocide, but the latter were slaying their own people. In analyzing Jewish anti-Semitism, Lifton speaks of an aversion to whatever has promised life and has subsequently failed. He points out, for instance, that money's tainted promise of immortality becomes revolting when riches fail to give eternal life; that is why money is associated with feces.[8] The Zealots' attack on their own people, therefore, becomes more understandable when viewed as an expression of a similar revulsion against those whose claims to superior value have failed to protect the community from fatality. The Zealots sought to eliminate, as though tainted by death, a god that had failed.

I interpret this penultimate destruction of the sacred, this secularization-by-the-sword, as a pathological attempt to preserve the self in the face of death. Lifton reviews, for instance, the account of a fifteen-year-old boy, a Viennese Jew, who was taking refuge during the war in a Holland occupied, domi-

---

[6]Lifton, *The Broken Connection*, pp. 301ff.
[7]*Ibid.*, pp. 309ff.
[8]*Ibid.*, p. 320.

nated, and terrorized by Nazis, where Jews were marked for death. The whole world seemed mobilized against Jews and, to live, one had to associate himself with a world hostile to everything Jewish. "The victim's temptation," concludes Lifton, "is that of cultivating hatred for his own group as a means of dissociating himself from its death taint and embracing not so much the victimizers as their 'life-power' and immortalizing claim."[9]

The Zealots may well have identified with the Roman aggressors. It is a sign of individual "emptiness," as Lifton points out, that individuals seek to incorporate external figures and so to transcend their own nothingness. When those external guarantees fail, it is no wonder that they seem not only empty but revolting. The empty self then turns to the last remaining symbols of power over death—the aggressors themselves.

Step 5: Destroying the Last Sanctuary of the Sacred

The first century in Palestine pitted two systems against each other. On the one hand, the ensigns of Rome promised immortality to the faithful and threatened the enemy with summary proceedings or bloody reprisals. The Temple and the Law promised a victory over death that could be achieved only through sacrifice—sacrifice at the Temple, the giving of tithes, the purification of one's daily life, and finally, if necessary, the immolation of the body by fire or the sword.

Of course, war is only the court of last resort when all other rites have failed; that is precisely my point, that by the time of the Jewish civil war, 66–70 C.E., the rites for celebration of symbolic victory over death had already failed. Rites provide symbolic tests of supernatural endowments; they provide demonstrations of the gift of divine grace, of life itself, and of immortality. Ritual therefore creates a sacred time and space in which the end, death itself, is experienced symbolically and then postponed—but not forever. When one can no longer celebrate the postponement of death, one may submit to the fact of death in hope of divine favor and rescue—a submission that Josephus has recorded in excruciating detail.

---

[9]*Ibid.*, p. 327.

In this light one can understand the pathological, destructive aspect of secularization. The fine line of sanity separates secularization from desecration. Note that the Zealots were defending the Temple. The Zealots began their desecration by entering the holy places reserved for the purified; in the sanctuary their blood flowed in unsanctified sacrifice on the floor. The Zealots completed their desecration of the Temple by melting down its treasures for weapons. Josephus notes that their self-justification was simple enough: that the defenders of the Temple have a right to use its treasures, and those who are defending the divinity are entitled to the use of divine things (*War* 5.6.564). Many of the gifts had been provided by Roman emperors as offerings of good will to the Temple. The pathology emerges in the Zealots' desire to control and possess what only the pure and the powerful formerly had a right to touch.

Radical acts of secularization turned pathological are magical, counterphobic defenses against the charismatic attraction and power of those who have monopolized the production of the sacred. The wish to transcend death leads at first to the desire for ritualized contact with purity and power, but the underlying drive is to manipulate, to take the sacred into one's own hands so as to possess and consume the sacred for oneself. The desecration of the Temple was therefore not merely a grab for power but an attempt to take into one's own hands the sources of life and immortality. At the same time, however, the Zealots held in contempt the very authority that had hitherto kept these symbols of the sacred at a safe distance from the relatively unclean and expendable, because that authority had failed to protect the community from death. In the end, the rebels poured contempt on all their pride in the Temple.

Conclusion

The unconscious rage against death underlies every holocaust. That rage may be turned outward toward those who seem to shatter our own dreams of immortality, or it may be turned—in identification with aggressors—against our own sanctuaries. The beast, in either case, is within. Not only the desire but the capacity to separate ourselves from those outside our own sanctuaries, rites, and social systems will persist so long as the latent rage against death is indirectly expressed in ceremonies or in regulations. Rituals provide symbolic victories over death and symbolic triumphs over others in the struggle for immortality. In the absence of a spiritual cure for our unconscious rage against death, rituals provide the functional alternative to political and military contests for the prize of immortality. They provide a symbolic arena in which contests are waged against death.

If we assume that unconscious rage against death will persist, that the demand for symbolic victories over death will continue, and that symbolic victims are preferable to the actual victims of state terror, it will be necessary to contain the capacity for violent expression to the arena of ritual. Until Christians and Jews are capable of joining together within a single liturgical context to express their anguish over death and their common hopes for triumph, they will remain tempted to declare each other beyond the pale and to project their internal rage, the beast, on the Gentile or Jewish other.

My second conclusion concerns the pathological elements of Christianity as symbolic defenses against desperation, grievous loss, and death itself. The Christian community developed in a catastrophic century. Famine and drought threatened the life support of Palestinian communities; Roman garrisons, bandits, and guerrillas inflicted random terror on the population; political and military occupation by the Roman forces created despair over the very survival of the Palestinian community. It would not be surprising under these circumstances for an entire nation to engage not only in wishful or imaginative but in regressive and magical thinking. It would not be surprising to find a wide range of pathological belief systems or rituals in any society exposed to the acute and pervasive suffering to which Israel was subjected in that period. Here I am primarily concerned with whatever residues of delusional thinking and practice may have been carried over into the early Christian community.

Here I can only call attention to some of the pathology already described in this brief essay. The desire to force the hand of God in a decisive test of a nation's supernatural endowment or divine favor may have survived in Jewish-Christian versions of apocalyptic literature. The belief that one is aided in such a battle by supernatural power may have survived in Christian triumphalism. The notion that believers have access to supernatural powers in their fights against disease and death as well as against the enemies of the faith may also reflect similar residues of magical thinking in early Christian popular piety. In the claims of Zealots and of Roman generals we encountered the notion that others of differing faith are more vulnerable to mortality than one's fellows and followers who are supernaturally endowed with power over death. The same delusion and grandiosity can be found in a variety of Christian claims of the period as well as in contemporary Christian orthodoxy. The docetic and anti-Semitic elements in these claims of victory over death are the by-product, I am arguing, of the underlying delusion of magical power over death itself.

My second conclusion, then, is that the primary task of theology should be to divest Christian faith and practice of these residues of magical thinking. There is nothing new in this recommendation, of course, except to link demythologizing with the survival of nations. Sociologists have been investigating the relation of Christian myths to anti-Semitism for some time and with somewhat inconclusive results. It is not certain whether Christian orthodoxy causes, reinforces, legitimates, or transmits anti-Semitism. Certainly there are other—ethnocentric and non-Christian—sources of anti-Semitism. The problems are partly theoretical, partly methodological, and they remain intractable. On the strength of relatively well-established findings, however, I am confident of one conclusion: that tendencies to magical thinking find legitimate expression in Christian orthodoxy, and that the same orthodoxy may also focus these tendencies on imaginary spiritual or political triumphs over differing religious, ethnic, and national groups. To the perennial human tendency towards grandiose and delusional thinking in the face of death, Christian belief may add intensity, the veneer of legitimacy, and an acceptable outlet focused on Jews. The TV evangelists who clamor for an Armageddon in Israel simply provide the most disgraceful and potentially destructive case in point. Their legitimacy derives from the cultural pattern that I have been attempting to describe in this essay. It is up to theologians to finally repudiate any traces of triumphalism from Christian expectation and to state clearly that the Christian faith provides no privileged access to supernatural powers or victories over death for the faithful few.

My third conclusion concerns the tie between nature and society; clearly that tie must be cut if racism and ethnocentrism are not to have at their disposal either the engines of a Roman seige or the advanced machinery of the modern military. To some extent the tie between society and the state is genetic. To some extent, of course, that tie is psychological and cultural—the belief in a connection between social life, race, blood, and soil. Fascism—whether Christian, Jewish, Islamic, or Zionist—will disappear when the cultural, psychological, and legal connections between nature and society are broken once and for all.

Both the holocaust of the first century and that of our own time encapsulated individuals within a territory; without passports they could not get out. There is ample documentation on the fate of Jewish refugees who were declined entry into the United States and other countries for lack of such a passport and were returned to the Nazi ovens. There is documentation also of the rescue of Jews by one bearing Swedish passports in their name. The simple and obvious lesson is that dual citizenship is a viable—if not the only—way out. Under the laws of the United States, however, only those who have genetic ties to two countries—those whose parents are of different nationalities—can hold dual citizenship. I recommend that this right be extended to all citizens of this country and of any other whose legislature can be so persuaded. I would urge the relevant Christian and Jewish organizations to promote the legislation necessary to secure this right in our time.

When society and nature are intertwined, individuals personify the society in totemic symbols from nature. Consider both Jewish Christians and Jews who personified the state of their time as the beast, only to find the beast within themselves in the form of a towering rage at their enemies. The enemy, of course, not only is death; the person's rage against the dying of the light is itself "the beast." It is the desire to make one's life count for more than another's in the eternal scheme of things that makes the beast devour those others whose dreams of glory threaten one's own. Call the beast narcissism and the hunger for power or by other more theologically pertinent terms. We are now hostages of our own states, encircled not by Roman walls but by barriers to our free passage, barriers of our own making. As I have just argued, we need passports not only for refugees but for ourselves. To immigrate and emigrate at will has become absolutely necessary for survival. Appropriate legislation to guarantee these rights should be very high indeed on the political agenda of every religious community.

In the long run, however, there is no escape from "the beast" short of a renunciation of the state itself, a renunciation of the political means to psychological satisfaction. My fourth conclusion is that the naton-state must die. The state will not even wither away, however, until the people withhold from the state every psychological investment, every anxious desire for control or domination, and every narcissistic, vainglorious wish for symbolic victories over death. Cultural and psychological disinvestment of the state is the urgent task of both Jews and Christians.

In the past the tie between the citizen and the state has been challenged by insisting that Jews and Christians have a higher citizenship, a loyalty to a heavenly ruler, and a source of transcendental power that eclipses every imperial claim to glory. The cure for the disease of imperial power has thus been a heavy potion of magical thinking on the part of the faithful who are still hungry for power and for the victories over death. To decapitate sacred statues, to destroy sanctuaries, or to behead kings in a reign of terror by the faithful is the "madness" deplored by Josephus. The term is appropriate, whether the zealotry is Galilean, Cromwellian, or contemporary Christian apocalyptic enthusiasm for a final test of spiritual and military power with the enemies of God. To demythologize both the Jewish and Christian faiths has become a necessity for survival and may at least deprive this "madness" of the supports of religion.

My last point concerns the link between society and time. I agree with the sociological viewpoint that argues that modern societies are perennially running out of time. They are under pressure to make decisions, pressures intensified by mass communications as well as the inevitable course of events. To buy time has become a crucial element in the survival of entire societies, lest they make precipitate decisions and galvanize an entire nation in the response of total mobilization. An extended present of indefinite duration, on the other hand, allows debts to be recycled, faith in leaders to be renewed, and claims for justice to be made without holding the entire society hostage to particular demands. When religious leaders, of whatever tradition, constantly remind the present of past grievances, the present is always burdened by the pressure for payment and satisfaction. When religious leaders, of whatever persuasion, insist that promises for a new order or for simple reform have become due and payable, the future must begin in the present, and there is no further room for experimentation, for what we call—quite rightly—"temporizing." Zealots have always been impatient with temporizing; Josephus nonetheless tried to buy time with them. The Jewish-Christian faith has enormous resources for building reservoirs of time: Sabbaths, Jubilee years, the time between the times, and a prayerful insistence that we not be brought to the time of trial. From these reservoirs have come the ability to suspend judgment, forgive debt, postpone claims for damages, trust promises, and to be agnostic about the particular days and the season of revelation. Those reservoirs are now dangerously low, in part because the times of Jews and Christians are out of joint. A sacred chamber on which we could all agree might not prevent the worst disasters of a nuclear age, but it is an essential place to begin.

DISCUSSION

ECKARDT: In your paper you refer to the Holocaust as a pathological act of secularization. Does the identity of the Holocaust lie in pathology, in the secularization, or in both?

FENN: Not in the pathology. Even if it's going to be benign, a lot of societies still have to deal with the magical thinking, triumphalism, death anxiety, narcissism—all these code words for what ails us.

ECKARDT: But it does happen?

FENN: The pathological can be an undercurrent in simply the routine of orderly administration of welfare aid or Medicare or anything else. But I think you can secularize it in a way that doesn't put people beyond the welfare payroll or beyond any political payroll. It can be a way of saying goodbye to a past without wrenching loose, a sort of slow erosion of the past where you never really break loose. We drift; we're always paying off increasing amounts of national debt and remembering slavery. It can be benign but it's got to be done carefully because the genie may get out of the bottle.

BEKER: I am so influenced by the dullness or routinization of life that I think we need a little bit *more* madness. I don't see why you find charisma to be madness, but I think that without a certain charismatic leadership, we won't get anywhere. Now you want to contain it by ritual, and that's a wonderful Catholic, Anglo-Catholic option. But it seems to me dubious.

FENN: I like it better than red flags and torches burning in the streets.

BEKER: There are other forms of charisma, I hope, that you also wrote about.

FENN: When charisma gets really trivialized then I begin to like it. And in a really secular society you can take the sting out of charisma and it becomes a matter of personal style. But you still have to keep a close eye on it because for some people it may be a matter of substance, that is, they may attribute it to Carter or Reagan—as if to say, This man really is as good as his word and he can protect us against the enemy and give us symbolic triumphs. But I'm not sure it's ever just a matter of style.

BEKER: It seems to me in the history of doctrine we have a very important analogue to your description. You talk about the struggle throughout church history and especially coming to the fore in the Reformation with people who live the whole relation between work and spirit. Now it seems to me that spiritual illumination which is not "checked by the Word," as the Reformation people put it, would put you in imminent danger.

FENN: I'm a little afraid that when you kick charisma out the front door, or when you kick magical thinking out the liturgical front door, it comes in again from the back door, especially in confessional tradition.

BEKER: I haven't seen much of it in our churches.

FENN: You think you can order the right words in the right sequence and have some sort of effect.

BEKER: I would like some more.

ZINN: I think if you look at the traditional liberal Protestant establishment, there is no charisma anywhere, or it's almost invisible. Where do you find charisma? It seems to me that it appears on the television between seven and twelve on Sunday morning and after 11 o'clock at night. These people show charisma and you can't trivialize it. The question is, Why do they appeal to some people? These evangelists are seen by their followers as mediators.

FENN: If it's on television and on the airwaves, then you can schedule it, right? But I'm a little afraid that we're looking at that as though that were the time when the genie gets out of the bottle. If it were liturgically framed, that would be the time you let the genie out of the bottle. But if it's over the airwaves from seven to twelve you just can't shut it off.

BEKER: Look at the larger light in terms of the history of religion. African society would not be able to function without the shaman. Neither would Asian society. It seems to me that the shaman is a typical charismatic leader. That seems to function pretty well.

FENN: That's the point. The priest-king or the priest who becomes the chief is just "hell on wheels." If you look at studies of ritual process, people—just as in our agonizingly long political campaigns—would hurl insults at the candidate chieftain, and there is no doubt in anybody's mind that when this person becomes chief, he or she will know that they're really human, who they belong to, and that they're no better than anybody else. And when they're really convinced of that, you throw excrement and verbal abuse on them, you untie them from the stake, and then you can put glorious robes on them and they won't forget who they are. But when those rituals fail and they get proceeded by a glorious procession of motorcycles, their arms outstretched like they're airborne, we're all in trouble because the liturgies fail and the genie is really out of the bottle riding motorcycles. And the only way you can get rid of a guy like that is through assassination. So yes, I share your fascination with shamans and charismatic figures and so forth. But in my fascination I worry whether we can contain it within the liturgy of tribes. I worry that if all those liturgies fail, and they get control of the military and start riding motorcycles, you're going to kill them.

I think that once you break the liturgical tie, that's the first step. Then you build a wall where you put them together. There was a study back in the sixties that proposed that canons be brought out to the lower end of Central Park so as to encapsulate Harlem—shut off the water supply and the electricity and bring out the artillery. That's what really worries me about our society. It has developed a capacity to encapsulate parts of itself and cut the symbolic and other exchanges and then destroy them while thinking that the system itself can continue intact. That was not in response to an external threat. Part of the system can be alienated from the rest of the system and stay within control of the system. Some of the feminist literature from Russia talks about the experience of supporting a system that crushes. And that's what I'm trying to get at here—when you are aliens in a system and you can't get out and you get crushed by it, yet you're required to work for it.

You go to work in the mines and you produce the coal that they use to gas you. Are you still part of the system? If there's a peculiar analogue in modern society for what I thought I was reading in Josephus, it's the capacity of a system to encapsulate part of itself and then destroy it in the process—still working for the system to serve the purposes of its own destruction.

CHAPTER NINE

The Christian Blasphemy: A Non-Jewish Jesus

Robert T. Osborn

Introduction

From its very beginning, Christianity has suffered from a persistent, chronic strain of hostility to Jews and Judaism.[1] One can find it, for instance, in the designation of God's covenant with Israel as the "Old" covenant and in the way the New Testament frequently makes "Jews" as such, and not merely elements of Jewish leadership, responsible both for Jesus' death and for the persecution of early Christian witnesses. The sad history of Christian anti-Semitism is well documented by Rosemary Ruether, who draws an unbroken line from the New Testament to the Holocaust. "The Nazis," she observes, "of course, were not Christians. They were indeed anti-Christian. . . . Nevertheless, the church must bear a substantial responsibility for a tragic history of the Jew in Christendom which was the foundation upon which political anti-Semitism and the Nazi use of it was erected."[2] Eberhard Bethge states that anti-Semitists like Hitler had "only secularized and thus provided a racial basis for what heretofore had been established upon a foundation prepared by religion and theology."[3] In view of this story the question persists, "Is the New Testament itself already anti-Semitic?"[4] Is the Holocaust an inevitable outcome—even if a *reductio ad absurdum*—of essential Christian faith? Rosemary Ruether comes close to this conclusion when she states that anti-Semitism is the left hand of christology, the negative side of the claim that Jesus was the Christ.[5] It must also seem so to

Jews. Bethge cites Golda Meier's autobiography, where she recalls that, even as a five year old, she was identified as a "Christ-murderer."[6] Must Christians, in order to be Christians, so understand Jews? To be pro-Christ, must one be anti-Jew? The *prima facie* evidence would suggest so, since a Christian hatred—or at least disrespect—for Jews and Judaism seems to be as old as Christian love of Jesus.

The Sin of Anti-Semitism

If it is true that Christianity is essentially anti-Jewish, then there is nothing more to discuss—at least theologically. Any criticism or judgment of such an intrinsic anti-Semitism from the perspectives of faith and theology would necessarily entail a compromise or rejection of both faith and theology. The only choice then open to Christians would be either to be anti-Semitic in the name of Jesus and in obedience to the word of God, or to cease to be Christian in disobedience to the word of God and Jesus the Christ. The theological overcoming of anti-Semitism is *a priori* impossible on the premise that Christianity as such is anti-Jewish.[7]

Alternatively, it is no solution to propose a non-Jewish Christianity that would acknowledge the Jews as Jews—in their self-understanding as God's chosen, covenantal people—and yet would understand itself apart from and independent of the Jews in a circumstance of mutual independence and indifference. Such a solution is impossible because an essential dimen-

---

[1]The immediate context of this paper is my exposure to the remarkable conversations which have taken place among some German Christians and between these Christians and Jews on the meaning of Judaism for Christianity and Christianity for Judaism. What differentiates these conversations from most of their American counterparts is that they have been carried on to a large extent within official ecclesiastical circles (the Rhineland Synod of the German Evangelical Church in particular) and are conversations with and within the church, and not just among individual Christians or academics. This German experience and my feeling that it is important for American reflection explain the preponderance of references to German discussions, as opposed to American.

[2]R. R. Ruether, *Faith and Fratricide* (New York, 1974) p. 184.

[3]E. Bethge, *Am Gegebenen Ort* (Munich, 1979) p. 196.

[4]C. Thoma, *Christliche Theologie des Judentums* (Aschaffenburg, 1978) p. 10.

[5]Ruether, *Faith and Fratricide*, pp. 64-65.

[6]Bethge, *Am Gegebenen Ort*, pp. 194-95.

[7]I am using the terms "anti-Semitism" and "anti-Judaism" interchangeably, recognizing that the religious and racial aspects of Christian hostility to Jews are inseparable.

sion of Jewish self-understanding is that as God's chosen people they are exclusive instruments of God's universal salvation.[8] A Christianity that acknowledges the Jews as Jews would
have to acknowledge not only this claim of Jewish faith, but
also Christianity's dependence upon Jews and Judaism for its
own self-understanding and for its share in God's salvation
history. Only if Judaism were redefined as a parochial religion,
valid for the Jews alone, could Christianity acknowledge the
tuth of this Judaic claim without a correlative dependence upon
it. But so to redefine Judaism is to reject it at its very heart.
This is precisely the route proposed by Rosemary Ruether in
her effort to avoid an anti-Jewish Christianity. Christians, she
suggests, can recognize themselves as "in the same historical
situation as the Jews, indeed as peoples of every culture,
making his way through the desert. . . ."[9] Similarly, she con-
tends that "the story of Jesus parallels, it does not negate the
Exodus. . . . When Easter is seen not as superceding or fulfilling
the Exodus . . . but as reduplicating it, then the Christian can
affirm his faith through Jesus in a way that no longer threatens
to rob the Jew of his past. . . ."[10] But Christians hardly need
to "rob" Jews of their past when that past has been robbed of
universal significance, when the Exodus is regarded as only a
symbol of a transcendental ideal that Christianity can realize in
its own way quite apart from Israel. According to Ruether,
both Christianity and Judaism should forgo pretensions to
exclusivity, because "a universal language which can unify all
mankind . . . cannot be the already established possession of
any one of these traditions. . . . The future point of unity exists
now only in the transcendent universality of God and in his
universal work as Creator, which gives us the basis for affirm-
ing universal human kinship."[11] Thus Ruether denies the very
essence of Judaism—its covenant relationship to God, upon
which the salvation and unity of all humankind ultimately
depend. Similarly, she denies the essence of Christianity—its
*christ*ological focus: on the Christ or Messiah of the Jews. A

---

[8]See Gen 12:3 and Isa 49:22-26, for example. See also S. Schechter, *Aspects of Rabbinic Theology* (New York, 1961) pp. 114-15.

[9]"An Invitation of Jewish Dialogue: In What Sense Can We Say that Jesus was 'The Christ'?" in *The Ecumenist* 10 (January–February, 1972) 23.

[10]Ruether, *Faith and Fratricide*, p. 239.

[11]*Ibid.*

non-Jewish Christianity is anti-Jewish and, for that very reason, also anti-Christian.[12]

Christianity can overcome its own anti-Jewishness only by recognizing that when true to itself it is in fact pro-Jewish. However, if this be the case, how is it that Christians have been anti-Jewish and anti-Semitic, apparently from the beginning? If, contrary to Rosemary Ruether, anti-Semitism is not the other side of christology, then why is anti-Semitism so chronic a dimension of Christianity? To answer this question I argue that Christian anti-Judaism has its roots not in Christian faith but in Christian faith*lessness*. Anti-Jewishness is the Christian sin, the sin of which Christians alone are so singularly capable.[13] The truth in Ruether's contention is that christological faith makes such sin possible, for through Christ Christians are the only Gentiles to have come to know the truth about the Jews and so to find themselves in a position sinfully to deny it. The truth revealed to Christians in Jesus is that the God of the Jews, the Lord God of Abraham, Isaac, and Jacob, as witnessed to in the Old Testament and as incarnate in the Jew Jesus, is the one, true God, and that this God comes to the world and reveals himself to all peoples only in and through this one people, the children of Israel (in our times, the Jews), and through one of them in particular, the Jew of Nazareth

---

[12]Ruether claims that Judaism avoids a "parochialism" in its view of election that would lead to a confusion of its own particular identity with that of the Ultimate, by distinguishing between the covenant with Israel and the covenant with Noah. (See *Faith and Fratricide*, pp. 235–37). This conclusion from the Noachide covenant will not wash. The Noachide covenant is the divine promise that the God of Israel will not destroy the world, but will sustain it and preserve it for its salvation through the covenant with Israel. Among the "fixed elements" that are to be found "in the Rabbinic literature of almost every age and date" is "the belief that the establishment of this new kingdom [the Messianic kingdom whose establishment follows the destruction of the enemies of God] will be followed by the spiritual hegemony of Israel, when all the nations will accept the belief in the unity of God, acknowledge his kingdom and seek instruction from his law" (Schechter, *Aspects*, p. 102). Thus Schechter can also properly suggest that rabbinic teaching (referring particularly to commentary on Isa 44:5) "becomes a sort of spiritual imperialism with the necessary accompaniment of the doctrine of the 'Open Door' through which the whole of humanity might pass into the kingdom" (*Aspects*, p. 106).

[13]"Real anti-Judaism with all its excesses existed only in Christian countries." H. Gollwitzer, "Die Judenfrage—eine christliche Frage," in W. D. Marsch and K. Thieme, eds., *Christen und Juden* (Mainz, 1961) p. 287.

[14]As Gollwitzer notes, "whoever speaks of Christianity must unavoidably speak of Judaism." *Befreiung zur Solidarität: Einführung in die Evangelische Theologie* (Munich, 1978) p. 121. So having to speak of the Jews, Christians can speak either faithfully and truly or faithlessly and falsely.

called "Jesus." Precisely this knowledge distinguishes Christian faith[14] and also makes possible the distinctive Christian sin of falsifying the truth of Christ (which is also the truth of the Jews).[15]

The form of sin we are talking about here, recognized by Karl Barth as "the specifically Christian form," is the sin of "lying," the evasion tactic employed by the sinner in the encounter with Christ.[16] If pride and sloth are the *works* of sin, falsehood is the *word* of the man of sin. In other words, lying is sin in its theological form (a sin at which professional theologians are therefore most adept).[17] "In the mouth of human teachers, in the ears of human listeners it [the truth] is always threatened by some measure of misunderstanding, deception, falsification and corruption." Indeed, Barth adds, "falsehood loves to take the garb of doctrine, ideal, principle and system."[18] The primary focus of this paper is on this theological form of anti-Semitism.

Lying, then, is the prerogative only of those who have encountered the truth and are thus in a position to falsify and distort it—i.e., lie about it. Their lying presupposes and feeds on the truth; "the devil has nothing of his own to oppose to God, but only his falsifying intimations. . . ."[19] The liar will not negate the truth; "on the contrary, he will affirm it emphatically." As only Barth might have observed, the liar "kisses the Master as Judas did."[20] Since this lie so feeds on the Christian knowledge of the truth of Christ, it is, as we have seen, "the specifically Christian form of sin."

What makes the truth of Christ so offensive, notes Barth, is simply that it is the truth of *Jesus* Christ, a truth that cannot be separated from a person—a particular, historical person.

> There would be no offence in the truth as such, in the idea of the gracious intercourse of God with man and the grateful intercourse of man with God. . . . Nor could there be any objection

---

[15]Christian falsehood, says Barth, is "the disguise or mask which the man of sin at once assumes when he is confronted by the true witness," namely, Jesus Christ. *Kirchliche Dogmatik* (Zollikon-Zürich, 1959) IV, 3, p. 434.

[16]*Ibid.*, p. 371.

[17]*Ibid.*, p. 373.

[18]*Ibid.*, p. 376.

[19]*Ibid.*, p. 373.

[20]*Ibid.*, p. 436.

to the existence of an extraordinary, authentic Proclaimer of this truth. . . . The painful and scandalizing thing which man wishes to avoid is the identity between this man and this truth, between this truth and this man. . . . Since this man is identical with the truth and the truth with Him, the encounter with the truth and therefore with Him . . . becomes an absolutely vital, binding, decisive and even revolutionary affair. That is why the man of sin would like to escape it.[21]

He can take the man or the truth, but not both. "He seeks to silence, suppress and eliminate their identity. This is the work of falsehood." The problem with the man Jesus, says Barth, is "Gethsemane and Golgatha, and therefore the truth as the truth of His death and passion."[22]

At this point that we must go somewhat beyond or behind Barth to recognize that *this man Jesus* and his cross are so offensive essentially because he was and remains *a Jew*—the quintessential Jew, the very Messiah of the Jews. It is as a Jew that Jesus is so wholly other. If the truth that we meet in Jesus is inseparable from his Jewish personhood, then we meet in him also the unacceptable and radical judgment that the truth is not in us, who are the children only of Adam. Were he one of us non-Jews, we could imagine the truth in him as a potential of us all, and thus not so wholly other or revolutionary. But the truth that he as a Jew brings and that the Christian encounters in him is itself a "Jewish" truth: the truth of the God of Abraham, Isaac, and Jacob, the God who is attested to *by* the Jews and who attests *to* the Jews. To know the Jews as they really are is to know their God, and to know their God inevitably entails knowing them as God's chosen sons and daughters.

If this is the truth as encountered in Jesus Christ, then Christian sinners who seek to avoid it have at least three possibilities. First, following Arthur Drews (*Das Markusevangelium als Zeugnis gegen die Geschichtlichkeit Jesu* [Jena, 1921]), they can seek to perpetuate the crude and unpersuasive lie that Jesus never existed and that he is at best a mythological expression of a truth that can be possessed independently of this mythical man. The second kind of lie is more indirect and more effective.

---

[21] *Ibid.*, pp. 440-41.
[22] *Ibid.*, p. 441.

It does not deny Jesus' existence; it affirms him, often en-
thusiastically, as a teacher or prophet in whom we do encounter truth, but a truth that is essentially separable from
him. The third lie, perhaps the most pervasive, is the least
recognized because it is the most subtle and convincing. Here
Christians directly deny neither Jesus nor his essential relationship to the truth, but only that he is Jewish. However, since
as a matter of historical fact *Jesus was Jewish*, a person who
existed and was human only as a Jew, this denial is tantamount
to a rejection of Jesus altogether, of his very historical, human
existence. Furthermore, since his God is the God of the Jews,
the falsifying denial of his Jewishness is also a denial of the
truth about God that we encounter in him. So to rid Jesus and
Christianity of their Jewishness is the most powerful way of
lying, for thereby we Christian sinners can *allege to confess Jesus*,
God, and the unity between them. We can have every semblance of the truth and yet effectively deny and seek to avoid
its reality.

For Christians, then, anti-Semitism is the quintessential sin
of lying—it is nothing less than *blasphemy*. In the Holocaust,
"all confessions of the God of Abraham, Isaac and Jacob who
elected these people are made a mockery, because for Christians the planned and executed rooting out of the elected
people of God is perfect blasphemy. . . ."[23]

The Christological Forms of the Lie
of Anti-Semitism

While the proclivity to engage in the lie of anti-Semitism is
ubiquitous in Christian thought, perhaps the two most crucial
points of contact are the christological—regarding the person
and work of Christ—and the theological—concerning the nature and knowledge of God. Of these, primary is the christological, since it provides the basis for the theological. The first
deception at the christological level is the claim, despite the
New Testament witness, that in reality, in the mystery and
truth of his own person, Jesus was not Jewish,[24] he just *seemed*

---

[23]From the Synodalbeschluss der Rheinischen Landessynode in B. Klappert and H.
Starck, eds., *Umkehr und Erneuerung* (1980) p. 268.

[24]"The person of Jesus does not permit being isolated either from the Old Testament
or from the Judaism of his day." C. Thoma, *Christliche Theologie des Judentums*, p. 167.

to be. Since Jews cannot separate or distinguish their humanity as such from their Jewishness, the denial of Jesus' Jewishness is tantamount to a *docetic* denial of the reality of his very human existence—his concrete, historical, and only real humanity.[25] The second falsification maintains that it does not matter whether Jesus was Jewish or not, since the resurrected Christ and Lord of the Church certainly is not Jewish.

"Jesus is not Jewish"

Perhaps the most common and influential case of the first form of the christological falsehood is the negative application of the *criterion of dissimilarity* to identify the authentic sayings of Jesus. This principle, widely employed by biblical scholarship, holds that sayings attributed to Jesus that are not dissimilar to Judaism (and to Christianity) cannot be regarded as authentic. Following this principle, E. Käsemann concluded that "only in a few instances are we standing on more or less firm ground; that is, where the tradition, for whatever reason, can be neither inferred from Judaism nor attributed to earliest Christianity. . . ."[26] The principle has had fairly wide adoption, especially by scholarship in the tradition of Bultmann and, if we were to go back further, also in liberal theology, as reflected, for instance, in the writings of Schleiermacher and Harnack. Harnack assumed that historical, critical scholarship would reveal that the essence of Christianity has to do with "something which is common to us all." Accordingly, he was persuaded that "Jesus Christ's teaching will at once bring us by steps which, if few, will be great, to a height where its connection with Judaism is seen to be only a loose one, and most of the threads leading from it into 'contemporary history' become of no importance at all." Harnack entertained no doubt that "the founder [Jesus] had his eye upon man . . . upon man who fundamentally always remains the same."[27] The essential

---

[25] As L. Keck observes, "It was as a Jew that Jesus trusted God and not as a man in general believing in the divine in general." *A Future for the Historical Jesus* (Philadelphia, 1981) p. 219. Schechter makes the point more radically when he notes that "according to some Rabbis, Israel's election was, as it would seem, predestined before the creation of the world. . . . Israel was there before the world was created." *Aspects*, p. 59.

[26] E. Käsemann, *Exegetische Versuche und Besinnungen* (Göttingen, 1965) pp. 206–07.

[27] A. von Harnack, *What is Christianity?* (New York, 1957) pp. 9, 16–17.

Jesus, from this perspective, is every man, not the Messiah of the Jews; he only appears to be a Jew. For his part, Bultmann pointed to this negative application when he stated that "where opposition to the morality and piety of Judaism and the specifically eschatological tone, which constitutes what is characteristic of Jesus the preacher, are expressed, and where on the other hand there are no specifically Christian features, it is easiest to conclude that there is an authentic parable of Jesus."[28] The trouble with this negative criterion, which Schillebeeckx says "must not be employed,"[29] is that it assumes that the differences between Jesus and Judaism are alone determinative of his relationship to Judaism, so that the distinctive and essential Jesus is *a priori* not Jewish. As Bultmann understands it, the essential Jesus is in "opposition to the morality and piety of Judaism."

In American biblical scholarship, perhaps the most consistent application of the principle of dissimilarity is to be found in the writings of Norman Perrin.[30] Since it is the nearly unanimous consensus of biblical scholarship that the "Kingdom (or Rule) of God" is the theme of Jesus' ministry, scientific scholarship as pursued by Perrin must show that (and wherein) Jesus' employment of this kingdom language was in fact dissimilar to Jewish (and also Christian) practice. Perrin did this by demonstrating to his own satisfaction that Jesus, in non-Jewish fashion, employed the word "kingdom" as a *"tensive symbol."* As such it is not a "concept," a "well defined understanding of the nature and form of the activity of God,"[31] but a symbol "standing for some larger meaning or set of meanings" which it mediates for human experience.[32] As a tensive symbol it is one whose "meaning could never be exhausted or adequately expressed by any one referent,"[33] as for instance an event in Israel's history. Perrin contrasts a tensive symbol to a *"steno symbol,"* what is generally understood as a "sign," such as is

---

[28]R. Bultmann, *Die Geschichte der synoptischen Tradition* (Göttingen, 1931) p. 227.

[29]E. Schillebeeckx, *Jesus: An Experiment in Christology* (New York, 1979) p. 93.

[30]It is important to note here that I am not implying or stating that Perrin or any other scholar whose works are cited in illustration of Christian anti-Jewishness is in any way personally anti-Semitic, but only that the tradition of scholarship in which they find themselves has fundamental anti-Jewish dimensions.

[31]N. Perrin, *Jesus and the Language of the Kingdom* (Philadelphia, 1980) pp. 29–32.

[32]*Ibid.*, p. 39.

[33]*Ibid.*, p. 22.

predominant, according to Perrin, in traditional Jewish apocalyptic, and which unlike the tensive symbol, has a one-to-one
relationship to the specific reality (event) which it represents.
When one knows the event, then the steno symbol itself can
be abandoned and the story retold in terms of critical historiography.

Perrin recognized that the symbol "kingdom" as employed
by Jesus appears to refer to the history of Israel, but that for
Jesus this history is conceived in a most un-Jewish fashion as
"myth." The announcement of the coming of the kingdom
becomes then a "challenge to the hearer to take the ancient
myth with renewed seriousness, and to begin to anticipate the
manifestations of the reality of which it speaks in the concrete
actuality of their experience."[34] The petitions of the Lord's
prayer, all of which are contained in the one, "thy kingdom
come," are not invocations of a divine action, but mythical
evocations of a human experience. They "represent realistic
possibilities for the personal and communal experience of God
as king. . . . God is to be experienced as king in the provision
of daily bread, in the forgiveness of sins. . . ."[35] Jesus' procla-
mation of the kingdom thus bestows on his hearers "the responsibility to explore the manifold ways in which the experience of God can become a reality to man" and to understand
the Kingdom of God not as a "single identifiable event which
every man experiences at the same time," but as something
"which every man experiences in his own time."[36] Israel, with
its history of salvation (Heilsgeschichte), and its apocalyptic
hope, is abandoned, and the particular is replaced with a universalism so that every man and his "experience" becomes
normative.

This approach to the gospel tradition of Jesus not only alien-
ates Christianity from Judaism by separating God from the
history of Israel (as meaning is separate from the myth which
symbolizes it); it also separates Christian "truth" from the event
of Jesus. If Jesus did understand the kingdom as a tensive
symbol of an inexhaustible "existential reality" and not as a
steno symbol of a specific, concrete historical event, then the

---

[34]*Ibid.*, p. 43.
[35]*Ibid.*, p. 47.
[36]*Ibid.*, pp. 198-99.

New Testament community could not, in faithfulness to Jesus, have done what it in fact did, and interpret the "kingdom" as a steno symbol of the particular event of Jesus himself or perhaps of his promised second advent. The Fourth Gospel is clearly out of order with its *ego eimi* ("I am"), with its substitution of Jesus himself for the Kingdom of God as the focus of Jesus' own witness. That Christians should make anything of Jesus at all, that they should have written gospels, is a bit mystifying on these premises.

"Christ is not Jewish"

The second christological misrepresentation is that Jesus in his flesh may well have been Jewish, but that as the resurrected Christ he certainly is not. The argument here, drawn from the tradition of Christian theology, tends to appeal especially to an interpretation of *Romans* 9–11, in which Paul explores the significance of Jesus' life and death for the Jews and for the relationship between the Jews and the church. The gist of this line of reasoning in its varied expressions is that Jesus entered the camp of the Jews not in order to save them, as appearances might suggest, but in fact to wrest the covenant from them and give it to the church. This "Trojan horse" theory takes a variety of forms. Bertold Klappert in his analysis of these, each of which tends to eliminate the particularity of Israel, designates the first as *"the substitution model."*[37] His example is the Berlin court preacher, Adolf Stöcker (1834–1909), who made three basic points: (1) Before Christ, the history of Israel is the history of denial and disobedience against God's patient efforts to call this people to himself. (2) After the crucifixion of Jesus, the children of Israel are no longer to be regarded as the elect, for "with the rejection of Christ the Jewish people have forfeited their calling to the Church."[38] (3) The only hope for Jews is for the individuals among them who become baptized Christians. By giving himself to be rejected and crucified by the Jews, Jesus in fact became the occasion of their rejection of the covenant and their yielding it up to the church. They were deceived, it would appear, into thinking that by denying Jesus

---

[37] Klappert and Starck, *Umkehr und Erneuerung,* pp. 18-19.
[38] *Ibid.,* pp. 14-15.

they could and would maintain their calling and their identity as God's people, whereas in fact in that very denial they who sought thus to save themselves instead lost their souls as God's elect and chosen people.

Second is *"the integration model,"* based upon a reading of *Romans* 11:1–6, according to which the church has replaced Israel as God's people, so that Israel's future as God's people now depends on the integration of a remnant into the church, and the church becomes a church of both Jews and Gentiles. Paul catches this notion in his two-fold view that the church is based in Israel and Israel matures in the church, to which Klappert responds: "It never occurred to Althaus that *Romans* 11:25 in no way speaks of the coming entrance of the whole of Israel into the Church, but to the contrary, of the entrance of the eschatological, full number of heathen into the elect people of Israel."[39] Essentially a variation of the substitution model, this one also denies to Judaism any significance after the crucifixion.

A third model, which can be interpreted either as substitutionary or integrational, is *"the typological model,"* according to which "Israel, its history and institutions are . . . the type of the church and of the salvation ultimately represented by the church."[40] Klappert sees this model implicit in the text of Vatican II, *Nostra Aetate*, in which the exodus of Israel from Egypt is conceived as a mysterious anticipation of the salvation of the church. As in the preceding models, with the coming of the church as a benefit of the work of Christ, Israel loses any significance and importance of its own and instead finds its significance after the cross and only as it is integrated into the church.

The fourth, *"the illustration model,"* is the "negative form" of the other models sketched above, in which Israel is understood as "the negative foil for the church."[41] In explanation, Klappert recalls the reaction of Rabbi K. K. Geis to the view of Judaism in Harnack's *Das Wesen des Christentums*—"the one sad justification for the existence of Judaism is that it can serve as the dark background for setting forth the full light of Christian-

---

[39] *Ibid.*, p. 17.
[40] *Ibid.*, p. 18.
[41] *Ibid.*, p. 20.

ity."[42] As Helmut Gollwitzer has observed, from this perspective God seems to have reserved "judgment for Israel and grace for the church." A most influential spokesman for this view is Ernst Käsemann who, in his exegesis of *Romans*, states that "Paul must shatter Israel's claim based on its own history just as he must that of the individual person who makes a claim based on his piety. That Paul does so expressly, proves that Israel has exemplary meaning for him, namely, that in and with Israel the Jew which is hidden in all of us is confronted— the man, that is, who makes claims and demands against God and to that extent serves an illusion instead of the true God."[43] Klappert notes in response that "here Käsemann stands in the tradition of his teacher R. Bultmann, for whom the particular history of Israel becomes the illustration and example of the fall of human existence-as-such under the power of the law."[44]

The final model identified by Klappert is the *"subsumption model."* He finds it somewhat surprising that according to this model it is the negative "privilege" of Jews to "illustrate the existence of the person under the law, the self-righteousness of that person, and his or her consequent fall, but not also the corresponding positive privilege of Israel and the Jews to be the primary example of the person under the gospel, the recipient of the divine justification and the covenant. Rather, we find that it is godless humankind as such that is first elected and justified only insofar as it is subsumed within the general category of humankind."[45] Rejecting Bultmann's teaching that election pertains not to Israel but to the existing individual, Käsemann claims that "justification alludes . . . primarily to God's lordship over the world and only therefore over the individual."[46] Paul "breaks the covenant with Israel . . . insofar as he challenges its exclusive connection with Israel and comprehends it anew by deriving its validity from the creation."[47] After Christ, God's covenant is with creation rather than with Israel; the "theology of the cross and the eschatology of creation shatter the election and the covenant of Israel," says

---

[42] *Ibid.*
[43] *Ibid.*, p. 41.
[44] *Ibid.*, p. 23.
[45] *Ibid.*, p. 22.
[46] *Ibid.*, p. 252.
[47] *Ibid.*

Käsemann. "The God who is bound by his covenant partner cannot be the God of the cross and of the Godless."[48] Accordingly, Israel can be saved only as are the Gentiles, only as they deny their Jewishness and are subsumed under the universal justification that is in Christ and available in the Church.

Before we turn to the next section we must be reminded of an earlier statement that the theological sin of lying occurs primarily at the methodological or hermeneutical level, where choice and decision are still operative in the determination of presuppositions, and not primarily at the subsequent level of research, exegesis, and application, where scholarship and the data allege to determine the results. In the above cases I have contended that the functonal anti-Semitism of the kind of scholarship represented by Perrin is based on the elected presupposition of the anti-Jewish principle of dissimilarity. The various models of Christian-Jewish relationship discussed by Klappert all presuppose that Christianity has replaced Judaism and has no need for it. It remains now only to demonstrate how this position is manifest in the text and to draw out its inexorable implications. That there are other possible presuppositions in both cases is clear. I cited Schillebeeckx and Keck as examples of scholars who have rejected as categorical the negative employment of the principle of dissimilarity; Klappert continues his exposition by presenting "models for the determination of the relationship between Israel and the church which tend toward an acknowledgement of the continuing election of Israel."[49] Klappert's own interpretation moves in this direction.

The Theological Falsification

Necessarily, the misrepresentation of Jesus as not Jewish and as having separated the church and Israel by taking the covenant from Israel and delivering it to the church, leads to a similar misconstruction and falsification of the church's understanding of God. When Jesus' witness to God and the Christian confession of him as the Son of God are thus abstracted from their original Old Testament and Jewish context, they

---

[48] *Ibid.*
[49] *Ibid.*, pp. 26–37.

necessarily fall into the context of the general human situation, where the word "God" no longer refers to the God of Abraham, Isaac, and Jacob who *acts* to fulfill the promises he makes to Israel, but to the God of religion who *is* the alleged presupposition of and answer to the universal human quest. Similarly, theology remains no longer a radical "biblical" theology, which seeks to understand Christian faith in God in terms of the existence and history of Israel and of the Jew—Jesus—but tends toward a Christian "natural" theology, which seeks to interpret Christian faith with reference to human nature and history as such. The difference between these methods is radical; as Pascal has reminded us, there can be no confusion between the God of Abraham, Isaac, and Jacob, and the God of the philosophers (and the natural theologians). Hans Joachim Kraus quotes the distinguished Berlin Rabbi, Leo Baeck, who observed that God is not God because he is more than but because he is other than the gods; "in relation to them he is incomparable."[50] The God of the Bible, Jesus' God, is the God of Israel, and because, as Kraus notes, "God's existence is self-determined as an existence-for-Israel . . . , all ontological speculation is excluded; the self-revealing God of the Bible withdraws himself from the world of religion, from that autonomous, anthropomorphic 'middle ground' between God and the people. . . ."[51]

The themes of creation and exodus are specific foci of the biblical contradiction of the religious perception of life and the world. Since the God who exists for Israel is the creator of the world and the world is God's creation, the creating and sustaining power of the world and its ultimate authority are not to be found in or of the world, whether as its height or depth; all the demons of the world are denied their authority and the numina of nature lose their power. As creatures of this God, humankind is not to be the religious slave of the deities, but the free lord of all, created in the very image of God. As for the exodus, it is an earthly, political event that at the same time established and inaugurated the holy history of Israel. In Kraus' words, it is "the radical new in the world of religion," in which religious salvation becomes a political liberation. "At the beginning of

---

[50]H. J. Kraus, *Theologische Religionkritik* (Neukirchen-Vluyn, 1982) p. 103.
[51]*Ibid.*, p. 229.

all Israel's ways there stands not a mysterious experience of revelation or a holy place, but a profane, this-worldly action of the God of Israel . . . in which God steps forth as a fighter for his people and for humankind."[52]

The Biblical God

There are four dimensions of this biblical view of God that I would emphasize, and I would do this in terms of some of the traditional attributes of God. First is the love or the grace of God, what we might call the attribute of immanence. We recognize, to begin with, that the immanence of the creator God of the exodus cannot be conceived ontologically or metaphysically. Rather, God must be understood historically by referring to those events within history in which God comes to us, in human form, on our level, in the flesh-and-blood history of a particular people. God is not the God who eternally is with us, but the God who temporally comes to us. With the coming of this God to earth the heavens are effectively emptied and the spirits of the earth exorcised. God is *God with us*—not as a spiritual height or depth—he is a person among us.

Correlatively, the divine transcendence, the holiness of God, is found not in the metaphysical difference between time and eternity, but in the wholly otherness of the concrete particularity of that history in which God comes among us. As Bonhoeffer wrote, "God is beyond in the midst of our life."[53] God is as other from the world, as transcendent and holy, as are the Jews, the children of Israel, and as is the church, the branch grafted onto Israel. Thus God's holiness, his very deity, is at stake in the destiny of his people. God has promised to redeem Israel "for the sake of my holy name" (Ezek 36:22), to raise up the dry bones of an exiled and scattered Israel, not for Israel's sake, but, as God says, so that "you shall know that I am the Lord" (Ezek 37:6). Deutero-Isaiah made the same point when he promised that God would be revealed to the nations as "the Holy One of Israel" (e.g., Isa 45). It is as the God who redeems and cares for Israel, as the Holy One *of Israel*, that God has

---

[52]*Ibid.*, pp. 231-32. Kraus quotes Kierkegaard to this point: "Therefore my soul ever returns to the Old Testament and to Shakespeare. There one feels that it is human beings who are speaking" (*ibid.*, p. 87).

[53]D. Bonhoeffer, *Widerstand und Ergebung* (Munich, 1970) p. 308.

revealed himself also to the nations as the one and only God. God is "wholly other" from the Christian, and from the world as such, because and as God has been "Jewish," and Jewish is precisely what Gentiles are not. If God has been "Jewish," and therein holy, then God has been, for instance, not Aryan, not even American, not Black, Latin, or feminine, and not simply and universally human (were there such). Rather, God has been the God of Israel—the holy God who transcends and judges all, the God whom the world can know and of whom it can speak only insofar as it first knows and can speak of this wholly other people, the children of Israel.

A third attribute is the divine goodness or righteousness. Because the transcendence and immanence of God must be understood historically, so must the righteousness of God be understood politically. From this perspective, at issue in the knowledge and obedience of God is less a spiritual salvation than a political deliverance. The biblical God is a partisan of the oppressed underdog; he liberates Israel, and through Israel humankind, for a true community of justice and peace; he calls his followers less to acts of religious devotion than to individual and corporate responsibility for the politics of God. Those who by God's grace are forgiven and "justified," who are reconciled and set right with God and so find themselves on God's side, are those who in that very event of their justification are also called and liberated to *work with God* in the establishment of the divine justice.

The experience of Dietrich Bonhoeffer illustrates how the recognition of God as the God of Israel reveals the political nature of the divine righteousness. Bonhoeffer was the first—and for a time the only—major voice of the Confessing Church in Germany to grasp the political implication of the Barmen Declaration of 1934. Bonhoeffer's early recognition appears to be grounded in his singular openness to the Old Testament and his consequent conviction that God has an essential stake in the destiny of his chosen people.[54] This concern for the Jews, and therefore for the eminently political Jewish question, led Bonhoeffer to call the church to its political obedience and

---

[54]H. E. Tödt, "Judendiskriminierung 1933—der Ernstfall für Bonhoeffers Ethik" in *Ethik im Ernstfall: Dietrich Bonhoeffers Stellung zu den Juden und ihre Aktualität*, ed., Wolfgang Huber and Ilse Tödt (Munich, 1982) p. 155.

brought him directly into conflict with the Third Reich. Bonhoeffer recognized that in the political reality of the Jewish people, Germany and especially the church were confronted with the historical and political reality of the wholly other God, to whom Bonhoeffer—and in his mind, the church—could be faithful ultimately only in a political way.

Finally, I would ask about the unity and universality of God. There is *only one God, the God of Israel*. His integrity, what I have called his holiness, is disclosed as he keeps his word and promises to Israel and proves himself to be their faithful and only God. He is not the champion of any and every revolutionary cause; he is a partisan of his own cause—the cause of Israel. Only as this particular God also becomes the God of all does he become the universal God that he is. The universality of God, the final meaning of his unity, is an eschatological reality—the *telos* ("end") of his history with Israel. For Christians, this universality is assured and promised to all through Jesus Christ. With the Rhineland Synod, Christians confess Jesus Christ, the Jew, "who as the Messiah of Israel is the Christ and savior of the world who binds the peoples of the world with the people of God."[55] In Jesus Messiah the one God of Israel becomes the universal God, the God of all.

The Religious God

The basic contention of religion—as opposed to biblical faith—the proposition that determines all others, is that God has not revealed himself primarily or exclusively within the history of Israel, and thus does not take us Gentiles out of our own history to become co-actors in God's covenant history with Israel. The God of religion is not conceived of in historical terms; indeed, the very notion of such a God evokes the satire of God as the mythological "large being acting in space and time."[56] Rather, the God of religion is understood much more "profoundly" and "spiritually" as a metaphysical, transhistorical, and ontological depth, as the presupposition and potentiality of reality, which confronts us at the boundary of existence

---

[55]Synodalbeschluss, p. 54.
[56]L. Gilkey, *Message and Existence* (New York, 1980) p. 186.

and is revealed especially in the universal history of religion and in modern religious pluralism.

Whereas the "Jewish" God of the Bible is the liberator who strives in the divine history with us to create a new world of love and justice, this higher, more spiritual God of religion may be understood as a "savior" who saves either by delivering one from this evil world of time and history into a spiritual unity with the transcendent being of the divine itself, or by upholding and sustaining the present world through a reaffirmation of the divine as the immanent truth, depth, and ground of all being. In both cases, the religious God is found, on the one hand, wholly "outside" or beyond history and the material realities of existence, and on the other hand, wholly "within" the spiritual depths of the inner person. Salvation therefore entails a primarily inward, spiritual unity with the wholly external spiritual depth. As Kraus states, a "decisive characteristic of religion is the coincidence of inwardness and transcendence."[57]

Thus, the religious quest for salvation can move in either of two directions. In the first instance it is directed toward deity in itself and as such, and the goal is a unity with the divine that "saves" and rescues one from the disunity and estrangement threatening human existence. Salvation is then a deliverance from the fragmented surface of life through a new integration with its ground and depth. As suggested by Tillich, in its highest form it is "absolute faith," a union with Being-itself in which all the ambiguity and alienation of a life menaced by nonbeing, death, and meaninglessness are overcome. "It is," he says, "nothing separated and definite. . . . It is the power of being. . . ."[58] Insofar as it offers this kind of escape from life, from all that is "separate and definite," religion can be said to have its roots in a sinful human laziness.[59] Too tired of the struggle, one seeks in religion to flee the world in a saving experience of the transcendent God of religion.

Alternatively, religious salvation may focus not on God as such, but on God as the ground and possibility of universal

---

[57]Kraus, *Theologische Religionkritik*, p. 70.

[58]P. Tillich, *The Courage to Be* (New Haven, 1952) pp. 188-89.

[59]See Kraus, *Theologische Religionkritik*, p. 456, where he also cites Barth, *Church Dogmatics*, IV, 2.

human existence and history. Here religion as salvation alleges to reveal in a saving way the meaning and purpose of human existence, and the power of its divine depth; it thus claims to give a viability to life, which otherwise is threatened with meaninglessness and futility. Insofar as it thus pulls life together, as it were, it has what Kraus designates an "integrating function." This type of religion can be said to be "historical" and even "political" to the extent that it provides not an escape from this world but instead a spiritual foundation and justification of it, including its history and its politics. By explaining human existence and history, by revealing their immanent meaningfulness, religion justifies and "saves" this world and life in it. This form of the religious falsification nevertheless also serves the lazy insofar as it legitimates a satisfaction with this world and discourages one from taking up, in the power of the Holy Spirit, the struggle for the new world promised with the coming of God's Rule.

We might say that religion and its promised salvation provide in the first case a saving escape from the world and, in the second, a saving legitimation of it. In either case, Karl Barth's observation that "religion" in no way contradicts the world is correct.[60]

The God of religion is certainly not "political" in the partisan sense of the biblical God. Viewed religiously, God does not even "exist" at the historical level, where politics is at home. Moreover, unlike the God of the exodus, who elects Israel and those who through Jesus Christ join the Israel party, the God of religion is non-partisan. As the ground of all being and history and, as it were, all politics, the divine plays no favorites and is immediately universal and impartial. At least this is the claim. The actuality, however, is that the God of religion is in fact quite partisan. While the biblical God has his own party and program—Israel and the Kingdom of God—the religious God serves the political interests of whatever party prevails in any particular place and time. In the Germany of 1933 "God" was manifest in the so-called German hour, in the German nation and folk, in the pure Aryan, and in the leadership of Adolf Hitler. Karl Marx's observation that there is no humanity-as-such is true, provided we understand that "classes" in-

---

[60]Barth, *Kirchliche Dogmatik*, p. 711.

clude not only economic divisions but also races, sexes, nations—a variety of parties always ready (and apparently able) to claim the God of religion as their advocate, or perhaps, in the name of religion, to keep God, the true God, from interfering with their causes.

Finally, a word should be said about the holiness or transcendence of God in the religious perspective. We have seen that the biblical God is *holy* because of the *wholly* otherness and particularity of his politics and because of that history with humankind in which he judges this world and creates a new world. He is transcendent precisely in this election of Israel, in his condescending to enter into the midst of our history in solidarity with Israel and the poor and oppressed of our world. With the gods of religion it is otherwise; they are, like the Olympians, beyond and above life. "These gods," says Kraus, "are the ambitious gods, the conceptions of human, all-too-human, ideas of domination and of strivings for superiority projected into transcendence, and who run counter to the direction of the one true God who descends into the depths of human existence."[61] The gods of religion are, for all their alleged transcendence, nevertheless finally quite earth-bound in their apparent willingness to become captive to any prevailing political program, either directly in advocacy, or indirectly in otherworldly indifference.

The preceding interpretation of "religion" and natural theology refers implicitly and explicitly to a Christian use of these categories and not to non-Christian religions or their theologies. My argument is that a sinful Christian anti-Judaism that separates Jesus and Christianity from Judaism necessarily leads to a so-called "Christian" natural theology and a religious understanding of God, and thus to a falsification of the Christian revelation. What remains to be demonstrated is precisely how and wherein this process is "sinful." On the assumption that Christians lie in order to cover and legitimize their sins, how is sin served by this pattern of "lies"?

The Resulting Sin

When "the church" is truthful it knows itself to be the com-

---

[61]Kraus, *Theologische Religionkritik*, p. 42.

munity of those who through Jesus Christ have been and are being called into the covenant between God and Israel. Only in *this* sense is the church the New Israel, the community of God's adopted children, the wild branches grafted on to the living root. In answering its call, the church, in the power of God's grace, faces and overcomes its sin, its proud separation from God, and its "natural" enmity to God's will. But although sin is thus confronted and overcome, it nevertheless exists on borrowed time and will seize every opportunity to reinforce itself. Typical of the effort of sin to prevail is the Christian lie which maintains that, after all, Jesus is not really Jewish and that the God he reveals and who calls the Church is not the God of the Jews. The consequence of this falsehood is that the church is delivered from the humiliation of having to become Israel's adopted ones in order to be saved. It can disregard Calvin's injunction that "when we seek salvation we have to go to the promise which was given to our father Abraham; we must be his spiritual children if we would be servants of the church of God, members of our Lord Jesus Christ."[62]

The Sin of Pride

By avoiding the fact of Israel's primacy in the covenant the church can subsequently and proudly turn the tables and claim that Israel and the Jews must come to the church for its salvation. The promises that Christ fulfills belong to the church first of all and to the Gentiles who come into the church rather than to the elect of Israel. Christ does not call people to become Israel's adopted ones but to become children of the church itself. Of course, the resulting claim is that the Jews can also become Christians if they should so choose to continue to enjoy the blessings of the covenant.

This move in the interest of human pride occurred very early in the life of the church, when it construed the separation between Jesus' followers and Judaism as evidence that God had rejected Israel as his partner and given the covenant to the church. Frank Mussner, following the Jewish scholar Jules Isaac, shows how such anti-Judaism exploited this separation

[62]*Commentary on Isaiah*, cited by E. Osterhaven, "Calvin on Covenant" in A. O. Miller, ed., *A Covenant Challenge to Our Broken World* (Atlanta, 1972, 1982) p. 120.

to insinuate itself into the early church's self-consciousness as it formulated the gospel tradition. According to Isaac and Mussner, the early conflict between Christianity and Judaism was the *Sitz im Leben* ("setting in life") of the gathering and redaction of the Jesus materials, which led "with almost natural necessity to an increasingly anti-Jewish accentuation of these materials and to the construction of *'Feindbilder'* [a portrayal of the enemy] (especially of the Pharisees)."[63] The allusion to "an almost natural necessity" recognizes the necessity or logic of nature (or sin), not of faith. The Christian truth of Jesus as the Messiah of Israel through whom Gentiles are called into covenant between Israel and God, which the Jews finally could not accept and which led to the separation between Judaism and Christianity, becomes the opportunity for the Christian lie that God has rejected the Jews and established the church as a justly proud and *independent* institution of salvation.

This boastful contention likely occasioned Paul's warning in the *Epistle to the Romans* of the danger of boasting: "If some of the branches were broken off [alluding to Israel's refusal to accept Christ] and you, a wild olive shoot [the Gentiles], were grafted in their place to share the richness of the olive tree, do not boast over the branches. If you do boast, remember that it is not you who support the root, but the root who supports you" (Rom 11:17-18). In and of itself the wild branch has no life and is without the knowledge of God; it has no grounds for boasting except in the root from which it receives its life. In language reminiscent of Second Isaiah, Paul must remind the Corinthians, who also were chronically disposed to boasting, that "God chose what is foolish in the world to shame the wise, God chose what is low and despised in the world, even things that are not, to bring to nothing things that are, so that no human being might boast in the presence of God" (1Cor 1:27). Endemic and natural to the church as such, regarded apart from Jesus Christ, is only its sin, which, apart from the grace of the God of Israel, is always there and looking for its opportunity, as in the church at Corinth. The truth that God comes to Gentiles through the Messiah of Israel, through the one who breaks down the wall between Jews and Gentiles so

---

[63]F. Mussner, "Israel und die Enstehung der Evangelium," in Martin Stohr, ed., *Existenz und die Erneuerung der christlichen Theologie* (Munich, 1981) p. 53.

that Gentiles may be included in Israel's covenant, as Paul so well recognized, is in the world's eyes "foolishness." It was and remains a consummate offense to human pride that in order to be God's people the church must identify with God's chosen people, whom other peoples and nations can but recognize as "despised and rejected," and especially with their Messiah. Nothing better serves human and ecclesial pride and resists this humiliation than the lie that separates Jesus as Christ and Lord of the church from the Jews and their messianic hope. This self-deception allows the church to imagine itself to be a free, independent, self-conscious institution of salvation that can boast of itself over the root in which it lives and without which it has no life.

Thus, from its beginning the church reveals a tendency toward a sinful self-centered ecclesiasticism, and this pride is rationalized by anti-Semitism, which denies the dependence of the church on Jesus the Jew, as well as on his Judaism. The coincidence of anti-Jewishness and ecclesiastical pride is nowhere so painfully manifest in modern times, or in any time, as in the German Church during the period of national socialism. In 1928, on the eve of the rise of Hitler, Bishop Dibelius triumphantly declared the twentieth century "the century of the church." "The Christian Churches," he wrote, "stand at the beginning of a new epoch. They are gathering their strength. They dare to undertake new tasks. They are driven forward by new responsibilities. The spiritual situation of the world demands its labors. . . . We have only to ask what is God's command for this hour which is given to us. And we hear as his command just one word, and that word is 'Church.' "[64] In this same spirit, just a few years later, German Christians were united in their enthusiasm for the establishment of a new united evangelical (Protestant) church, one that was to have the backing and support of Hitler himself. "The goal of the faith movement, 'German Christians,' is an evangelical German state (Reich) church. The state of Adolf Hitler calls for the church, the church must hear this call."[65] And this was to be a "German" church, proud and independent. Therefore,

[64]K. Kupisch, *Quellen zur Geschichte des Protestantismus, 1871-1945* (Berlin, 1960) pp. 230, 234.

[65]E. Wolf, *Barmen: Kirche zwischen Versuchung und Gnade* (Munich, 1970) p. 50.

according to the so-called Aryan paragraph of the German Christian platform (which became the law of the Prussian Church), it was to be a church that excluded "non-Aryans"— i.e., Jews, who were not really Germans and would prevent the church from being truly and proudly German and independent.

Even the Confessing Church, established in 1934 at Barmen, did not escape ecclesiasticism. It addressed itself only to the question of the integrity and truth of the church and initially attempted to avoid political questions. Not coincidentally, therefore, the Barmen Declaration failed to address the Jewish question; it ignored both the Aryan paragraph, which excluded Jewish Christians from service in the church, and the situation of German Jewry as such.

The Sin of Indolence and Sloth

The ironic other side of the sin of a prideful, self-conscious ecclesiasticism is the sin of laziness, in which the church does not even begin to rise to the heights of its calling as Christ's Church. Inwardly, this sin is experienced as a quiescent, conservative satisfaction with and consent to the status quo, whether explicitly and actively or tacitly and passively, whether as a sin of commission or as a sin of omission. Outwardly it results in and is expressive of the church's bondage to the world in which it finds itself. If those who come into the church do not find themselves transposed into the covenant with Israel, if the situation of Israel before God is not the situation of the church, then the church finds itself enslaved by the world. If it is not called out of its own history as a part of the world's history, into the revolutionary, world-changing history of God and his people, then it is "free" only to live out the story of the world, either silently by default or confessedly in abject support of that world. Similarly, as we have noted, so-called natural theology tends to rationalize the status quo of human existence and history and, at best, fails to help the church understand and rise to its calling as God's exodus people. Those "gods" natural to this world, who are construed as the final truth of the world, scarcely occasion the church's rising to the cause of a new world. An independent and self-conscious ecclesiasticism, together with its correlate of either an abstract ecclesiastical or natural theology, immediately becomes a hopelessly dependent church—too tired, too indolent, and too captive to live up to its mission as the people of Jesus the Messiah.

This other side of the coin is again apparent in the case of the German Church, especially during the period of national socialism. In 1925 Bishop Dibelius argued that to answer its call, the church "cannot be an international society of a Christian sort, but a humanity that builds itself up out of the nations, in which every national group comprehends Christian faith in its own way and stamps it with its own style. The commitment to love the neighbor makes the national community (*Volkgemeinschaft*) the obligation of everyone, since for us the brother in one's own people is always the neighbor."[66] Similarly, we recall that the German Christians defined the goal of the faith movement as "an evangelical German state Church. . . . ," which would be truly "German," exclusive of non-Aryans. The church, they contended, is not subject to God's law as exemplified in the Old Testament because the Old Testament is, in fact, not the law of God for everyone, but only for Israel; it is merely an example of the way that God calls every nation and people. "He called Israel to its particular history. . . . He calls each people to its particular mission."[67] A gospel that is not stamped by Jesus Christ with the experience and history of Israel can only bear the mark of the nation. In pre-war Germany, the church necessarily became German. Instead of being subject exclusively to Jesus Christ, it fell subject to the will of the "creator," to his law as manifest in the history of the German nation and Volk. Even the Young Reformers, who were not numbered among the German Christians, could state as a part of their guiding theses that the Evangelical Church should, "in full freedom from all political influences and in a joyful yes to the new German state, fulfill its God-given duty and bind itself at the same time in an indissoluble service to the German Volk."[68] The will of God was thought to be heard in this German hour, "in the particular historical moment of the family, the people and the race, that is, in a particular

---

[66]Kupisch, *Quellen zur Geschichte des Protestantismus*, p. 232.

[67]H. Sasse, "Das Volk nach der Lehre der evangelischen Kirche," *Bekennende Kirche*, Heft 20. Cited by E. Busch, *Juden und Christen im Schatten des Dritten Reiches: Theologische Existenz Heute* (Munich, 1979), no. 205, p. 28.

[68]Wolf, *Barmen*, p. 101.

moment of their history."[69] The church was to shoulder the destiny of the German people. "Germany is our task, Christ is our strength."[70]

Is it formally different when a modern American theologian claims that "it is necessary to appropriate God's acts from our situation," or that "our theology must make sense of our experience, of the world we live in"?[71] Is not the world, our present historical situation, then dictating the task of church and theology, for which Christ may then be invoked as the source of strength? Whereas the German theologians of 1933 saw the fulfillment of the will of the Creator in the German hour and the rise of national socialism, a contemporary theology can claim to "have seen in the advent of secularism the fulfillment of the will of the creator." The church "must learn to listen to secular man, and must listen to him honestly . . . with a willingness to learn both about the world (*and about the meaning of the faith it confesses*).The view that sees revelation as "channelled through Scripture and the institutional churches" is too narrow and restricted; "it fails to take seriously the work and purpose of the Creator."[72] In the name of the Creator, then, the church must listen to the world, and let the world set the agenda, speak for God, and determine the criteria of the church's relevance in the modern world. Is this kind of natural theology any more able today than it was in 1933 to call the church to itself, to call it out of its situation in the world so as to take its place in God's struggle in and against the world on behalf of a new world? Is the Church of God served by a theology that deliberately seeks to "move outside the walls of the church and into the broad arena of the world, where our deepest attitudes about what is real and true are formed"?[73] Doubtless the church must move outside its walls, but is it "into the broad arena of the world" that it should move? Actually, of course, it cannot so move. As Dibelius perhaps unintentionally observed, a church that does not move into God's historic struggle with the world, moves and must move into a particular part of the world itself—which for Dibelius was the

---

[69]*Ibid.*, p. 101.
[70]*Ibid.*, p. 109.
[71]E. C. Gardiner, *The Church as Prophetic Community* (Philadelphia, 1967) p. 214.
[72]*Ibid.*, p. 213. The emphasis is mine.
[73]Gilkey, *Naming the Whirlwind*, p. 232.

nation, the Volk. Does the modern church fare any better? Abstracted from the people of God, does it become free in the name of God to serve all, or does it not in fact become the dependent voice of the dominant powers of the status quo, serving them either directly and intentionally, or indirectly and implicitly by its irrelevant and pointless abstraction into "the broad arena of the world"?

In itself and by itself the church is an abstraction. Its actuality and existence are found in the service it renders: the church either in the name of Christ serves the cause of God and his kingdom as revealed and realized in the history of his chosen people, or—ostensibly in the name of Christ, but actually by falsifying his truth—serves the world. In fact, the church exists only in the struggle for its truth against this lie. The lie serves sin and the devil well. By appearing to legitimate a self-conscious ecclesiasticism, it effects a church which either by its ecclesiastical preoccupation leaves the world alone or with its so-called natural theology provides a tacit—when not explicit— legitimation of this world as it is. In both cases the church denies and defies the new for which God in Christ and through his chosen people has been and is still struggling. The anti-Jewish fabrications of the church serve the sinful pride and the indolence of the church, both of which render it subject to the principalities and powers of this age and contradict its true being and calling as the New Israel, as the adopted children of God and covenant partners with God in Jesus Christ in the fight for a new world, a new humanity, a new heaven, and a new earth.

DISCUSSION

Robert T. Osborn's paper is deemed a significant statement, and one that completes the discussions of the symposium; it focuses on a major challenge to the continuation of the power, truth, and integrity of Christian theology. We are delighted to include it here with the other papers from the symposium of May 1987. I am pleased to state that the members of the symposium would have been challenged and pleased by the acute insights and careful reflections offered by Professor Osborn. He was not present during the discussions, hence, we did not discuss his paper. [J.H.C.]

List of Illustrations

(All illustrations appear following page 126.)

1. Reims Cathedral.
   Juxtaposition of the Church and the Synagogue.
   (Kunstgeschichtlichen Institut der Philipps-Universitaet, Marburg, West Germany.)

2. Strassbourg Cathedral.
   Depiction of the Church.
   (Kunstgeschichtlichen Institut der Philipps-Universitaet, Marburg, West Germany.)

3. Strassbourg Cathedral.
   Carving of the Triumphant Church.
   (Kunstgeschichtlichen Institut der Philipps-Universitaet, Marburg, West Germany.)

4. Church of the Abbey of St.-Denis near Paris.
   Christ with the Church and the Synagogue.
   (William W. Clark.)

5. Notre Dame de Paris, north entrance
   (J. H. Charlesworth.)

6. Notre Dame de Paris, main doors
   Flanking depictions of the Church (left) and the Synagogue (right).
   (J. H. Charlesworth.)

7. Notre Dame de Paris
   Sculpture of fallen Synagogue.
   (J. H. Charlesworth.)

8. Freiburg Cathedral
   Carving of disheveled Synagogue.
   (Directors of the Cathedral, Freiburg im Breisgau, West Germany.)

9. Detail of medieval manuscript drawing (early eleventh century).
   Church (left) and Synagogue (right) flanking the crucified Christ.
   (Librarian of the Bibliotheek der Rijksuniversiteit te Leiden.)

A Selected Bibliography on Jewish-Christian Relations

Jeffrey S. Siker

Bibliographic Resources

Blewett, R. P. *Annotated Bibliography for Jewish-Christian Relations.* Anoka, Minn., 1987.

Celnik, M. *A Bibliography on Judaism and Jewish-Christian Relations.* New York, 1965.

Fisher, E. J. *Seminary Education and Christian-Jewish Relations.* Washington, D.C., 1983.

———. "A New Maturity in Christian-Jewish Dialogue: An Annotated Bibliography 1973-83," *Face to Face* 11 (1984) 29-43.

The Study of Judaism: Bibliographical Essays, vol. 1 and 2. New York, 1972, 1976.

Marcus, I. G. "The Jews in Western Europe: Fourth to Sixteenth Century," *The Study of Judaism: Bibliographical Essays in Medieval Jewish Studies*, vol. 2, edited by Y. H. Yerushalmi. New York, 1976. Pp. 17-108.

Stow, K. R. "The Church and the Jews: From St. Paul to Paul IV," *The Study of Judaism: Bibliographical Essays in Medieval Jewish Studies*, vol. 2, edited by Y. H. Yerushalmi. New York, 1976. Pp. 109-68.

Wood, J. E., ed. "A Selected and Annotated Bibliography on Jewish-Christian Relations," *Jewish-Christian Relations in Today's World*. Waco, Texas, 1971. Pp. 139-62.

Periodicals

Christian-Jewish Relations: A Documentary Survey (American Jewish Committee)

Explorations: Rethinking Relationships Among Jews and Christians (American Institute for the Study of Religious Cooperation)

Face to Face: An Inter-Religious Bulletin
  (Anti-Defamation League)
Immanuel
Interreligious Bulletin
  (American Jewish Committee)
The Journal of Ecumenical Studies
S.I.D.I.C.
  (Service International de Documentation Judéo-Chrétienne; English
  Edition)

General

Bea, A. C. *The Church and the Jewish People.* New York, 1966.
van Buren, P. *Discerning the Way.* New York, 1980.
Cohen, A. A. *The Myth of the Judeo-Christian Tradition.* New York, 1971.
Croner, H., ed. *Stepping Stones to Further Jewish-Christian Relations.* New York, 1977.
————, ed. *More Stepping Stones to Jewish-Christian Relations.* New York, 1985.
Croner, H., and L. Klenicki, eds. *Issues in the Jewish-Christian Dialogue: Jewish Perspectives on Covenant, Mission and Witness.* New York, 1979.
Eckhardt, A. R. *Elder and Younger Brothers: The Encounter of Jews and Christians.* New York, 1973.
————. *Your People, My People: The Meeting of Jews and Christians.* New York, 1974.
————. *Jews and Christians: The Contemporary Meeting.* Bloomington, Indiana, 1986.
Fisher, E. J. *Faith Without Prejudice.* New York, 1977.
————. *Homework for Christians Preparing for Christian-Jewish Dialogue.* National Conference on Christians and Jews, 1982.
Fisher, E. J., A. J. Rudin, and M. H. Tanenbaum, eds. *Twenty Years of Jewish-Catholic Relations.* New York, 1986.
Flannery, E. *The Anguish of the Jews: Twenty-Three Centuries of Anti-Semitism,* rev. ed. New York, 1985.
Forster, A., and B. R. Epstein. *The New Antisemitism.* New York, 1974.
Hay, M. *The Roots of Christian Anti-Semitism.* New York, 1981.
Isaac, J. *The Teaching of Contempt.* New York, 1964.
————. *Jesus and Israel,* trans. by S. Gran. New York, 1971.
Klenicki, L., and G. Wigoder, eds. *A Dictionary of the Jewish-Christian Dialogue.* New York, 1984.
Küng, H., and W. Kasper, eds. *Christians and Jews.* New York, 1974.
Lapide, P. *Israelis, Jews, and Jesus.* New York, 1979.
Long, J. B. *Judaism and the Christian Seminary Curriculum.* Chicago, 1966.

Oesterreicher, J., ed. *The Bridge: A Yearbook of Judaeo-Christian Studies*, vols. 1-5. New York, 1955-1970.

———. *The New Encounter Between Christians and Jews*. New York, 1986.

Parkes, J. *Judaism and Christianity*. Chicago, 1948.

———. *The Conflict of the Church and the Synagogue: A Study in the Origins of Antisemitism*. London, 1934; New York, 1974.

———. *Prelude to Dialogue: Jewish-Christian Relationships*. London, 1969.

Pawlikowski, J. T. *What Are They Saying about Christian-Jewish Relations?* New York, 1980.

———. *Christ in the Light of the Christian-Jewish Dialogue*. New York, 1982.

Poliakov, L. *The History of Anti-Semitism*, vols. 1-4. New York, 1965.

Prager, D., and J. Telushkin. *Why the Jews? The Reason for Antisemitism*. New York, 1983.

Rousseau, R. W., S.J., ed. *Christianity and Judaism: The Deepening Dialogue*. Scranton, Penn., 1983.

Sandmel, S. *We Jews and Jesus*. Oxford, 1965.

Swidler, L., ed. "Jews and Christians in Dialogue," *The Journal of Ecumenical Studies* 12 (1975) 471-642.

———, ed. "From Holocaust to Dialogue: A Jewish-Christian Dialogue between Americans and Germans," *The Journal of Ecumenical Studies* 18 (1981) 1-216.

Tal, U. *Christians and Jews in Germany: Religion, Politics, and Ideology in the Second Reich, 1870-1914*. Ithaca, N.Y., 1975.

Talmage, F. E., ed. *Disputation and the Dialogue: Reading in the Jewish-Christian Encounter*. New York, 1975.

Thoma, C. *A Christian Theology of Judaism*. New York, 1980.

Thoma, C., and M. Wyschogrod, eds. *Understanding Scripture: Explorations of Jewish and Christian Traditions of Interpretation*. New York, 1987.

World Council of Churches and International Jewish Committee on Interreligious Consultations, *Jewish-Christian Dialogue*. Geneva, 1975.

Zeik, M., and M. Siegel, eds. *Root and Branch*. Williston Park, N.Y., 1973.

New Testament and Early Christianity

Baum, G. *Is the New Testament Anti-Semitic?* New York, 1965.

Beck, N.A. *Mature Christianity: The Recognition and Repudiation of the Anti-Jewish Polemic of the New Testament*. London and Toronto, 1985.

Boadt, L., H. Croner, and L. Klenicki, eds. *Biblical Studies: Meeting Ground of Jews and Christians.* New York, 1980.

Bowman, J. *The Fourth Gospel and the Jews.* Pittsburgh, 1975.

Callan, T. *Forgetting the Root: The Emergence of Christianity from Judaism.* New York, 1986.

Charlesworth, J. H. *Jesus Within Judaism.* Anchor Bible Reference Library 1; Garden City, New York, 1988.

————. "The Need for Explorations," *Explorations: Rethinking Relationships Among Jews and Christians* 1.1 (1987) 1-2.

————. *The Old Testament Pseudepigrapha and the New Testament.* Society for New Testament Studies, Monograph Series 54; Cambridge, 1985, 1987, 1988.

————. "The Prayer of Manasseh: The Classic Jewish Penitential Prayer," *Explorations: Rethinking Relationships Among Jews and Christians* 2.1 (1988) 2.

————. "Unprecedented Leadership From Scholars," *Explorations: Rethinking Relationships Among Jews and Christians* 2.2 (1988) 1,4.

———— ed. *The Old Testament Pseudepigrapha,* 2 vols. Garden City, New York, 1983-85.

Cook, M. J. *Mark's Treatment of the Jewish Leaders.* Leiden, 1978.

Davies, A. T., ed. *AntiSemitism and the Foundations of Christianity.* New York, 1979.

Gager, J. G. *The Origins of Anti-Semitism: Attitudes Toward Judaism in Pagan and Christian Antiquity.* New York, 1983.

Hare, D.R.A. *The Theme of Jewish Persecution of Christians in the Gospel According to Matthew.* Cambridge, 1967.

Koenig, J. *Jews and Christians in Dialogue: New Testament Foundations.* Philadelphia, 1979.

Martyn, J. L. *History and Theology in the Fourth Gospel.* Nashville, 1968.

Meeks, W. A., and R. L. Wilken. *Jews and Christians in Antioch in the First Four Centuries of the Common Era.* Missoula, Mont., 1978.

Nickelsburg, G.W.E., and G. MacRae eds. *Christians Among Jews and Gentiles.* Philadelphia, 1986.

Richardson, P., with D. Granskou, eds. *Anti-Judaism in Early Christianity,* vol. 1, *Paul and the Gospels.* Waterloo, Ontario, 1986.

Ruether, R. *Faith and Fratricide: The Theological Roots of Anti-Semitism.* New York, 1974.

Sanders, E. P. *Paul and Palestinian Judaism: A Comparison of Patterns of Religion.* Philadelphia, 1977.

————. *Paul, the Law, and the Jewish People.* Philadelphia, 1983.

————. *Jesus and Judaism.* Philadelphia, 1985.

————, ed. *Jewish and Christian Self-Definition,* vol. 1, *The Shaping of Christianity in the Second and Third Centuries.* Philadelphia, 1980.

Sanders, E. P., with A. I. Baumgarten and A. Mendelson, eds. *Jewish and Christian Self-Definition*, vol. 2, *Aspects of Judaism in the Greco-Roman Period*. Philadelphia, 1981.

Sandmel, S. *Anti-Semitism in the New Testament?* Philadelphia, 1978.

Schüssler Fiorenza, E., ed. *Aspects of Religious Propaganda in Judaism and Early Christianity*. Notre Dame, 1976.

Segal, A. F. *Rebecca's Children: Judaism and Christianity in the Roman World*. Cambridge, Mass., 1986.

Sloyan, G. *Is Christ the End of the Law?* Philadelphia, 1978.

Stendahl, K. *Paul Among Jews and Gentiles*. Philadelphia, 1976.

Vermes, G. *Jesus the Jew*. Philadelphia, 1973.

Wilson, S. G., ed. *Anti-Judaism in Early Christianity*, vol. 2, *Separation and Polemic*. Waterloo, Ontario, 1986.

Church Fathers

Braude, W. G. *Jewish Proselytizing in the First Five Centuries of the Common Era*. Providence, 1940.

de Lange, N.R.M. *Origen and the Jews. Studies in Jewish-Christian Relations in Third-Century Palestine*. New York and Cambridge, 1976.

Neusner, J. *Aphrahat and Judaism. The Christian-Jewish Argument in Fourth-Century Iran*. Leiden, 1971.

———. *Judaism and Christianity in the Age of Constantine: History, Messiah, Israel, and the Initial Confrontation*. Chicago, 1987.

Simon, M. *Verus Israel*. rev. ed. and trans. by H. McKeating. Oxford, 1986.

Stylianopoulos, T. *Justin Martyr and the Mosaic Law*. Society of Biblical Literature Dissertation Series; Missoula, Mont., 1975.

Wilde, R. *The Treatment of the Jews in the Greek Christian Writers of the First Three Centuries*. Washington, D.C., 1949.

Wilken, R. L. *John Chrysostom and the Jews: Rhetoric and Reality in the Late Fourth Century*. Berkeley, 1983.

———. *Judaism and the Early Christian Mind*. New Haven, 1971.

Medieval and Reformation

Berger, D. *The Jewish-Christian Debate in the High Middle Ages*. Philadelphia, 1979.

Chazan, R. *Church, State and Jew in the Middle Ages*. New York, 1980.

Cohen, J. *The Friars and the Jews: The Evolution of Medieval Anti-Judaism*. Ithaca, 1982.

Grayzel, S. *The Church and the Jews in the Thirteenth Century*. Philadelphia, 1933.

Katz, J. *Exclusiveness and Tolerance: Studies in Jewish-Gentile Relations in Medieval and Modern Times.* Oxford, 1961.

Lasker, D. J. *Jewish and Philosophical Polemics Against Christianity in the Middle Ages.* New York, 1977.

Oberman, H. *The Roots of Anti-Semitism in the Age of Renaissance and Reformation,* trans. by J. I. Porter. Philadelphia, 1984.

Synan, E. *The Popes and the Jews in the Middle Ages.* New York, 1965.

Trachtenberg, J. *The Devil and the Jews: The Medieval Conception of the Jew and Its Relation to Modern Antisemitism.* New Haven, 1943.

Williams, A. L. *Adversus Judaeos: A Bird's Eye View of Christian Apologiae until the Renaissance.* Cambridge, 1935.

Theology

Bokser, B. Z. *Judaism and the Christian Predicament.* New York, 1967.

Borowitz, E. *Contemporary Christologies: A Jewish Response.* New York 1980.

Brueggemann, W. *The Land.* Philadelphia, 1977.

van Buren, P. *A Theology of the Jewish-Christian Reality,* 3 vols. San Francisco, 1980-88.

Cohn-Sherbok, D. *On Earth as it is in Heaven: Jews, Christians, and Liberation Theology.* Maryknoll, N.Y., 1987.

Davies, W. D. *The Gospel and the Land.* Berkeley, 1974.

Klein, C. *Anti-Judaism in Christian Theology.* Philadelphia, 1978.

Klenicki, L., and G. Huck, eds. *Spirituality and Prayer: Jewish and Christian Understandings.* New York, 1983.

Lapide, P. and J. Moltmann. *Jewish Monotheism and Christian Trinitarian Doctrine.* Philadelphia, 1981.

Mussner, F. *Tractate on the Jews: The Significance of Judaism for Christian Faith,* trans. and introduction by L. Swidler. Philadelphia, 1984.

Olson, B. E. *Faith and Prejudice.* New Haven, 1963.

von der Osten-Sacken, P. *Christian-Jewish Dialogue: Theological Foundations,* trans. by M. Kohl. Philadelphia, 1986.

Parkes, J. *The Theological Foundations of Judaism and Christianity.* London, 1960.

Rahner, Karl, and P. Lapide. *Encountering Jesus—Encountering Judaism: A Dialogue,* trans. by D. Perkins. New York, 1987.

Schoeps, H. J. *The Jewish-Christian Argument: A History of Theologies in Conflict.* New York, 1963.

Strober, G. S. *Portrait of the Elder Brother.* New York, 1972.

Thoma, C. *A Christian Theology of Judaism,* trans. and ed. by H. Croner. New York, 1980.

Holocaust

Cargas, H. J. *A Christian Response to the Holocaust*. Denver, Colo., 1982.

Dawidowicz, L. *The War Against the Jews*. New York, 1975.

Eckardt, A. L. and R. A. *Long Night's Journey into Day: A Revised Retrospective on the Holocaust*, rev. ed. Detroit, 1982.

Fleischner, E., ed., *Auschwitz: Beginning of a New Era?* New York, 1977.

Helmreich, E.C. *The German Churches Under Hitler*. Detroit, 1979.

Lifton, R. J. *History and Human Survival*. New York, 1970.

Littell, F. *The Crucifixion of the Jews*. New York, 1975.

Littell, F., and H. Locke, eds. *The German Church Struggle and the Holocaust*. Detroit, 1974.

McGarry, M. B., *Christology After Auschwitz*. New York, 1977.

Morley, J. F. *Vatican Diplomacy and the Jews During the Holocaust 1933-1943*. New York, 1980.

Pawlikowski, J.T. *The Challenge of the Holocaust for Christian Theology*. New York, 1978.

Peck, A. J., ed. *Jews and Christians After the Holocaust*. Philadelphia, 1982.

Rausch, D. A. *A Legacy of Hatred: Why Christians Must Not Forget the Holocaust*. Chicago, 1984.

Zahn, G. *German Catholics and Hitler's Wars*. New York, 1963.

Index of Names

(Page numbers in parentheses refer to the Italian version of Cardinal Martini's article.)

Aaronson, L. (Rabbi), 169
Abbot of Cluny, 125
Abelard, 108
Abraham, 24, (31), 48, 112, 171, 172, 214, 216, 217, 225
Adam, 59, 112, 216
Adler, R., 168-169, 169n
Agus, I.A., 121, 121n
Alcuin, 114
Allen, W.C., 50n
Althaus, P., 142, 222
Ambrose, Saint, 20, 25, 26, (28), (32), (33)
Anderson, G.H., 153n
Andrew of St.-Victor, 13, 103, 108, 115-120
Ashton, J., 77n, 92n
Augustine, 20, (28), 102, 112, 115
Avigad, N., 37n

Bach, K.O. v.d., 142n
Baeck, L. (Rabbi), 225
Bainton, R.H., 130, 130n
Baldwin, J.W., 101n

Bammel, E., 52n
Bar Kokhba, 38, 94
Barlow, F., 117n
Baron, R., 103n
Barrett, C.K., 89, 92, 93n
Barth, K., 19, (27), 127-128, 215-216, 215n, 216n, 230, 230n
Barton, B., 155
Baumann, A., 128n
Beasley-Murray, G.R., 92n
Beck, N.A., 96n
Becket, T., 13, 117, 119, 123
Bede, 112
Beker, J.C., 47, 47n, 54, 70
Benson, R.L., 101n, 102n
Berkovits, E. (Rabbi), 161, 162n
Bernard, Saint, 22, (29)
Bethge, E., 153n, 211, 212, 212n
Bienert, W., 134n
Bismarck, 138, 148, 149
Black, M., 40
Blisard, F., 15
Blumenkranz, B., 101n, 104n, 105n
Boccaccio, 21, (29)

Bonhoeffer, D., 152, 153, 153n,
  154, 226, 226n, 227-228
Borg, D.R., 141n
Borowsky, I.J., 15
Borowski, T., 158, 158n
Brandon, S.G.F., 43, 43n
Brosseder, J., 128n, 135n
Brown, R.E., 49, 49n, 84n, 92,
  96n, 162n
Buck, E., 52n, 53n
Bultmann, R., 50n, 78-79, 78n,
  84, 91-92, 92n,, 93, 181, 218,
  219, 219n, 223
Busch, E., 236n

Cahn, W., 106n
Caligula (Emperor), 188
Calvin, J., 232
Carter, J., 207
Charles V (Emperor), 133
Charles, R.H., 39, 39n, 64, 89n
Charlesworth, J.H., 36n, 37n,
  38n, 39n, 40n, 44n, 45n, 46n,
  50n, 157
Charny, I.W., 160n
Chatillon, J., 103n, 107n
Chazan, R., 101n
Chenu, M.-D., 101n, 108n
Chrysostom, John, 12, 86
Clark, K.W., 51n
Clark, W.W., 16
Cleopas, 182
Cohen, A.A., 152n
Cohen, J., 101n
Collins, J.J., 40
Comestor, Peter, 118
Constable, G., 101n, 102n
Constantine "the Great", 13
Conzelmann, H., 45, 45n, 46, 96
Cook, M.L., 155, 155n
Cornfeld, G., 185, 186, 186n
Cullmann, O., 43n, 92
Culpepper, R.A., 50n, 77n, 92n,
  93n

Dahan, G., 118n
Daly, M., 175
Daum, A., 168n, 171
David, 112
Davies, A., 86n, 159n
Davies, P.R., 37n
Davies, W.D., 47n, 50n, 85, 85n,
  98
Denifle, H., 128
Dibelius (Bishop), 234, 236,
  237-238
Dobschutz, E. von, 50n
Dodd, C.H., 92, 92n, 93
Drews, A., 216
Dundes, A., 166n

Eckardt, A.L., 152n, 157n, 160,
  160n, 163
Eckardt, A.R., 152n, 154n, 156n,
  159n, 161n, 163n
Ehlers, J., 103n
Ehrlich, E.L., 128n
Ephraem, Saint, 20, (28)
Epp, E.J., 76, 77n
Erasmus, 133n, 146
Ericksen, R.P., 142, 142n
Eusebius, 111n, 112, 113
Evans, G.R., 101n
Everett, R.A., 152n, 163, 163n,
  167

Fackenheim, E.L., 153n, 154n,
  160, 165, 165n
Falk, H., 45, 45n
Falwell, J., 169, 170
Fiorenza, E.S., 152n, 159n
Fleischner, E., 158n
Fortna, R.T., 84, 84n
Fraikin, D., 48n
Freud, S., 189
Friedmann, J., 135n
Fromm, E., 128-129, 129n

Gager, J.G., 171

Gamaliel (Rabbi), 74
Gamaliel II (Rabbi), 85
Gardiner, E.C., 237n
Gaston, L., 48n, 71
Geis, K.K. (Rabbi), 222
Gerson, P.L., 104n
Ghellinck, J. de, 101n
Gilkey, L.B., 237n
Ginzel, G.B., 142n
Gollwitzer, H., 214n, 223
Goulder, M.D., 50n
Grabois, A., 101n, 114n, 115n
Graetz, H., 141
Granskou, D., 48n, 52n
Green, W.M., 108n, 109n
Greenberg, I., 156n, 158, 158n
Greenburg, S.T., 178
Gregory the Great (Pope), 109
Grisar, H., 128
Gritsch, E.W., 128n, 131n, 132, 132n
Grodecki, L., 104n, 105n, 106n

Haile, H.G., 133n
Hailperin, H., 115n, 120n
Halperin, J., 128n
Harding, S., 114
Hare, D.R.A., 50n, 52n
Häring, N., 101n
Harnack, A. von, 14, 142, 218, 218n, 222-223
Hartman, G.H., 159n
Hasan-Rokem, G., 166n
Heer, F., 101, 101n
Hemer, C.J., 89n
Hengel, M., 43n, 45-46, 46n
Henry of Cornhil, 118-119
Henry II (King), 117
Hentoff, N., 159n
Herbert of Bosham, 13, 115, 117-121, 123, 126
Herod [the Great] (King), 188
Hill, D., 50n
Hillerbrand, H., 13, 157

Hillel (Rabbi), 12, 42
Hirsch, E., 142
Hitler, A., 11, 128, 152, 162, 211, 230, 234
Hoffmann, K., 105n
Horsley, R.A., 43n
Hotchkin, J.F., 14, 26
Huber, W., 227n
Hugh of St.-Victor, 103, 104, 106-115, 111n, 119, 123
Hurd, J.C., 48n

Isaac, 171, 214, 216, 217, 225
Isaac, J., 23, (30), 40, 161, 232, 233
Isidore, 112

Jackson, J., 169, 170
Jacob, 214, 216, 217, 225
James, 182
Jeremiah, 160
Jerome, 112n, 115, 117, 119
Jesus, 10, 11, 12, 13, 14, 19, 24-25, 26, (27), (32), (33), 36, 39, 40, 42-47, 49, 50, 51, 52, 53, 54, 55, 56, 57-59, 62, 65, 66, 72, 74, 75, 77, 78, 79, 80, 81, 82, 83, 84, 90, 91, 92, 93, 94, 98-99, 129, 131, 136, 147, 154, 155, 156, 162, 163, 164, 165, 166, 167, 171, 175, 179, 180, 181, 182, 211-213, 214-225, 232, 233, 234, 236, 238
John (Evangelist), 88-89, 91-92, 99
John the Baptist, 62, 79, 80
John Paul I (Pope), 26, (32)
John Paul II (Pope), 23, 24, (30), (31), 174
John XXIII (Pope), 24, (31)
Jones, W.R., 166, 166n
Jonge, M. de, 92
Joseph, 13

Josephus, 93-94, 115, 185, 186n,
    188, 190, 191-193, 195, 197,
    198, 199, 201, 205, 206, 210
Judah the Prince (Rabbi), 42
Justin Martyr, 85

Kampe, N., 128n
Kant, I., 140
Käsemann, E., 47, 47n, 218,
    218n, 223-224
Katz, J., 101n
Katz, S.T., 86n, 87
Keck, L., 218n, 224
Kellner, M.M., 169n
Kierkegaard, S., 226n
Kimelman, R., 86n, 87, 97-98
Kirchhoff, H.G., 140n
Kisch, G., 133n
Kittel, G., 142
Klappert, B., 217n, 221-224,
    221n
Klein, C., 159n
Klijn, A.F.J., 39
Knibb, M.A., 37n
Köhler, W., 133n
Kraus, H.J., 142n, 225-226, 225n,
    226n, 229, 229n, 231, 231n
Kremers, H., 128n, 135n, 142n,
    144n
Kupisch, K., 234n, 236n

Lamparter, E., 142, 142n
Langton, S., 118
Lanham, C.D., 101n
Lapide, P., 165
Lazarus, 58-59, 82
Lessing, A., 139, 160
Levinson, P., 165
Lewin, R., 132n
Lifton, R.J., 193, 193n, 199-200,
    199n, 200n
Lindner, H., 128n
Littell, F.H., 152n, 159n

Loewe, R., 117, 117n, 119, 119n,
    121
Lombard, Peter, 117, 119
Louis VI (King), 107
Luscombe, D., 118n
Luther, M., 13, 72, 127-150

McCauley, D., 168n, 171n
McGarry, M.B., 161n
Maier, P.L., 186n
Marsden, G.M., 141n
Marsch, W.D., 135n, 214n
Martha (Sister of Lazarus), 58,
    82
Martini, C.M. (Cardinal), 14, 34
Martyn, J.L., 49, 49n, 83-84, 84n,
    85-87, 86n, 92, 97, 98
Mary (Mother of Jesus), 13, 106n
Mary (Sister of Lazarus), 82
Mary Magdalene, 182
Marx, K., 230-231
Matthew (Evangelist), 51-53, 65
Maurer, W., 129n, 139n
May, K., 143
Mazar, B., 186n
Meeks, W.A., 86, 92
Meier, G., 212
Melchisedek, 39
Metz, J.B., 24, (31), 152n, 159,
    159n
Miller, A.O., 232n
Mirandola, P. della, 117
Moltmann, J., 156, 156n, 163,
    163n
Moses, 112
Moule, C.F.D., 52n
Mussner, F., 232-233, 233n

Nathanael (Apostle), 82
Nations, A.L., 86n
Nepper-Christensen, P., 51n
Neusner, J., 37n, 62n
Nicholas of Lyra, 120

Nickelsburg, G.W.E., 40
Nicodemus, 82
Niebuhr, H.R., 152n
Noah, 112

Oberman, H.A., 128n, 132n,
133n, 134, 134n, 135n, 146
O'Connor, J. (Cardinal), 158-
159, 159n
Origen, 115
Osborn, R., 13, 14, 16
Osten-Sachen, P. von der, 152n
Osterhaven, E., 232n
Oyer, J.S., 131n

Panofsky, E., 104n
Parkes, J., 156, 156n
Pascal, 225
Paul (Apostle), 20, 25, (28), (32),
42-43, 47-49, 53, 56, 65, 67-69,
70, 71, 72-75, 80, 172-174, 180,
182, 221-224 (see also Saul [of
Tarsus])
Paul VI (Pope), 24, (31)
Pawlikowski, J.T., 152n
Peck, A.J., 152n
Perkins, Ph., 162n, 165n
Perrin, N., 219-220, 219n, 224
Peter (Apostle), 182
Peter the Chanter, 118
Peter the Venerable, 116n, 125
Petronius, 188
Pius XI (Pope), 23, (30)
Pogrebin, L.C., 169-170, 170n
Poliakov, L., 21, (28)
Priest, J., 14
Przybylski, B., 53n

Rademacher-Chorus, H., 106n
Ralph of Diceto, 111n, 113-114,
119
Rashbam, 114
Rashi, 101n, 114, 115n, 119, 120,
121, 125, 126

Rausch, D.A., 159n
Reagan, R., 207
Reiter, P.J., 128, 129n
Rendtorff, R., 152n, 159n
Reuchlin, J., 117, 129, 146
Rhoads, D.M., 44n
Richard of St.-Victor, 103, 108,
116, 116n
Richardson, P., 48n, 52n
Richter, G., 92
Rivkin, E., 52n
Rosenfeld, A.H., 156n
Rosenzweig, F., 156n
Roth, C., 101n
Rouse, M., 101n
Rouse, R., 101n
Rubenstein, R., 178, 185-186,
186n, 190
Ruether, R.R., 76-77, 77n, 159n,
163, 176, 211, 212n, 213-214,
213n, 214n
Rupp, G., 128n

St. Chamberlain, H., 36, 43
Samuel the Small, 84n, 85, 86
Sanders, E.P., 44, 44n, 45, 48n,
72, 74, 75, 86n, 172n
Sanders, J.A., 152-153, 152n
Sasse, H., 236n
Saul (of Tarsus), 87 (see also
Paul [Apostle])
Schaeffer, E., 142n
Schechter, S., 213n, 214n, 218n
Schillebeeckx, E., 219, 219n, 224
Schilling, H., 139n
Schlatter, A., 50n
Schleiermacher, F., 218
Schniewind, J.D., 50n
Schorsch, I., 141n
Schottroff, L., 152n
Schürer, E., 14, 35-36, 36n
Seeberg, R., 142, 142n
Segel, A.F., 42n
Segovia, F.F., 90n

Seiferth, W.S., 104n
Shirer, W., 128, 128n
Siegele-Wenschkewitz, L., 128n, 152n
Signer, M., 111, 111n, 116, 116n
Siker, J., 15
Singer, H., 137n
Sloyan, G.S., 155, 155n, 165n
Smalley, B., 102n, 103, 103n, 107, 109n, 114, 114n, 115, 115n, 116, 116n, 117n, 118n 119, 119n, 120, 120n, 121, 126
Smith, D.M., 49, 49n, 54, 77n, 88, 157
Smith, M., 86
Sölle, D., 175, 175n
Song, C.-S., 153-154, 153n
Southern, R.W., 101n, 113n
Sovik, A., 128n
Sparks, H.F.D., 40n
Spinoza, B., 140
Spivey, R.A., 77n
Stanton, E.C., 170-171
Stanton, G., 50n
Starck, H., 217n, 221n
Stegemann, E., 159n
Stendahl, K., 48n, 51, 51n
Stock, B., 121, 121n
Stöcker, A., 141-142, 221
Stöhr, M., 135n
Stone, M.E., 40
Stransky, T.F., 153n
Strauss, H., 128n
Strecker, G., 51n
Sucher, B.C., 128n
Suetonius, 12
Suger of St.-Denis, Abbot, 105, 106-107
Suter, D.W., 40

Tacitus, 12
Tal, U., 143n

Thieme, K., 135n, 214n
Thoma, C., 212n, 217n
Tillich, P., 164, 229, 229n
Titus, 186, 192, 193, 195
Tödt, H.E., 227n
Tödt, I., 227n
Townsend, J.T., 86n
Tracy, D., 151, 152-153, 152n, 156, 156n, 159n
Tracy, J.D., 139n
Trever, J.C., 37n
Trilling, W., 51n
Troeltsch, E., 152n

Uhlig, S., 40

van Buren, P.M., 152n
VanderKam, J.C., 40
Vermes, G., 44, 44n
Vespasian, 186, 195
Vogelsang, E., 142n

Walde, U.C., von, 82n
Wallace-Hadrill, D.S., 112-113, 113n
Walsh, K., 118n
Weber, M., 36n, 195, 195n, 196
Wellhausen, J., 84
Wengst, K., 92
Wiener, P.F., 128
Wiesel, E., 178
Wilken, R.L., 151, 152-153, 152n
William of Champeaux, 107
Willesme, J.-P., 107n
Wilson-Kastner, P., 172, 172n
Winter, P., 52n
Wolf, E., 234n, 236n
Wood, D., 118n

Zechariah, 51
Zikmund, B.B., 171-172, 171n
Zinn, G., 13, 16, 21, 103n, 107n, 108n, 113n, 114n

Index of Biblical, Ancient, and Medieval Texts Cited

SCRIPTURES

OLD TESTAMENT

Gen	110
12:3	213n
17:10	173
Ex	110
Lev 11:45	24, (31)
Josh	110
Judg	110
Isa	110, 116, 125
4:1	110
7	116, 123
7:14ff	13, 116
8	116
9	123
11	123
28:16	69n
44:5	214n
45	226
49:22-26	213n
Kings	110
Chronicles	110
Job	110
Ps (s)	110, 119, 129
2:4	166
Song	110
Ezek	110
36:22	226
37:6	226

Hos 11:1	46
Zech 9:9	51

NEW TESTAMENT

Mt	39, 42-43, 50, 51-53, 54, 56, 57, 65, 81, 98, 110
2:2	79
2:15	46
5:17	77
5:43	90
5:44	90
21:7	51
21:33-46	65
21:41	66
21:45	81
27	181
27:15,24	66
27:24-25	51
27:25	66
27:62	81
Mk	44, 50, 51, 54, 65, 81
7:3	79
8:27-30	83
12:1-12	65
12:9-12	66
12:31	90
Lk	50, 54, 55, 56, 65, 66, 81
6:15	79
15:18-24	164

19:26-27	66n	17:20-23	91
20:9-19	65	18:13	81
20:16	66	18:15	80
Jn	19, (27), 42-43, 49, 50,	19:3	82
	54-55, 56, 58, 65, 76, 77,	19:39	82
	79-93, 95, 98, 99, 110, 221	20:30-31	84
1:12	90	Acts	12, 65, 66, 80, 110
1:35	80	1:13	79
1:45	13, 80	5:34	81
1:47	82	23:6-9	81
1:49	82	23:6-10	66
3:1	82	28:26-28	66
3:16	90	Rom	12, 20, 49, 88, 223
3:22	98	1:16	67
3:26	98	2	173
4:1	98	2:1-29	69
4:9	80	2:9-10	67
4:22	65, 80	2:17,28,29	88
4:23	22, (29)	2:26-29	173
6	81	3:1	88
7:45	81	3:3	68
7:50	82	3:9	68
8:31	82	3:28-31	68
8:40, 44	76	3:31	25, (32)
8:44	10, 88	8	149
9	80	9-11	67, 144, 221
9:16	82	9:4-5	48
9:22	50, 81, 82, 84, 85, 86	9:30-33	68-69
9:28	95	9:31-33	69n
10:34	65	9:33	69
11	58	10:2	68
11:47	81	10:4	68
12:42	50, 81, 82, 84	10:11	69n
13-17	88, 90	10:17-24	25
13:33	90	10:21	68
13:34	96	11	48
13:34-35	90	11:1-2	48
14:16	95	11:1-6	222
15:12	91	11:17-18	233
15:12-13	90	11:18	154
15:18-16:4	90	11:24,28	67
15:18,19	90	11:25	222
15:23	50, 91	11:25-26	67
16:2	84, 90	11:26	48

1 Cor 1:27	233	1Jn	90
7:19	173	2:7	96
15:14	165	2:15	90
Cor	12	3:23	90
Gal	12	4:3,5	89
Eph 2:12,19	154	4:10,14,16	90
1Thes 2:14-16	54, 67	4:20	90
Heb	65, 66	2Jn5	89, 90
8:13	67	Jude	65
10:1	67	Apoc	110 (see also Rev)
10:9	67, 67n	Rev	65, 88, 89
Jas	65	2:9	88, 89
1Pet	65	3:9	88, 89 (see also Apoc)
2Pet	65		

OLD TESTAMENT PSEUDEPIGRAPHA

Apocalypse of Baruch, 93
Apocalypse of Ezra, 93
2 Baruch 30:1, 39
2 Enoch, 39, 39n
4 Ezra, 55
Joseph and Aseneth, 40
Martyrdom and Ascension of Isaiah, 38
Odes of Solomon, 40
Parables of Enoch (1En 37-71), 40
Prayer of Manasseh, 40
Testaments of the Twelve Patriarchs, 38

EARLY JEWISH HISTORIOGRAPHY

The Jewish War, 186n, 188-189, 191-192, 193, 198, 201

RABBINIC PRAYERS

The Eighteen Benedictions (*Shemoneh Esreh*), 13, 36, 58, 85
The Twelfth Benediction (*Birkat ha-Minim*), 85, 86, 86n, 97-98

EARLY CHRISTIAN LITERATURE

The Apostolic Constitutions, 40
Chronicorum, 112n
De paenitentia I.ii, 26, (33)
Dialogue with Trypho, 85, 86
Hebraica, 119, 119n
Homilia adversus Judaeos, 12

MEDIEVAL CHRISTIAN LITERATURE
Chronicon, 108, 108n, 109, 111, 112, 113, 113n, 119
Cum nimis absurdum, 22, (29)
De gradibus ascensionum, 103n
De sacramentis christianae fidei, 110, 110n, 113n
De vanitate mundi, 113n
Decameron I.3, 21, (29)
Didascalicon, 108-109, 109n, 110, 110n
Magna glosatura, 119